Our Transformative Journey – A Gift of Healing to The World

An Integrative Holistic Health Coach Collaboration

Compiled by Karen Y. Moore

Twenty-one authentic, inspirational transformational journeys that move beyond pain and despair and into triumph, health, healing, and purpose. Stories that will inspire, motivate and empower every reader.

Copyright © 2019 by Karen Y. Moore

Our Transformative Journey – A Gift of Healing to The World

www.ourtransformativejourney.com

All rights reserved. No part of this publication may be reproduced, distributed, or transmitted in any form or by any means, including photocopying, recording, or other electronic or mechanical methods, without the prior written permission of the publisher, except in the case of brief quotations embodied in critical reviews and certain other noncommercial uses permitted by copyright law.

ISBN For this edition: 978-1-7335168-2-2

Published by Karen Y. Moore Lifestyle, Inc.

Savannah, Georgia 31415-8905

www.karenymoorelifestyle.com

Cover Design by: Emilybrandz

Page Design and Formatting by: Last Mile Publishing

First Edition Published: May 1, 2019

Printed in the United States of America

With appreciation to Joshua Rosenthal, Founder, Marcello Anzalone, President and Chief Financial Officer, and Marco A. Anzalone, EVP, Chief Legal Officer of the Institute for Integrative Nutrition.

Table of Contents

Dedication _____ *v*

Acknowledgments _____ *vi*

Forward _____ *viiii*

Introduction _____ *1*

Chapter 1 Overcoming: From Breakdown to Breakthrough _____ *5*

Chapter 2 The Strength Within _____ *20*

Chapter 3 Challenges Are What Make Life Interesting _____ *34*

Chapter 4 Listening to Your Gut _____ *47*

Chapter 5 A Life Evolving-Growing, Changing, Living _____ *60*

Chapter 6 Coming Full Circle and Finding True North _____ *73*

Chapter 7 Journey to the Other Side of Fear _____ *86*

Chapter 8 In the Garden, He Met Me _____ *99*

Chapter 9 From the Darkest of Nights, Emerged a Shining Star _ *113*

Chapter 10 Don't Like Your Story, Change It! _____ *127*

Chapter 11 Let it Happen Organically _____ *139*

Chapter 12 Me Vs. FGB (Fat Girl Brain) _____ *152*

Chapter 13 Restored-Healed Inside Out _____ *165*

Chapter 14 Tears and Goosebumps _____ *177*

Chapter 15 Follow the Lights _____ *190*

Chapter 16 The Metamorphosis of a Healthy Smile _____ *203*

Chapter 17 The Longest Goodbye _____ *215*

Chapter 18 Progress Over Perfection _____ *227*

Chapter 19 Learning to Love Myself While Managing ADHD __ *240*

Chapter 20 Awakening of My Inner Healer _____ 251
Chapter 21 My Growing Space _____ 264
Epilogue _____ 276
Bonus Material _____ 278

Dedication

The authors of *Our Transformative Journey* dedicate this book to the devoted champions, family, friends, and cheerleaders along our journeys. You have motivated, encouraged, guided, and inspired during trial and triumph. We take this moment to thank each of you, as your hand in the journey helped us create transformation. We also honor the individual experiences, obstacles, and acts of healing that brought us all together. The process of transformation, while at times crippling and gut-wrenching, is the ultimate act of self-love and is also saturated with joy, celebration, and new beginnings.

Acknowledgments

The authors of *Our Transformative Journey* wish to express our deepest gratitude and acknowledge those who believed in the power of our stories. Your astronomical support is evident as the first twenty-five purchasers of our book. Your confidence pushed us to work harder and pursue excellence in all aspects of this project, and for this, we are forever grateful.

As co-authors, we would be remiss if we failed to recognize our fearless leader, momma bear, mastermind and compiler Karen Y. Moore, without whom this book would not exist. The result of many prayers and thoughtful planning; her vision became a dream come true for twenty more. Karen's focused drive, attention to detail, and remarkable dedication to excellence have been our foundation. Under her leadership and guidance, twenty-one strangers shared their darkest moments, deepest fears, and monumental triumph. Through the sweat, tears, and laughter, we were all motivated and inspired. We value the incredible journey and lifelong friendships gained because you welcomed each of us into your dream. Thank you, Karen, for believing in us and trusting us to share your vision.

Thank you Emilybrandz for the gorgeous cover design. You were somehow able to capture twenty-one visions in one design. Thank you as well to the countless friends, neighbors, and family members who spent hours poring over our work, providing edits and feedback ensuring that we showed our best effort.

Courage and determination are unmistakable in the lives of our authors. Aristotle said, "You are what you repeatedly do. Excellence then is not an act, but a habit." Transformation is a lifelong journey in which we change our habits to improve ourselves. We thank you, the reader, for being a part of our transformative journey. We hope our stories inspire you to embark on a transformative journey of your own.

Our Transformative Journey

We also wish to thank our "first supporters" without whom none of this would be possible:

Shulamit Morris – Ventura, California

Melissa Amon - *Cushing, Oklahoma*

Tanya Riggan – Omaha, Nebraska

Ashely Lenn – Tacoma, Washington

Nichole Quayle - Chariton, Iowa

Gail Riela – Summit, New Jersey

Tiffany Loy – Rockledge, Florida

Joe Costarella – Staten Island, New York

Henry Ellsworth - Bristol, Rhode Island

Marilyn Shaw – Bristol, Rhode Island

Steven Alers - Raynham, MA

Brenda Herrera – St. Augustine, Florida

Judd DeWitt – Charlotte, North Carolina

Abby Eldridge – Shelby, Ohio

Ekaterini Kosmopoulos – Flushing, New York

Carl Rice – Antioch, Tennessee

Wendy Gunder – Shelby, Ohio

Nidia Rodriguez – New York, New York

Kassie Underwood - Mansfield, Ohio

Debbie Sallee – Shelby, Ohio

Edward Friebel – Shelby, Ohio

JoAnn Nelson – Shelby, Ohio

Cindy Lash – Shelby, Ohio

Amanda Rader – West Salem, Ohio

William Bianco – Staten Island New York

Stacey Wampler – Mansfield, Ohio

Forward

Our society is in desperate need of a healthcare revolution. In the United States alone, billions of dollars are spent each year on "sick care" – the focus on treating and managing illness rather than preventing it in the first place. All it takes is one look at the current rate of obesity, heart disease, and other health issues to realize that our current system isn't working and it's time for a massive shift. Our lives literally depend on it.

When I started the Institute for Integrative Nutrition (IIN)®, I was just one person with the simple idea that if I could change what people ate, I could change the world. I became motivated by the idea that every person is unique and there is no "one-size-fits-all" approach to health. My dream became even bigger as I came to understand that food is only part of the equation. Many doctors and health practitioners in the Western world are trained to treat patients' symptoms rather than treating the whole person. I wanted to train people to do something different – to listen. The power of listening is so incredible to me. By simply listening and being present with another human being, you can help them heal. You can help them transform their bodies, their lives, and the lives of those around them.

At IIN, we teach that people need more than the food on their plate to be healthy; they need love, movement, purpose, creativity, and connection in order to thrive. In IIN's Health Coach Training Program, we call this primary food. Primary food refers to the things in your life – career, relationships, spirituality, physical activity, and environment – that nourish you beyond food. Secondary food refers to the food we have on our plate. The food we eat is critically important, but primary food plays an equal if not more significant role in the quality of our lives and our health. Together, primary and secondary food fuel our bodies, minds, and spirits, impacting the way we feel about ourselves and the energy we put out into the world.

More than 25 years later, Integrative Nutrition has grown into the largest nutrition school in the world, with over 100,000 graduates worldwide. Integrative Nutrition Health Coaches are part of a growing revolution to transform our planet for the better. The mission of the school is to play a crucial role in improving health and happiness and, through that process, create a ripple effect that transforms the world. Each of us has the power to impact the lives of those around us. It begins with one person deciding to take control of their health. Then their family, friends, neighbors, etc., notice a change in them and start asking questions. That is the ripple effect in action.

In Our Transformative Journey, you'll hear stories from twenty-one Integrative Nutrition graduates who made the commitment to transform their lives from illness and disease to well-being and healing. The stories of these courageous men and women demonstrate that sometimes life gives us challenges in order to gain strength and grow into the people we are meant to become. Their journeys will inspire you to rethink everything you know about health and go deeper into how you can begin to repair the root causes of your own health imbalances.

As you read each story, I challenge you to reflect on the positive changes you would like to make in your own life. The clearer your vision, the more likely you will be to create it. No matter what your goal is, it's very important that you remember that your journey will not look like anyone else's. We are all unique in what we need to achieve balance. Being healthy is about moving beyond a limited view of nutrition and creating your own larger vision for your health and happiness.

I often get asked what my greatest inspiration is, and my answer is always the same. It's the students and graduates of Integrative Nutrition who inspire me year after year. They come from many different backgrounds and countries around the world, and their stories are powerful. Our students and graduates collectively create the larger ripple effect I have always dreamed IIN would have on the world. They embody the school's mission, beginning with themselves, and I am truly amazed by their passion and devotion to making the world a healthy and happy place. Together, we are stronger.

Bio:

For over 20 years, founder Joshua Rosenthal has been the director of the Institute for Integrative Nutrition®, a school at the forefront of holistic nutrition education that offers comprehensive, cutting-edge training to enrich minds, careers, and personal lives. His revolutionary approach introduces a wide variety of dietary theories – from Eastern to Western, ancient to modern, and everything in between. Joshua is a highly sensitive healer with a master's in education and 30 years in the fields of whole foods, personal coaching, and teaching.

Introduction

Before you begin, I want to take a moment to commend you for taking the first step to transforming your life. It's easy to become fearful, complacent or decide to sweep change under the rug and say, *"It's too late or too hard to transform my life."* Wrong. You can create a brand-new chapter in your life's story at any moment. What do you want to write? What goals do you have? What are your dreams and aspirations?

In *Our Transformative Journey* you will meet twenty-one authentic and diverse individuals who decided that "Enough Is Enough." Each of us decided to transform our lives. We made an intentional decision to move beyond pain and despair and into triumph, healing, and purpose. Each of us has decided that we would no longer be victims but become VICTORS! We hope that our stories will inspire, motivate and empower you to change.

I don't believe that any of us were put on this earth to merely exist. We were meant to thrive, to fulfill our purpose, and to become more. YOU have the power to transform your entire life at any given moment. Change is a choice, but a lot of people don't want to do the hard work to get there. They hit a plateau, shift into dabbler mode and never accomplish their goals in life. They get overwhelmed by the magnitude of it all and forget that change begins with a single step. If you want to transform your life, you need to become the master of your destiny.

Transformation doesn't happen by accident or pure luck. It requires that you do the work. You alone are responsible for the changes that you make in your life. The first step to change is making the realization that you want to. It starts by shifting the way that you think.

Our Transformative Journey

Yes, transforming your life can be scary and challenging, but it can also be exciting and massively rewarding. It's a process that starts and ends with you. In the words of Dr. Judith Wright, *"When you transform, you do something that you could never have imagined yourself doing, become something you could never have imagined yourself becoming, and, ultimately, live a life greater than you could have ever imagined yourself living."*

If you are reading this book, I'm assuming that you have a desire to change and transform your life. Close your eyes and imagine what your life would look like if you had everything that you've ever imagined. Tap into your emotional state. How does the environment look?

How is your health? How do you feel? What do you smell? What do you hear? Visualize what transformation feels like and activate all of your senses. Now hold onto that vision.

Transforming your life starts with committing to change your beliefs and your behaviors. If changing your life was easy, everyone would do it. It requires patience, discipline, motivation, confidence and an unwavering belief in your ability to create a better experience for yourself; one that allows you to be in alignment with your purpose and your higher self.

Before you start reading, I want you to understand what transformation stories are and why we need them for inspiration and motivation. Transformational stories are stories that report the process of changes that occur. They exemplify through true-life stories and events and they help to shine the light on different situations of life and how we can improve, overcome or emerge from each one of them.

As we contemplate on the changes needed in our collective attitudes and behavior to meet the complexities of day to day life, it becomes clear that we need a whole new way of thinking, eating and acting. A quantum change, something outside the box, a paradigm shift–a profound transformation to bring us into a sustainable relationship with that beautiful life we deserve. It is true that optimists, or positive thinkers, are at an advantage in life compared to pessimists because of the effect your mindset and attitude have on everything that you say or do.

With each story, you will see how transformation is associated with the mind and soul's determination. Your social relationships, your job and also your health are an integral part of your daily life and you can feel how negative and positive thoughts can have a domino effect on everything you do.

The way you choose to think, positive or negative, has a great impact on the final outcome and, is reflected in everything you do. Hence the importance of having a balanced outlook on life.

Three questions you have to answer on your transformational journey:

- Are You Doing What You Love To Do?

- What Is Stopping You From Being The Happiest Version Of Yourself?

- Are You Settling For Less In Any Aspect Of Your Life?

Are you doing what you love to do?

This might be a tough question to answer for the simple fact that most people don't know what their dream is until they have found it. However, if you aren't excited to do that job every day (or at least most of the time), then you are likely stuck at a dead-end job or at least one you do not fancy.

Everyone's pursuit of happiness is different (some people simply want wealth in the form of an endless amount of money, while others want a family and financial security), but if you are not doing what you love to do, then you aren't going to be as fulfilled as you would like to be. If you aren't doing what you love to do, then it is up to you to make the necessary changes. No one can follow your dreams for you, after all. Only you can.

What Is Stopping You From Being The Happiest Version Of Yourself?

Unfortunately, we all face this question at one point or another. Is your negative attitude stopping you from being the happiest version of yourself? Perhaps it is a harmful habit or negative people in your life. Maybe you just know there is something better out there for you, but it's up to you to search for it. The sooner you find an answer to this question, the sooner you will be the happiest version of yourself.

Our Transformative Journey

Are You Settling For Less In Any Aspect Of Your Life?

If you want to be the happiest person, you can possibly be, and if you want to take your pursuit of happiness to the ultimate level, then you can never settle. Don't settle with people, whether it comes to a romantic relationship or friendships, don't settle until you achieve optimum health, or your fitness, financial or life goals.

The moment you settle is the moment you are telling the universe you are happy with not getting everything you want/deserve. You are the only person who truly knows what you are worth and what you want. Go out and get those things and never settle.

Many of us, after experiencing setbacks and failures, emotionally give up and stop trying. We believe that because we were unsuccessful in the past, we will always be unsuccessful. In other words, we continue to see barriers in our heads, even when no 'real' barrier exists between where we are and where we want to go.

It's time to achieve that breakthrough and become the person you were meant to be. In a triumphant spirit of this, we have compiled these stories for you to learn, grow and gain inspiration from so that you're able to transform YOUR life and achieve your goals and dreams.

As part of a social revolution against life stagnancy, and as Holistic Health Coaches we are bound by our passion to help people heal and transform. We are butterflies that have transformed and undergone a life-changing *metamorphosis*, and now we are ready to share our transformations as our gift of healing to the world.

Human beings are capable of so much greatness. You have the freedom to do whatever you want. Life transformation is bringing qualitative change into your life. Once you transform your life, you will feel a lot different. So, it's time to get focused, motivated and hungry! There is no limit to what you can accomplish. We did it and so can you!

Best Wishes on your transformative journey,

Karen Y. Moore

Compiler

Chapter 1

Overcoming: From Breakdown to Breakthrough: The Evolution of a P.H.A.T (Pretty, Healthy and Transformed) Girl

By: Karen Y. Moore

Have you ever felt like you are drowning and there is no lifeguard, lifeboat, or lifeline anywhere in sight? Tomorrow looks blurry and you feel like you are about to let everyone down. You become angry, scared, fearful and anxious. You can't sleep at night because your mind is racing and you can't perform during the day because your body is crashing.

Has any of this ever happened to you? If so, know that you are not alone. I have been where you are now. Life happens to all of us. We all experience the ups and the down, the loves and the losses, the good times and the bad. There is no area of life that is immune to adversity. You can face challenges physically, emotionally, spiritually, in your career, your business, financially, in your relationships, and the list goes on and on.

I have experienced my own fair share of adversity; loss of a spouse, bad career choices, foolish business decisions, extreme financial difficulties, ideas that just did not work, and hard work that just did not pay off. On more than one occasion, I have crawled out on a limb to get the ripest fruit only to have the branch give way and send me free falling to the ground.

You will probably think I am crazy for what I am about to say, but in the end, I'm thankful for each and every challenge and adversity that I've faced in life as well as for every fall I've ever had.

My transformational story is written to appreciate everyone that has ever crawled in or out of bed and wept uncontrollably because the pain in their chest was just too much to bear. It is dedicated to men and women whose suffering is beyond anything he/she has ever known, the kind of suffering that makes you scream out and surrender it to God as you know that if you don't, you will be crushed and consumed by the adversities and challenges of life.

My story is also a labor of love for everyone that has paced and rolled on the floor in the middle of the night screaming out of desperation for God to bring peace to their quivering and questioning soul. It doesn't matter what challenges, adversities or blockages you are experiencing I want to encourage, motivate, inspire and provide a blueprint of success for positive effective change and transformation.

I will share with you my real life story of how I moved from tragedy to triumph. The loss of my spouse, best friend, and business partner started an avalanche of heartache, despair and brokenness.

Mourning the loss of my husband James gave birth to a plethora of unresolved issues and wounds from my past that were never healed. My darkness intensified when I realized that my life had been a succession of pyrrhic victories and living in a constant and perpetual state of ambiguity.

My healing process didn't happen overnight. It has been a journey of more than ten years and counting. From my breakdowns, break-outs to breakthroughs, I have been able to emerge and evolve as a woman of wisdom, power, grace and influence. I have re-written and redefined the rules of engagement for my life and have now learned how to play out loud without asking for permission, validation or acceptance.

In order to understand how I have arrived at where I am, we must travel back to where I was before now. My life has been filled with unusual twists and turns and by returning to my past with me is the only way that you can adequately understand the miracle of my journey.

Stepping Back in Time to A Carefree + Happier Life

Turning a few pages back in time, I remembered when my career started as a loan officer before moving on to open my private mortgage brokerage firm some years later. My life was comfortable, or so I thought, and I didn't have much to complain about. I had a loving family and made a good living as a broker. I lived the most normal life that I could, fulfilling expectations placed upon me by loved ones as a dutiful wife, mother, daughter, sister, aunt, and friend who never complained. I remained committed to all of the expectations that were placed upon me.

A few years later I never envisaged that a major change was about to happen, there was a sharp decline in the mortgage and housing market so I decided to make a change. My husband was an Executive Chef, we were always throwing parties and entertaining in our home, and I began to think about how I could monetize it. And the rest was history. I shut down my mortgage company as I found a new love and passion for planning special events.

In 2001, I launched a successful destination wedding and special event planning company. The focus of my company was on planning multi-faceted events that created memorable client experiences for my clients. In many ways, I had a fulfilling career. I became an award-winning wedding planner. I wrote my first book and I was surrounded by people who looked up to me for my professional knowledge and wisdom.

I had the best Husband any woman could wish. Our journey together was really amazing. From our first hello on January 1, 1999, to our engagement 17 days later, and our wedding February 27th wedding. Things were pretty close to perfect! It was obvious that God ordained our union and put us together on a unique fast track. James and I shared a lifetime in the span of ten short years.

What we achieved in 10 years of our marriage is more than what many couples could complete in 20 or 30 years. James gave so much and asked for so little in return. Whenever I asked him for something, his response to me was always the same, "Do whatever you want as long as it makes you happy." Often times in response I would ask the question "Well, what would make you happy?" and he always replied "Seeing You Happy." He loved me so much! He loved me unconditionally. Despite all my faults and idiosyncrasies. He loved me! And he made sure that everyone else knew it as well.

Even after all of these years it still feels surreal, and there isn't a day that goes by that I don't miss his presence. On May 5th, 2009 my sweetheart made his transition.

The Beginning of The End

I remember the days leading up to it like it was yesterday. Friday, May 1, 2009 started like any ordinary weekend for us. James was an Executive Chef by day and moonlighted as a photographer on the weekend. Photography was one of his loves and favorite pastimes. Plus, it gave us the incredible opportunity to spend our weekends doing what we both loved. Seeing people happy. We had a full weekend of events, meetings and time scheduled to spend with friends and family.

I noticed that James wasn't quite himself as his eyes were watering and his nose was running. We just attributed to allergies. James had gone to our primary care doctor two weeks prior. He had gotten blood work done and it was all normal. His blood pressure was good, and he had lost 75 pounds. We chalked it up to allergies and went about our weekend. James was selfless and was a real trouper. Never in a million years would I have ever dreamt that this would be our last weekend together. What I'm most grateful for is that our last weekend together was nothing short of incredible.

Sunday came, and we still had one last event for the weekend. We got up and went about our day preparing for the event. By the time we got back home, James had developed a high fever. I asked him to let me take him to the emergency room, but he insisted that he was fine and that we would get up early on Monday and go see our primary care physician. His fever finally broke at 2:00am and he said he felt better. When James woke up early Monday morning, he started vomiting and developed diarrhea. Thirty minutes after him waking up he was so weak that I had to call EMS to get him to the hospital. After spending several hours in the ER, I was told that he had an infection in his blood. By this time James started to lose the feeling in his legs and he kept telling me that he couldn't see. By 4:00pm they decided to move him to ICU. Because they had prepared a sterile environment for James I couldn't go into ICU with him. I kissed him on his forehead and they wheeled him away.

Our Transformative Journey

I never dreamed that this would be the last kiss and the last time that I would see him alive. I was told that if he did survive that he may have brain damage and the quality of his life would be severely diminished. I was advised to go home and get some rest. How could I? My whole world was collapsing right before my very eyes. I arrived back home around 10:00 pm, took a shower, crawled into bed hugging my bible and my favorite picture of James.

At 1:00 am I got the dreaded call. The summons back to the hospital. The birds were chirping as I left to go back to the hospital; at that point, I knew James was gone because birds don't chirp at 2:00am.

I didn't find out the cause of James death until two days later when I got a phone call from our primary-care physician. I was told that James had Meningococcal meningitis, and he had gone into septic shock. His sudden death yanked the rug right out from under me.

Although I miss him terribly I'm happy James lived a happy and fulfilled life as he would be remembered for all his incredible deeds.

Our life together was nothing short of amazing. Our marriage was filled with happiness, joy, admiration, mutual respect, devotion and an incredible amount of love. We had some rough times, some ups and downs, and some highs and lows, but with God we emerged victoriously each time. The amount of growth that I experienced is immeasurable. Through James, I experienced God's unconditional love and grace. James not only changed my life but the lives of countless others. He had left and incredible legacy and a giant footprint of his time here on earth. He led by example and his legacy brings life, hope and promise to a dark and gloomy world. What we experienced was rare and will be cherished by me forever. I will forever carry him in my spirit. What a privilege it has been to be a part of his life. And an even greater honor and privilege to have been Mrs. James D. Moore.

Sepsis Knocks Twice

James' transition was the first time I had ever heard the word "sepsis" and unfortunately it wouldn't be my last. Sever years after the death of my husband, sepsis reared its ugly head again in my life.

In 2016, my life was interrupted and altered yet again as I was staring this ugly illness square in the face. The only reason that I'm here today is that I fought like hell for my life. My kidneys started to fail and shut down, my blood sugar level shot through the roof! My blood count was abnormal. Fevers, chills, diarrhea, depression, decreased urination as my kidneys were starting to fail, extreme weakness and the worst pain imaginable! All I could do is lie on the hospital bed weep and cry out to God asking him to help me.

I don't recall when I became full blown septic. I remember that I got a cold on Christmas day in 2015. That cold progressed into bronchitis, which I fought all of January. Then an unexplained abscess reared its ugly head. I have had a couple in the past but none that every grew almost to the size of a grapefruit.

I tried treating it at home with natural remedies. They had worked in the past and I felt that they would work again. Boy was I wrong. Finally, I went to the ER on February 1st. Within two hours they had diagnosed and admitted me. Later that evening I was rushed to the operating room for surgery.

When the nurses informed me that I was septic, I lost it. My husband died from it and surely I was going to lose my life as well. My body felt as if a major world war had been released on it, leaving nothing but charred, and smoking ruins.

For days I laid in the hospital bed and engaged in a war with my body. The pain coupled with uncontrollable diarrhea, which was a reaction to all the antibiotics and other medications, were enough to send anyone over the edge. I could barely walk or sit up in bed as the symptoms gripped me so tightly. My son came home on leave. At that time, he was in the Air Force. He tried is best to motivate and encourage me to not give up the fight.

I felt hopeless, helpless, and trapped! Although I had the best doctors and people around me, I still felt alone. The heaviness of my heart stifled me

Our Transformative Journey

with fear and kept me from moving forward. My confidence and self-esteem were at an all-time low. To look at me smiling from my sickbed, no one would never know the things that were going on inside my head. I concealed it with grace. I continued to press onward in spite of my pain. I realized that I was no longer living but simply existing from day to day. I was, in fact, wasting away to oblivion. Something inside of me wouldn't allow me to give up.

Like most people, we long to see our kids get married or see our grandchildren born. Deep inside I knew I wanted to live, but I wasn't able to figure out the why.

Upon my discharge from the hospital my daily routine schedule was replaced with doctors' appointments, follow up tests and post recovery. All my plans and dreams were put on hold as I fought to find a new healthy life after sepsis. I spent nine days in the hospital and 15 days at home attached to an infusion pump that administered unusually high doses of antibiotics 24/7.

Once I returned home all I could do was take baby steps towards recovery. As I settled into being back at home, I was able to truly appreciate the small things in life that I had been taking for granted. While this was an extremely difficult period in my life, it was also a time I was able to reflect on where I came from and where I was now headed. Everything becomes more pronounced when you feel you're on a time clock. Nature, the sunset, family; everything became much more meaningful to me. I decided I needed to rejoin life.

I also started thinking about self-healing. As I reflected on everything I have achieved so far, I began to believe that perhaps I could heal my life starting from the inside out. I began to think about the future I wanted to have. Although I faced a very deadly illness, I knew deep inside that it wouldn't be the end of me. If God spared me, there must be a greater good and purpose that I needed to fulfill.

Surprisingly, I started getting better. I grew a little stronger each day. My immune system was strengthened, the fever went away, and the diarrhea ended. The excruciating pain in my muscles subsided. Almost a year later and I was able to declare a partial victory as I finally started over and beat most of the lingering effects of sepsis.

Life hasn't been fair or pretty, but I lived to be able to tell my story and share my testimony. It's not something I like to talk about, because the aftermath still affects me daily and some days hurts me to the core. Especially when I think that I survived and beat sepsis, but my beloved did not. Today, I still wrestle with the overwhelming ordeal. And, at times, the emotional turmoil that is inherent with sepsis still knocks me for a loop. But all in all, I healed quite well. I'm grateful to be alive.

A New Beginning

A little over a year passed, and some of the after-effects of sepsis still remained. I found myself tired, experiencing cognitive issues, and couldn't get my blood sugar back under control. I realized that to live, I had to make a drastic change. I decided that enough was enough and embarked upon a personal journey in search of optimum health and wellness. Little did I know that transitioning to a vegan lifestyle would be the catalyst that would change my life forever.

I decided to stop eating animal-based products, often it was difficult to cope with my new regime. It was one of the best decisions I've made in my life. I tried not to rush things, I went about it at my own pace. I realize that like any other lifestyle change, going vegan not only takes getting used to, but it takes time to determine what worked best for me.

My official process started in April of 2017 when I started removing pork from my diet. Slowly I began to transition to a diet that was healthier and less processed. Making small changes to my everyday meals was the easiest way for me to make permanent, sustainable changes. I increased the amount of plant-based foods in my diet. Sometimes, I would change from one product to another; trying to determine what worked best for me. While doing this, I realized there's a plant-based alternative for almost everything.

I left my food comfort zone and took myself on a voyage of discovery of new cuisines. There are thousands of vegan recipes out there from every corner of the globe. I encountered amazing new dishes and interesting variations on my old favorites.

With all of this experimentation and the delicious recipes, the urge to eat meat still comes in once in a while. I am breaking life-long habits. I always have to remind myself of the reason why and all of the benefits that I have received since being on a plant-based diet which kept me accountable as I decided that nothing could derail me from my transitioning process. Anytime I was having a bad day or felt the whole plant-based lifestyle was too much like hard work – I would take a deep breath and reflect on my healthier lifestyle and how amazing I now felt.

I have become so in-tune with my body and by paying close attention to what my it tells me, I have been able to figure out what works for me and have improved my health. June 14th, 2017 I officially transitioned to a plant-based diet, and I couldn't be happier.

During my time transitioning to a plant-based diet, I discovered my passion for cooking. In the past, I cooked out of necessity but now I cook because I enjoy it. I have become so enamored with cooking that I started posting photos on social media to share my excitement for my new creations and to express how much I love and enjoy my food.

P.H.A.T (Pretty, Healthy, and Transformed) Girlz Thrive.

A few months after my transition into a plant-based lifestyle, I began to notice colossal changes. I started feeling better, I had more energy, and my feet stopped swelling. I was able to manage my diabetes more effectively by paying attention to my diet, and my blood sugar levels have gone back to normal.

All these changes inspired me to write and document my transformation process. I started journaling and chronicling what I was eating and paying attention to what effect it had on my body.

With all the wonderful changes I've experienced, I decided that it was time to pay it forward. I launched a project which teaches women how to have and maintain a healthy lifestyle. I started a wellness group called P.H.A.T. Girlz "Pretty, Healthy, and Transformed" Thrive. In 2012 I received my certification as a life coach, but I wasn't sure of what to do with it. But with PHAT Girlz Thrive, I was finally able to start putting my training to use.

P.H.A.T. Girlz Thrive, which is open to vegans and non-vegans alike, encourages a healthy attitude towards food and a focus on improving health, rather than losing weight. I used to be so worried about numbers on a scale rather than my health. Now I'm working out not to get to a number, but to enhance everything I've done to improve my health. And this is what I try to instill into my tribe.

The community offers a space for women to voice their challenges and successes, along with sharing recipes and cooking tips. The P.H.A.T Girlz Community has organically grown to over 160 women.

I am so happy that our community is bearing amazing fruit: Here is what one member said about PHAT Girlz. "There aren't enough words to express what this community of like-minded women have done for me and my family," said member Yolanda Mitchell. "The health of myself and my family has increased significantly. The wealth of knowledge and focus on overall health has made me more conscious and not so much focused on losing weight but how my body feels."

It is these kinds of comments that keep me motivated and moving forward. There is no greater feeling than helping a woman go from surviving to thriving.

Over the last five years I have diligently worked to reshape, redefine, and transform my life. Today, am proud to share that my life has greatly transformed to a new and better version of me. I am now a stronger, healthier, powerful, confident version of myself - Karen 5.0 as I like to call her.

Rock Bottom Doesn't Mean It's Over

In retrospect sepsis has been my greatest source of pain but also my greatest strength because it brought out resiliency, tenacity and purpose in me. This dreadful illness forced me into taking responsibility for my health. As my life started to improve my interest in wellness and healthy living started gathering momentum. Now I feel it is my calling to help educate and teach others about living a healthy lifestyle as well as bring awareness to sepsis. I have completed my training at the Institute of Integrative Nutrition®, and I'm now a Holistic Health and Wellness Coach. And in case you're wondering I officially hung up my wedding and event planning hat to follow my passion and my purpose.

One valuable lesson that I learned during my transformation process was to always to keep an open mind and free myself of any negativity. I began studying other successful people who had faced the most prolific tragedies imaginable. A commonality is they were able to keep a positive and determined outlook, even in the most horrendous situations. We should always look at every area of life with a positive mental attitude.

When you change your mental attitude, the world around you will change accordingly. Your world will become what you choose to make it. You can reach great heights of success, or you can settle for a miserable life that is devoid of hope. The choice is yours.

When you choose a positive course, you set in motion an unstoppable force that will allow you to have a fulfilling career, the love of your family and friends, good physical and mental health, and all the other true riches of life.

To transform your world, you must change it from the inside out. You must begin with yourself. When you choose the course that puts your life on a positive track, you will change your life for the better, and you will also positively influence the people with whom you come in contact. When you close the door of your mind to negative thoughts, the door of opportunity opens to you.

It is the nature of opportunity that it merely refuses to attach itself to negative thinkers. Negative minds cannot conceive exciting new business opportunities, invent innovative new products, solve difficult problems, or create beautiful music or works of art.

Our Transformative Journey

All of these activities require a positive belief in yourself and your abilities. When you approach every challenge with a positive mental attitude, you will always discover opportunities that others have overlooked. Relish your achievements and recall them when the going gets tough. Take comfort in the knowledge that you have succeeded in the past, and you can do it again. You can do it if you think you can! Trust yourself and most importantly trust the process.

We all have choices when disaster befalls us, and we can either focus on the negative or we can focus on the positive. This was not an easy journey as it was filled with great loss, pain and suffering. I suddenly lost my spouse in 2009. In 2016 I became septic and almost lost my life. I could have easily given up. I felt I hit an all-time low. It felt like I hit rock bottom.

Due to my resiliency and the resolve of not wanting to stay in a dark place, I found life. My life or my middle as I call it was messy, but it was during this time I transformed into the best version of myself, found my passion and purpose. I've learned that to gain any traction or momentum, you must give up the victim status, have the courage and be willing to take massive ACTION. That action requires developing, exercising and being able to flex your bounce back muscles.

Life is full of rapids, obstacles, roadblocks, negative emotions, and circumstances that will derail even the best-laid plans. Life is not smooth sailing, but an adventure full of rivers, valleys, and victories.

I may get knocked down 999 times, but you'd better believe that I'm getting up 1000. People shouldn't view crises as insurmountable problems. We can't change the fact that highly stressful events will happen, but we can change how we interpret and respond to these events.

Life events and challenges shouldn't derail or cripple us. Most people believe that when they hit rock bottom, it's the end. It's not the end; it's the beginning. Rock bottom is the foundation that can form the most significant growth of a person's life. It forces you to dig deeper. It forces you to let go of someone you pretended to be so you can work towards someone far more significant — the most excellent version of yourself. When a person becomes the greatest version of him or herself, they can move in a forward motion knowing that any and everything is possible. Rock bottom catapults you forward. Once you have momentum, you become unstoppable.

Become an expert in dealing with adversity, learn to triumph over tragedy, and rise above the challenges of day-to-day life. Keep your thoughts on where you're going, not on where you've been. Keep your eyes on your goals, and keep your chin tilted upward toward the sunshine. Resolve in advance that you will meet and overcome every difficulty, and then, no matter what happens, don't give up until you do. You can do it! You are an OVERCOMER!

God's grace, his transformational power and all sufficiency he has blessed me to ascend to my best and highest self. While on my journey I found my true identity and my authentic voice and now I passionately live my life out loud boldly, courageously, passionately and unapologetically.

About Karen Y. Moore

Karen Y. Moore is the founder of P.H.A.T (Pretty, Healthy, and Transformed) Girlz Thrive and the CEO of Karen Y. Moore Lifestyle, Inc. a premier health, wellness and lifestyle brand that is dedicated to educating, supporting and inspiring women to live happier healthier, more meaningful lives through an assortment of products, online courses, programs, coaching services, and live events.

Karen is a Wellness Advocate, sepsis entrepreneur, keynote speaker, a recently retired award-winning event planner (19 years) and the author of The K.I.S.S (Keep It Sweet & Simple) Method of Wedding Planning.

In 2019 Karen founded the James D. Moore Memorial Foundation for Sepsis Awareness to honor the life and legacy of her husband.

She is a Lisa Nichols Superfan, a modern health enthusiast, and a novice chef. Karen serves as a Vegan Mentor for PETA and loves helping women ascend to the best version of themselves.

Emerging from the battle and effects left behind by Sepsis and armed with the success of her transformation Karen set out on a mission to coach, motivate, inspire and empower women to take back their lives and their health. She teaches women how to regain control of their health, wellness, and well-being.

Karen shares her message of hope, triumph, and transformation globally with candid presentations, content-rich workshops, and a humanistic web presence. Her desire to be a global change agent in the earth was a determining factor in creating the P.H.A.T Girlz Thrive Movement, where she invests in the positive nourishment of women all over the world.

She provides encouragement, motivation, and information to assist in creating a wellness plan that works for any lifestyle. She is dedicated and committed to helping others realize how walking in optimum health is vital in becoming the greatest version of ourselves. Karen takes a holistic, integrative approach to wellness, which involves focusing on the whole person — the physical, psychological and emotional self.

Karen currently resides in Savannah, Georgia and is a 2019 graduate of The Institute for Integrative Nutrition®. She is widowed and has two sons Christian and her fur baby Harley Davidson.

In her spare time, she retreats to the beach, enjoys reading, street festivals, long walks, camping, traveling, and the cultural arts.

Contact Information

Karen Y. Moore
Karen Y. Moore Lifestyle
Website: www.kymlifestyle.com
Website: www.phatgirlzthrive.com

Facebook Community: www.facebook.com/groups/phatgirlzthrive
Email: karen@kymlifestyle.com

Chapter 2

The Strength Within

By: Kristie A. Alers

There's a famous quote by Fredrick Douglas that reads, "Without struggle, there is no progress." I like to add, "…thus no story of transformation to tell." My story of transformation doesn't follow the traditional blockbuster movie format wherein a traumatic event occurs, followed by one fell swoop of an epiphanic moment, and suddenly the protagonist can overcome the adversity, transform, and live happily ever after. My story is more of a compilation of non-stop obstacles that required me to access the strength within and keep moving forward.

I believe the amount of time spent in adversity during the first part of your life is about the same amount of time it will take to overcome said adversity in the second part of your life. It takes time to heal deep wounds, learn the importance of shedding layers that once served as protective barriers but no longer serve us as adults, shift mindsets and perspectives, and release from limiting belief systems that stunt growth and render our dreams impossible. Awareness alone makes a world of difference, but it is the mindful actions we take to change the unhealthy habits we've practiced for so long that will open our lives to an endless amount of possibilities. Transformation begins when you awaken and shift from being the victim to being the victor of your circumstances; from living in consequence to living as the creator of your life. For me, the awakening began on the worst day.

The Worst Day

You never know when the worst day of your life is about to unfold. They each begin the same way, with a clean slate full of hope. Despite my hopeful thoughts on that warm, autumn morning, I would not be able to maintain them by dusk. I never liked the smell of hospitals, and their bright fluorescent lights make me dizzy, sometimes even nauseous. Waiting hours throughout each step of the process of waiting to be seen by a physician is even worse. Hospitals in New York City are always full, and visits are at best a four to five-hour ordeal.

Nevertheless, I waited patiently until the sound of footsteps drew closer and the echoes reverberating through the hall reached into my stomach and twisted my internal organs. My heart raced, my right leg bounced up and down uncontrollably, and the only reason I didn't bite my nails was that I was more germophobic than anxious, these days. Heat rose from my feet as hot flashes washed over my entire body. After all that I had been through up to this twenty-fourth year on earth, I prayed for a break. I deserved one, but we all know that's not how life works. We aren't given what we deserve, we attract what we are, and I was broken.

All the trauma my life produced up until that point, fragmented my mind like the stained-glass windows of the Sainte-Chapelle; beautiful but broken. Not that I knew of this essential piece of wisdom as I sat uncomfortably fidgeting in my seat, but I knew I was never the one to get a break. The mental chatter was relentless in its mission to instill fear throughout my body, but as much as I knew I was a few seconds away from a full-blown panic attack, I could not stop it.

"What if it's positive? Am I going to die? Who's going to protect my Julie? How will I keep my job if I'm too sick to work? Where will I live if I'm evicted from my apartment? Am I strong enough to survive this? I've always had a weak immune system. Is this it? I can't believe I'm going out like this! Is this really it, God? What did I do that was so terrible in a past life, that I had to suffer my entire existence in this one?"

Suddenly, the negative dialogue in my head stopped at the very click of the doorknob's turn. In came a middle-aged man, with piercing eyes, wearing a white, monogrammed, lab coat. He walked directly to his computer, sat in his chair and immediately began typing away at the keyboard. After what could have been a minute, but felt more like an hour, his chair turned in my direction, and he smiled asking, "How do you feel, Kristie?"

I wanted to burst out and say, "How do I feel? Are you serious? I feel curse words bubbling to the surface, about to erupt from my mouth to burn you! You're beating around the bush, when you know damn well, I only want one thing from you, and only a cruel man would keep the answer from me for longer than a second after he walked through that door. DO I HAVE CANCER OR NOT, DOC? Are my ovaries covered in cancerous cysts or are they benign?"

Perhaps my nerves and inner yogi kept my tongue paralyzed at that moment because none of those words escaped my lips. Instead, I took a deep breath and said, "I'm feeling quite nervous, Doc and I would like to know the results to that very important test we completed last week, remember? My biopsy? Please. Don't drag this out any longer." Even in my states of panic, I could always be passive aggressive to get my point across without taking full responsibility of having been unnerved.

His smirk confirmed his understanding of my strategic reply, while also affirming I already knew what he was about to say; however, nothing could have prepared me for the actual words he delivered. "I'm sorry, Ms. Alers but you have a cancerous tumor in your left ovary, and we will schedule to have it removed immediately. We still have to run a few more tests to make sure it's stage one, but a few rounds of radiation therapy will follow, and we will take it from there with regards to the chemotherapy needed thereafter."

My eyes overflowed with tears as they streamed down my face like an open faucet. It hurt to breathe, and my chest barely expanded with each inhalation, but my mind was distracted by thoughts of my 3-year-old daughter without her mother. I envisioned Julie never remembering who I was or how much I loved her. I lost my own mother to drugs around the same age and granted she didn't die, but her abandonment changed the course of my life forever. I didn't want history to repeat itself, where a little girl loses the one person who is supposed to be there for her as she grows up; the person that's meant to protect her even when it's unjustifiable; the person that loves her unconditionally throughout her entire journey towards becoming a woman in this great big world.

I didn't hear the next words out of my oncologist's mouth. Time stopped, and I retreated into a deeper space of being. All my senses suspended as I rose from my seat, grabbed my black leather purse and walked out of the office in a daze. The tears were on autopilot as I continued through the halls towards the exit of the hospital. With each stare and perplexed face, I passed, I felt more and more out-of-my-body and less and less human. That day, I'd walk over 200 city blocks and across two small bridges to get home, all the while talking to God about how I needed to heal so that my daughter would not have to endure a life like mine.

Awareness of the Unresolved

"So, what's so bad about having a life like yours, Kris? Looks like you turned out okay." said a young, sassy girl named Tasha, who in recent months earned a place in my tiny circle of trusted friends. We were inseparable since the first day I met her at a bartending school I was attending, a few months back. However, it was quite clear I hadn't opened up to her as much as I imagined. That's a lie, scratch that. I never believed I had opened up to her because I built a fortress around my past. I deflected personal questions by asking others to talk about themselves. I did the same with her until that day.

"What's so bad about having a life like mine? I repeated. "Well let's see, shall we? I was born to Puerto Rican baby boomers who fell prey to the drug infestation of NYC in the 1980s; specifically, heroin. I was abandoned by them for a few days in our Bronx apartment at age 4, along with my two brothers, ages 10 and 2. On the last day, my older brother found my paternal grandmother's phone number and called her to pick us up. She instantly did. Without a mother or father to fight for us, the courts granted my grandmother custody of all three of us. We went to live in Brooklyn, NY where we attended elementary school in Bay Ridge.

Because several of my grandmother's kids were drug addicts too, we often moved to avoid their problems. We lived in a few different neighborhoods in Brooklyn, El Paso, TX, and New Bedford, MA, but always returning to NYC in between. By the time I was 13, I had been to eight different schools and learned to be a loner, as I couldn't keep any long-term friends for more than a year or two because of all the moving. And the moving wasn't even the hardest part of that time. I was raped and molested by a family member at age 6, lost my uncle (the only person that actually fought to protect me) to the jail system, robbed of everything of value by the people I loved, visited jails to have a few hours with my parents and developed anxiety, depression, extreme panic attacks and high cholesterol - all by age 12.

Then I moved back with my mother, who petitioned for us but was not quite done with drugs. I dated the neighborhood heroin dealer who was 11 years my senior and a cocaine addict, and I was so lost, alone, wounded, afraid and confused, that I craved any human attention. I was 15 when he went to jail, and I spent half a year visiting him at Rikers Island and another taking a bus from NYC to upstate NY when he was transferred, sending him money and letters just like I was used to when I was a little girl, sending them to my parents and my uncle.

When he was released, he continued with his drug habit, became physically and mentally abusive, and I was isolated from all my friends and family. For six more years, I would be his sex slave and beaten for so much as arriving 2 minutes late from work. When I turned 20, I had devised a plan to escape, and just as I was ready to run, I fell ill. Turns out I was pregnant with Julie and was forced to stay, as it became a high-risk pregnancy and I had to remain bedridden for the first six months.

After Julie was born, he continued to abuse me and it wasn't until one night that he threw a remote control at my head and grabbed my daughter from her crib as if to drop her, that something clicked in me and I decided to fight back, escaping with nothing but the clothes on our backs.

But guess where we had to return? Yeah, there I was, knocking on the door of my mother's house again. I vowed to get out as quickly as possible, and as soon as I gathered enough money, I moved to Manhattan where no one knew my face or story. I managed to support us and raise my girl for three years until another bomb was dropped. I was diagnosed with ovarian cancer yesterday, and I'm afraid. Afraid that the only people in my life who can help me are the same ones that hurt me, and not that I haven't loosely mended the relationships over the years, but I don't want to have to give my daughter up and fear the lack of protection will leave her vulnerable to a life like mine."

Silence filled the air, and the clock ticks were suddenly audible. No one spoke for a few minutes, and then, her voice cracked as she said, "Damn, I'm sorry. I didn't know. I can't believe you are who you are after all that… come give me a hug, girl." Feeling her warm arms wrap around me right after bearing my soul, was like a safety blanket wrapped around young

Kristie; young Kiki. It was Kiki who needed the warmth of a woman's, motherly and nurturing arms. I found solace right then, as my tears fell and soaked her shirt. She never let go. It was as if she could hear little Kiki telling her to hold on forever.

The next day, I realized there were unresolved issues I suppressed for over twenty years, but I didn't know what to do with them. For twenty years, I was surviving life subjected to the wants and desires of others because the void left by my parent's abandonment stunted my ability to feel worthy, accepted, loved, and whole. The sexual abuse only added to those feelings, and the domestic violence of my first common law marriage was an inevitable result of what I had learned about relationships my whole life. It took many years before I was able to understand that I was wounded and needed to heal to be in a healthy relationship.

Round 1 – Fight!

My fight against cancer was long and brutal because after I survived ovarian cancer, I was diagnosed with Acute Myeloid Leukemia (AML), a type of blood cancer. I was told it was a rare occurrence but that it was possible the radiation therapy administered for ovarian cancer caused the AML. It was this cancer that led me face to face with my mortality. It was aggressive and ugly. It took my hair, my weight, my energy, my range of motion, my identity, my money, my job, my apartment, my daughter, and my dignity.

But for as much as it was ugly, it was equally beautiful, as it was this cancer that forced me to become aware of the strength I had within; the strength I had always used instinctively, to get through the adversity of my past. It was also this cancer that created a window of opportunity to meet a wonderful man, who became my best friend, in the midst of it all. It was in his demonstration of loving support, patience and generosity of his time and resources that I began to fall in love with someone worthy of all I had been giving to the wrong people.

My daughter came to visit me one weekend. I thought I was feeling strong enough to have her, but when she arrived, I could not function. I spent the entire night in the bathroom throwing up, while she watched TV in the living room. I threw up so much, my stomach cramped like a washing machine's spin cycle, unbearably wringing my intestines of every last drop of water. I curled into position around the outside of the cold bowl while thumping sounds in my head amplified with each eye-bursting pulse. The irritations were compounded by the bright light, the temperature in the room, the smell of ammonia, and the bitter-sour taste of bile.

There was nothing left in me, as I laid half naked in a fetal position, trying to find some relief on the cold, white, ceramic tiles of the bathroom floor. My four-foot three-inch frame was accompanied by 95 pounds of bones and organs, and I was losing the battle within. I said to God, "Take me! Take me because I have nothing left in me to fight anymore. I can't even take care of my daughter and if you are a merciful God, just take me!" Just as I said, "Take me!" for the last time, I heard a knock on the door. I dragged myself up to sit against the wall, and my daughter walked in saying:

"Mom are you okay?"

"No, honey, I'm not, and I think I have to call Nana to come to pick you up because I can't take care of you. You haven't even eaten a thing. I'm so sorry, baby."

"I did Mom, I ate a sandwich, and I made one for you too. When I'm sick, you make me better so now you're sick and I will make you better, okay Mommy?"

My heart broke. Here I was, lying on the floor ready to give up and my five-year-old daughter was in the other room making me a sandwich and thinking about how to make me better. I knew it was God telling me to get up off the floor and fight for her. I screamed as I uncurled my body, got up, washed my face and dug deep to muster the strength I needed to go lay on the couch with my daughter. From then on, I fought, digging for the strength within to fight the only way I could; with knowledge.

Round 2 – Fight!

Growing up, I was an excellent student, despite my troubles at home. I enjoyed school and learning. It not only gave me refuge, but I always wanted to learn about the world around me. My study habits and work ethic were impeccable, which I carried throughout my entire academic career. Up until this point in my life, I hadn't finished college. I was out of school for over six years, but I began studying and researching everything

I could get my hands on about cancer and soon enough, I was led to alternative therapies, curing cancer with nutrition, and lifestyle change.

During my research, I came across the Gerson Therapy and something about the extreme juicing of organic vegetables and fruits, resonated with me. It made sense that juicing would allow for the absorption of a concentrated amount of nutrition into my body, and a deeper intelligence within me knew it was what I needed to survive the extreme vomiting and loss of nutrients. Every complication, ache, and pain I was experiencing was coming from the fact that I could not nourish my body. It wasn't long before I reached out to the developer's daughter in California, Charlotte Gerson, and scheduled a visit.

She was brilliant, and after seeing me and mapping out a food/diet and supplement plan, I learned how to juice properly. I was careful not to mix fruits and vegetables, use only organic produce, make more than 20 different yet specific juices a day, and take enemas and supplements on a strict schedule. It was extreme, but I knew that extreme times call for extreme measures.

It helped to endure the chemo treatments, and I began feeling better. I was gaining weight, and my blood count was rising. From that point on, I kept juicing and eating optimally for my body, as it healed itself enough to qualify for a blood and marrow transplant. This gave me the motivation to continue.

Once I started to feel the amazing results, I had the energy to do more throughout the days, so I simultaneously began reading self-help books, participating in Oprah Winfrey's free meditation specials with Deepak Chopra, and naturally healing myself from the inside out.

Round 3 – You Win!

After the transplant, I spent the next ten months back and forth to the hospital, receiving better and better test results and ultimately given the talk I had been waiting to hear since the worst day; "Ms. Alers, it is my pleasure to safely say you are in remission."

We were ecstatic. Doctors couldn't believe that I had even stopped taking the immunosuppressants and my body never rejected the transplant. I was reunited with my daughter and brought her to live with me again, and by this time, the man I had fallen in love with, was now my husband and our blended family of four was whole and happy.

Five years later and we were cancer free and stronger than ever. We were living a health-conscious, vegetarian life and were so strong, we got pregnant. Doctors advised my chances were always slim to get pregnant, and after the whole cancer tribulation, I should not try to get pregnant, my reproductive organs may not be strong and healthy enough to carry a baby to full term. I assumed we were defying the odds again as I knew only God could give that kind of advice. When we passed the four-month mark, we began to share the news with our families. We picked out a name, Aiden Anthony, and I was falling deeper and deeper in love with the being growing inside me.

You're Never Done Growing

At 20 weeks I started spotting, so we went for a checkup and was advised all was well. "Just a bit of spotting was normal," they said. A week later, I started having contractions and almost immediately, blood flowed copiously down my legs. My husband rushed me to the hospital, running red lights as I cried for the blood to stop. Upon checking me into the emergency labor room, I was told I was having a miscarriage. My son was twenty-one weeks in utero. That's five months and one week in utero. He was a fully formed baby on the outside, but his internal organs were not fully developed. It was then that I was told, "You will give birth to a lifeless baby, Ms. Alers. Are you with me?"

I couldn't breathe, I started hyperventilating, and I passed out. I woke to the most excruciating pain I had ever experienced. I was going to give birth naturally but violently, as the body shows no mercy when rejecting a baby. The contractions were turbulent and destructive. I laid on the table being asked to push, but I couldn't believe what was happening. The pain my body and my heart were experiencing at the same time, sent me into shock and I didn't have to push, my body was doing it all by itself. I cried and screamed at the doctor, "Please save my baby! Stop the contractions! Do something!"

My body was pushing, and I was concurrently holding him inside. It was a surreal fight between my body's autopilot and me, as I screamed, "I can't lose my baby! Aiden is a miracle baby, and he can't leave me before I mother him!" My tears felt like blood streaming down my face as I watched every single person in the room cry while I begged God to save my son. Minutes later, he was born, and a member of the clergy asked to pray over us. I cradled my son's body praying he was alive. I couldn't let him go. I kept examining his features and kissing his still warm, tiny face. When they came to take him away, I begged to keep him. They soon took him from my hands but not without my husband releasing my grip to free him from my grasp.

Giving my son a proper burial was the single most painful day of my life. Accessing the strength within was difficult. Nothing has left a deeper gash imprinted on my soul than the loss of my baby boy. I wept at the funeral while the priest tried to bring light to the darkest day, but I could not grab hold of it and take refuge in its warmth. It wasn't until the ceremony was over that I looked to the sky and the sun's rays warmed my face. I felt Aiden at that moment, and I knew God would get me through this too.

There's a Method to the Divine's Madness

In the year to come, I would become pregnant again, and despite the scares of blood spots and preeclampsia, the high-risk pregnancy would go full term. We were blessed with the miracle of another son, whom we named Lucas Anthony. During that year, I returned to college, began seeing a psychosocial psychologist, and immersed myself in healing spiritually. In one of my sessions with my psych, he asked me a question I had never asked myself before. He said, "What do you want? For the past few weeks, you have shared with me what you don't want, why don't you tell me what you DO want?"

I was quiet. I couldn't think of anything other than, "I want to be cancer free, and I want my family to be happy, healthy and safe." To which he replied, "You already have that and if you haven't acknowledged that you have that, acknowledge it, be thankful for it, and let's move on. Now, what do you want?" For the first time, I realized I had been living my life from a victim's perspective, in fear, worrying, and making decisions that were based on what I didn't want.

It was an "AHA" moment. What did I want? I never realized I could ask that question much less devise a plan to take small steps towards achieving whatever it was that I wanted. I went home thinking of the kind of life I wanted to live. I created a list of what I wanted in life and went on devising a plan for each desire. Through the years, with each accomplishment I'd check off, I was moving more and more towards the life I had always dreamed of living. The path then became very clear and effortless to me as my purpose was revealed.

I have spent every day of my life, in training for the career I've chosen; better said, the career that has chosen me, as it aligns with my purpose. I realized my purpose was relative to the trauma I experienced. What I once thought was tragic and horrific, has turned into blessings and a resource of strength.

Once I began working on healing my wounds, I was called to continue down the path of helping others to heal theirs. I recognized this when my desires began shaping my intentions, which brought opportunities and resources to continue down that path effortlessly. I am excellent at coaching others towards their own transformations because of the adversity, not despite it, and as I move forward in life accomplishing goals and reaching levels of success and happiness I once prayed for, I thank God for every second of my life.

What I have learned is that life will always impart obstacles upon your journey for the purpose of transformation. The test is to tap into the strength that's already within you. Understand that life is a long journey, wherein each department of your life will be challenged with variously sized battles, but that with each triumphant lesson learned, and each victorious feat applied, the experiences will accumulate to bigger and more profound transformations, and the obstacles become opportunities for growth.

So, accept all your struggles, build an arsenal of lessons from which to draw strength and wisdom, become aware of the issues that need resolution, take action to develop and work through those issues personally, and ultimately implement a new way of living that's conducive to the life of your dreams. It's not simple, but it's worth it and if I can do it, so can you!

About Kristie A. Alers

Kristie A. Alers is a Holistic Health and Wellness Coach, Biomedical Engineer, Certified Yoga Teacher, Reiki Master, and founder of Hybrid Health & Wellness. As a women's personal development expert, she teaches women how to heal and draw strength from the parts of their lives that keep them from moving forward in their careers and personal lives. Her company's mission is to facilitate the awakening of the power that lies within each woman, so they can shed limiting belief systems, shift their mindsets, and become successful, proactive creators of the lives they desire to live. Her company's methodology consists of bridging the gap between the native and modern approaches towards health and wellness, using the best of both worlds to support her clients optimally. She believes that women become truly successful when they are whole, inspired, supported and encouraged to think outside the box for solutions to problems that plague their goals and dreams. Drawing from the eclectic disciplines in which she has earned her accolades, she is giftedly strategic at innovating effective health program packages for her clients and students that go beyond just the physical.

Adverse childhood experiences and trauma are what she calls the "stagnant double," as her research and experiences have proved that those who have suffered either of the two or both, harbor stagnant energy in their bodies and stunted development in their minds and thought processes. With more than 10 years of health and wellness experience and being on both sides of the spectrum as patient and health professional, Kristie believes that harboring such energy over many years causes the body to manifest dis-ease. Her own life began with adverse childhood experiences from abandonment by her drug-addicted parents at age 4, to childhood sexual abuse, to living as a raped and battered woman throughout her first marriage. By the time she was 24, she had suffered from high cholesterol, depression, anxiety, extreme panic attacks, battled ovarian cancer and shortly after that acute myeloid leukemia due to the protocol radiation therapy administered. Her determination to heal led her to extensively study the human condition, the body as a machine and its spiritual component, resulting in studying biomedical engineering and learning about alternative healing modalities. As she immersed herself in examining her ancestry in Puerto Rico, enrolling in a yoga teacher training in NYC and simultaneously stumbling upon a Reiki Master from Thailand, she came to the realization that good health is not only dependent upon the body's physicality but by the integration of the mind, body and soul's ability to cohesively exist in harmony and balance, as they are nourished with respect to individual needs, culture, and preconditioning.

As passion and purpose for her studies grew, Kristie was led to specialize in meditation and yoga therapy, graduating from a 200Hr Yoga Teacher Training at Pure Yoga in NYC and 300+ added certification hours through Savi Yoga & Tantric Meditation Master Trainer, Yogi Charu and Prema Yoga Institute, for yoga therapy discipline. She earned a BS and MS in Biomedical Engineering from DeVry College of New York and certified in Developing Psychic Awareness while ultimately becoming a Reiki Level III Master in Bangkok, Thailand. She is also certified by The Institute of Applied Holistic Health Sciences (IAHHS) and most recently certified as an Integrative Nutrition Health Coach from the Institute of Integrative Nutrition® in New York.

Kristie resides in New York City with her husband and three children. Aside from running a thriving wellness business, she home schools her 5-year-old son and volunteers time teaching yoga and meditation to the United States Military Veterans and trauma victims. She enjoys immersing herself in nature, continuing her development in energy healing, building women up, cooking healthier versions of her Spanish cultural cuisine, and bringing health and healing awareness to her community through her thought-provoking workshops and keynote speeches.

Some of her favorite things outside of delivering a kick-ass presentation at an all-male board meeting are; bare feet in the grass; Grey's Anatomy; 5am morning stillness; squatting 200lbs with her favorite spotter and body-builder husband; sporadic, midnight-park adventures with the kids; her "Mommy's Sippy Cup" labeled, wine glass filled with organic, Italian, Cabernet, after a long week and most recently, she aspires to train for the Rock's Titan Games, regardless of acceptance but more importantly to teach her teenage daughters that a healthy woman knows there are no limits.

Hybrid Health & Wellness (HHW) operates in the Bronx, NY but is equipped to handle private consultation anywhere in the world with reliable internet service.

Contact Information

Kristie A. Alers
Hybrid Health & Wellness
Website: www.hybridhealthandwellness.com
Email: KristieAlers@hybridhealthandwellness.com

Chapter 3

Challenges Are What Make Life Interesting; Overcoming Them Is What Makes Life Meaningful

By: Alais B. Reta

Life for me started as a premature baby. I was born six weeks early and weighed in at just 5lbs. 2oz., which earned me some time inside of an incubator for the first week of my life, while doctors evaluated me. It was a stressful time for both of my parents. The medical world back then didn't have the advancements it does now, so being six weeks early was a big issue back then. Once I was finally released from the hospital, my parents brought me home, and I began to lose more weight, eventually getting down to 4lbs. 8oz, just a few days after being back home. Thankfully, I finally started gaining weight, and there was no need for me to have another stay in the hospital.

Many factors contributed to my earlier than average start to my life. My mother smoking and consuming alcohol throughout her entire pregnancy with me were contributing factors to a less than ideal beginning for me. But, during the early 1970s, smoking, and drinking while pregnant wasn't as frowned upon, as it is today. They didn't have the knowledge or scientific studies that show these habits directly contribute to low birth weight babies and prematurity as we know today. So many mothers-to-be back then continued with these types of habits, their entire pregnancy. They didn't realize that everything they inhaled or consumed, was directly affecting their unborn child in very detrimental ways.

My gut health, vitamin and mineral levels as a newborn, were less than ideal, due to being born prematurely. Babies who are born with a compromised gut and immune system, tend to have health issues throughout their lives, which develop into more significant health issues later in their lives. This proved to be very accurate for me. Illness is something I have dealt with quite often throughout my life, especially during my childhood years and continuing into my young adult years. During my adolescence, I had several chronic bouts of strep throat that never seemed to end — even suffering through tonsillitis a few times. Bronchitis was another illness I went through very often. Although, I have often wondered if my bouts of bronchitis were due to both of my parents smoking and my inhaling the second-hand smoke throughout my childhood, especially since I already had a strike against me due to my lungs being underdeveloped at birth.

In addition to health issues, I also dealt with gut issues very frequently during my childhood. Which I feel could be attributed to many factors. Things like stress in my home environment, excessive antibiotics consumed for many illnesses, a poor diet consisting of primarily processed foods, not drinking enough water, consuming too many high sugar foods and drinks, the list goes on and on. My gut health was a mess as a child! But I wouldn't find out just how bad it was, until later in life.

The Processed Food Extravaganza!

In the early 1970s, the way people addressed their health, lifestyle choices and diet, was very different than today. What was accepted back then as healthy, is not even close to what is known to be healthy today? During this era, many people smoked, enjoyed their alcoholic beverages and loved processed food for the quick and easy prep that went with it. During the 1950s is when the processed food revolution began. Everyone loved the idea of easy prep from a can or a box. Long gone were the days of making healthy, closest to nature meals.

By the time I was born, it was not uncommon that most meals were created from cream-based soups in a can or meals made out of ingredients in a box. Cream of Mushroom, Celery or Chicken soup were staples of many meals. Casseroles were a huge hit back then. It was so easy to throw together a greasy casserole, filled with canned vegetables, cream soups, fatty meats, tater tots, etc. Although they were convenient, they were probably one of the unhealthiest things that people consumed, right next to foods fried in unhealthy oils.

My mother's southern grandmother taught her to cook. So, we ate a fantastic amount of fried and heavily creamed foods, with a serving of sodium filled, canned vegetables on the side. Although my dad always had a garden and my mom would spend time at the end of the season canning the harvest, they were both still guilty of cooking from processed food options, rather than going the fresher route. It was the thing to do back then. Everyone was doing it. Lifestyles were changing, and everyone was jumping on the quick and easy food prep bandwagon. There was a lot of time and money spent on marketing these types of foods to people back then. It was appealing to save time and still get a meal they felt was nourishing. Never questioning if this food was healthy for them or not. Unfortunately, nobody realized at the time, how detrimental this style of eating would be to their health in the long-term.

Decades of Health Issues

In my early 20's, I was diagnosed with scarlet fever after a long bout of strep throat that didn't heal completely. I remember feeling so confused, trying to figure out how I could have contracted an illness that was rarely even heard of anymore. The prescription that was given to me for this was a strong dose of steroids and antibiotics. After taking all the medication as I was directed to do; I ended up gaining thirty pounds from the steroids and felt miserable! Those pounds took a while to come off too.

Not too long after having scarlet fever, I was rushed to the hospital with severe stomach pain, nothing like I had ever felt before! It was excruciatingly painful! Within a few hours of being at the hospital, it was discovered that my appendix was very close to rupturing and I had to have emergency surgery to remove it. This was my first surgery and my first organ removal. The surgery went well, and I recovered well. Again, antibiotics and pain killers were prescribed during my recovery.

I met my husband when I was 24 years old. Not long after meeting him, I was diagnosed with Mitral Valve Prolapse, after experiencing some odd heart palpitations that would come and go periodically. MVP is an issue where the valve on your heart does not open and close correctly on its own. This can cause a fluttering feeling and skipped heartbeats. My cardiologist prescribed a beta blocker to control them, which I took for 17 years. Years later I would discover this was one of many misdiagnoses I had been given over the years.

My husband and I got married in November 1996. During the early years of our marriage, we ate a diet filled with high protein, low fat and had a consistent and tough workout schedule at the gym. We were both in excellent shape physically. Eventually, we decided we wanted to have a family and started trying to conceive our first child. Unfortunately, it was soon discovered that it wasn't going to be an easy process to get pregnant. Fertility became a big issue, after a little over a year of trying with no success.

My Ob/Gyn was concerned that my strict workout routines and limited diet were contributing to my issues. So, he told me to take some time off from the gym, to eat a healthy diet (also known as the standard American diet) and put me on the fertility drug Clomid. Of course, I immediately gained a lot of weight with the change in diet and reduced gym time. But after taking Clomid for a few months and a short getaway with my husband to relax, we were finally able to conceive.

The day after my 26th birthday, I gave birth to our son by emergency cesarean section. His birth was a very stressful time as he suffered a brain bleed at birth, due to the delivery doctor's negligence. The stroke he suffered at birth caused him to lose full function of the right side of his body and left him with only a partial function of his right hand, and tightness in his right leg. Our son was eventually given a diagnosis of Cerebral Palsy.

I was distraught over this experience, so my OB/GYN put me on the anti-depressant Paxil, to try to help with the sadness and overwhelming feelings. I remember it made me feel like I was floating in the clouds and I quit taking it after a week. The stress that I endured through this time was nothing any mother should have to deal with. But I eventually got through it, and our son has grown into an amazing young man.

By the time I was in my late 20's I had gone through two long bouts of pneumonia as well as many colds and other illnesses. Which, you guessed it, meant more antibiotics consumed and more destruction of my gut health. How I wish I knew then what I know now.

In my early 30's we decided we wanted to try and have one more baby. Once again, fertility was an issue. Back on the Clomid I went. This time it didn't seem to work well at all. It took almost two years of being back and forth on Clomid and being at a place in my life where I told my husband, "if I don't get pregnant by my 33rd birthday, I don't want to try anymore." The fertility treatments and the side effects that went with the Clomid were putting a strain on my body. I was okay with having one child at that point, and so was my husband. Thankfully, our daughter had other plans, and we found out about two months before I turned 33, that I was pregnant with her.

Everything went well with her birth but afterward is when my health started to take a significant decline. I developed odd allergies after her birth. One, in particular, stands out for me. I could no longer cut up hot peppers without plastic gloves. My hands would swell up and turn bright red if I touched the hot peppers. I found this out a few short weeks after she was born when I was trying to make some Pico de Gallo salsa. In addition to this odd allergy, the years of antibiotic use were finally catching up to me. I ended up seeing a gastroenterologist for the constant burning in my gut. He performed an endoscopy and a colonoscopy.

The results from these tests indicated chronic Gastritis, GERD and Duodenitis. He put me on potent doses of Proton Pump Inhibitors (PPI's), to reduce the excess acid he said was causing these chronic issues. I took these pills faithfully, every day, for seven years. Truly believing they were helping me, not realizing that these pills are intended only to be used at short intervals.

By my mid 30's I was starting to have peri-menopause symptoms; hot flashes, night sweats, etc. My OB/GYN decided it was best to put me back on birth control to help with these issues even though I had my fallopian tubes removed after the birth of our daughter and no longer needed birth control to prevent pregnancy. I believed my doctor was giving me good advice and went back on them. In total, off and on, I was on birth control for seventeen years.

In my late 30's, both of my parents passed away - my dad in 2007 and my mom in 2010. This was a tough time for me emotionally and stress-wise. My stress was through the roof! In addition to my parents, we also lost several family members on my husband's side of the family during this time. As well as my sister's kids being taken away by child protective services and our dog and cat died, all within a few short years. Being that I am the one everyone turns to in my family to deal with these things, this is an area of time that contributed significantly to my health crisis. I was forced to deal with everything that was involved with laying my parents to rest. This included the planning and the financial end of things.

Our Transformative Journey

To say I was stressed out, would be an understatement. I had hit my limit mentally, and my weak body had hit its max on what it could handle. I am so thankful for my husband, who was there for me when it felt like my whole world was crashing down on me. During this time my gut issues were becoming unbearable. Nothing was helping. My symptoms just kept getting more and more severe with each passing day. The extremely high amounts of stress were taking its toll and was a significant factor in my deteriorating health.

By the time I turned 40, I was a mess health wise and gut-wise. I was having chronic 24/7 nausea, dizziness, fatigue, all sorts of uncomfortable symptoms. After two more Endoscopy's of my gut and a HIDA scan, I was told by my gastrointestinal doctor that my gallbladder was only functioning at 33% and he recommended it be taken out. There were no stones present. It just wasn't functioning as it should be. When I spoke with the surgeon, I remember him telling me that I was right on the edge of whether it should be removed or not. He said he would remove it if I wanted him too. But, it wasn't in the medically necessary range. Because I trusted my gastrointestinal doctor, I opted to have my gallbladder removed. This is one of the biggest regrets and mistakes I think I made in my journey. I wish I could go back and think twice on my decision to remove it, knowing what I know now.

After my gallbladder was removed, it seemed like the removal had solved my issues. At least for a short time anyway. After about two months of recovery time, we ventured to California to enjoy some time at Disneyland, attend our nephew and nieces wedding and get away from the daily things for a bit. During the drive, I started to feel nauseous. By the time we arrived at Disneyland, I was feeling pretty sick. I was unable to spend time with my family enjoying the park. The nausea and stomach pain I felt, was worse than any flu I had ever experienced. I was completely convinced that I had food poisoning. By the time we got back home from our vacation, I was feeling much worse. All I wanted to do was lay down. At this point, I knew this wasn't food poisoning or the flu. It was something much worse.

I decided a trip to my gastrointestinal doctor was in order. This time he prescribed me a different PPI (acid reducer) to try because after all, my acid must be very high, even though the one organ, my gallbladder, that helped with boosting my bile levels and aid in digestion had been removed. Unfortunately, appointments with this doctor started happening much more frequently for quite a few months, as I tried to figure out what was causing all my horrific symptoms. He finally ordered another HIDA scan to see how fast I was digesting a meal.

The results from this test showed that I was digesting at only 50% of average. That was when I was diagnosed with Gastroparesis. He told me my gut had lost the ability to digest food and function normally. He prescribed something called Reglan, which carried a black box warning label on it, and told me to take this medicine. I took the medication for four days without any noticeable improvements. My intuition kept telling me that taking this medicine was a terrible idea, in addition to how horrible it made me feel. I decided to stop taking it.

So, I decided to make another appointment with my gastrointestinal doctor and asked him what my options were at this point. He indicated that the only other option was the UCLA medical center, where they could perform a surgery on me and install a medical device called a Gastric Stimulator, inside me. This device uses an electrical charge to stimulate gut motility. Which in theory, helps food digest properly. It is like a pacemaker for the gut.

The thought of this was overwhelming! I remember leaving that appointment with my husband, just feeling so defeated and exhausted. Not quite sure which way to turn next. I knew I wasn't going to allow myself to go through yet another surgery. That wasn't going to happen. All I knew at that point, was that I wanted to feel better quickly, and I had to figure out what was going on.

Sometimes You Need to Take Control

The next few months were filled with trips to many doctors, including my primary doctor. He ran all sorts of bloodwork, hoping he would be able to help me. He made a diagnosis of mononucleosis based on some of my symptoms and elevated titers on my bloodwork. Per his advice, I was to let the mono run its course, I went almost two months just sleeping and resting. But my symptoms never ceased. They just kept getting worse. Nausea, dizziness, extreme weight loss, headaches, shaking, hot and cold flashes, severe breathlessness, the list went on and on. Once he realized he didn't know and couldn't figure out what was wrong with me, he immediately pulled out the "you have anxiety" card and offered me some anti-depressants, of which I declined. I knew I didn't have anxiety or depression like he was trying to make me believe. Because it was all in my head, right? Wrong!

Thank goodness for decent insurance through all of this. In just one of the years I was sick, my medical bills were over $10,000 out of pocket for us. The worst part of it all was I still had no answers! At this point I was done with all the bloodwork, the nonstop tests, x-rays, CT scans, MRI's, HIDA scans, the condescending attitudes of medical professionals and unbelievable nausea, exhaustion, dizziness, always feeling like I was out of breath and just the feeling of complete despair. This same song and dance, with no answers, was getting old. I finally decided enough was enough! I was a smart woman, and I would figure this out myself. It had become evident to me that the doctors didn't have a clue as to what was causing me to feel so unbelievably sick. I decided to take on a holistic approach to my health, and this was where my healing journey began.

My Road Too Wellness

I joined a few groups on social media that were for people dealing with Gastroparesis. It was in these groups that I met two ladies, who have become great friends. They invited me to a group where I was taught how to manage the symptoms of GP, using a clean way of eating and essential oils to help manage the chronic symptoms. I was finally able to get some relief from the 24/7 nausea that wouldn't go away. I was also ready to start weaning off of my acid reducers. I remember how happy I felt, to finally get a bit of relief. But I still had many other symptoms that were hanging around and were still unexplained. Things like red dots on the roof of my mouth, always being out of breath after walking just a few steps, random bouts of dizziness, muscles aches, ringing in my ears, eczema and the chronic fatigue that was there, no matter how much I slept.

After doing a tremendous amount of reading and research on my own, I decided the first thing I needed to do was make an appointment with an allergist, to confirm food intolerances or allergies. Thankfully, this turned out to be an excellent thing. The allergist suspected Celiac, but because I told him I had been tested for that with a blood test and endoscopy and it had come back negative, he diagnosed me instead as being NCGS (Non-Celiac Gluten Sensitive).

I immediately went on a gluten-free diet. For the first time in almost a year, I finally started to get some relief from the chronic nausea I was having, my eczema disappeared, and some of my energy began to return. After being entirely gluten-free for a few months, I soon realized that this was not the only underlying issue with my health. I needed to dig deeper and find someone who could help me discover why I was still struggling with symptoms like breathlessness, dizziness, shakiness, occasional anxious feeling, etc... That was when I found a health coach who truly changed my life and helped me recover completely. He believed me when I told him what I was feeling. He didn't tell me I had anxiety or downplay my symptoms. He assured me this wasn't all in my head and that we would get to the bottom of things, which he did just that!

My health coach, with the help of his wife, who was a chiropractor, were able to get to the bottom of everything for me. They did hair testing, and they had me do specific bloodwork. I finally had real answers. The biggest thing I had been suffering from was a chronic magnesium deficiency. I also had deficient potassium and zinc levels and crazy high calcium levels. None of these levels were ever checked previously by medical professionals. My health coach also determined my thyroid was not operating efficiently. He explained to me that my gut health had been critically affected by years of antibiotics, acid reducers, other medications, and the chronic stress I had endured over the years. He also explained that because I was born premature, I was at least 50% deficient in the average levels of healthy gut bacteria, vitamins, and minerals, at birth. He created a specific protocol for me to follow, based on my results. Within a week or two of starting this protocol, I began to feel significantly better. By the time I was two months into the protocol, I was starting to feel good.

About six months after this all started with my health coach, I was able to finally begin removing prescription meds I had been on for years. No more birth control for hormones, and no more daily beta blocker pill for the Mitral Valve Prolapse I had been diagnosed with 17 years prior. My undiagnosed chronic magnesium deficiency caused my palpitations. Not once, in 17 years, did my cardiologist run bloodwork on me to test my magnesium levels. Not once! This issue could have been resolved by a simple blood test many years earlier. Instead, I was misdiagnosed for years and endured EKG's and Echocardiograms unnecessarily. I shudder to think of all the adverse effects the beta blocker had on my body all those years.

Once I started to feel much better and had regained my quality of health and life, I started reaching out to others who were struggling with unexplained health issues. I knew I had to help in some way if I could. So, I would tell people my story in hopes they could learn something beneficial from it, that would help them. I told my story to anyone who would listen. Sure, some people looked at me like I had ten heads, and that was okay.

I couldn't expect everyone to believe me when I told them I healed myself through clean eating, keeping a positive mindset, and a few specific supplements. Most people have been taught that western medicine is the go-to when it comes to being sick and trying to get relief. What people haven't learned is that Western medical doctors are taught in school to treat symptoms only. They are not trained to find the root cause, which is the basis of holistic healing; finding the root cause and healing with foods closest to nature, and a few supplements to rebuild and fill in nutrition gaps. Add in the power of positive thinking and maintaining a positive mindset. This is known as the "mind-body" connection, and it is very real.

My journey to becoming a health coach started after some pushing from a few family members and close friends, many of whom I had helped with health challenges. I decided the way I could give back to others was to pursue a career in health coaching. This is what led me to the Institute for Integrative Nutrition. Attending IIN has given me the extra tools to supplement my already vast knowledge of holistic health and look past symptoms and understand the importance of finding the "root cause." Because finding the root cause and addressing it is when true healing and health transformation begins. In addition to what I have learned at IIN; I have also met many amazing, like-minded people who have become friends. This adventure has been fantastic for me, both personally and professionally.

We all have it in us to make healthy decisions and to take control of our health. We are indeed our own best health advocates. Never underestimate your ability to heal yourself. Our bodies are amazing, in that when they are given proper nutrition, self-care and the nurturing they need, they can rebound and bounce back better than they were before. This is the truth.

Throughout my healing journey, I have learned to believe in myself, to trust my intuition, do not give up and always ask questions. I have also learned the importance and amazing healing powers of reducing stress, keeping a positive mindset and eating as close to nature as possible. As the saying goes, food is medicine in its natural form.

One of the greatest gifts I was able to give to myself, was finally achieving my health and wellness after struggling through years of illness. I feel very fortunate to now have the opportunity to share what I have learned with the world and to help as many people as I can, in achieving their optimal health and wellness. Leaving behind a strong "ripple effect" as I go. One of my favorite quotes by Gandhi is, "Be the change that you want to see in the world." I plan on doing exactly that!

About Alais B. Reta

Alais B. Reta is the founder and CEO of Alais B. Health and Wellness. The primary focus of her company is to help people achieve and maintain their health and wellness goals, through holistically based, health coaching services. She truly believes that a healthy mindset and a healthy body equals a happy life!

Alais earned her health coaching certification as an Integrative Nutrition Health Coach, from the Institute for Integrative Nutrition®, in March 2019. She is educated and certified holistically, to assist, teach and guide people in many areas of health and wellness. However, she specializes in helping her clients learn to heal and manage digestive health issues and gluten sensitivity issues. These are areas of her health she has struggled significantly within the past and was able to overcome using holistic methods, without the use of prescription medications.

She truly believes in the power of holistic healing. Helping her clients achieve truly sustainable, long term transformation, that starts by finding the root cause of their health issues, is where Alais excels as a health coach. She uses many techniques with her clients that assist in mindset, lifestyle and dietary changes. She offers a wide range of services that include, one-on-one coaching, group coaching, online groups, webinars, and she is happy to customize programs for her clients, as needed.

Alais's passion for health and wellness started after overcoming her significant health challenges a few years ago. Through these challenges, she witnessed the fantastic power of holistic healing that comes from a healthy and happy mindset, as well as a healthy diet filled with foods that are closest to nature. It was at this point in her life that she realized there was a significant calling on her to share her journey with others and guide them in the same, holistic, and healthy way she helped herself.

Our Transformative Journey

Throughout her life, she has always found great joy in helping others. Becoming a health coach has given her the tools, education, and confidence, to do her part helping to educate people on how to regain their best health and live their best lives. Through her health journey, life experiences and her story of triumph overcoming her debilitating health issues, she can relay to others that they too can overcome their health challenges. That even in the worst of times, there is always hope. Every tomorrow we are gifted is a new day to move in a positive direction, to always believe in ourselves and to never give up.

Before she opened her health coaching business, Alais enjoyed 14 years at home, raising her children. She is very proud of her kids and truly feels that motherhood has been the most rewarding job she has ever had. Her son Jason Jr, who is 20 years old, and her daughter Kayla, who is 13 years old, are truly her pride and joy. Before becoming a stay at home parent, she spent eight years, as a successful Assistant Escrow Officer in the Title/Real Estate Industry.

Alais currently resides in Henderson, Nevada. Where she lives with her two children and husband Jason Sr., with whom she has been happily married for 22 years. They share their home with their furry kids, and two goofy Boxer dogs named Shammi and Annabelle and her daughters two guinea pigs, Punky and Ginger.

When she isn't coaching clients, she can be found enjoying time with her family, relaxing outdoors by the pool, cooking up some delicious and healthy food, baking fantastic gluten-free desserts, exercising (yoga and weight training), or reading a good book.

Contact Information

Alais B. Reta
Alais B. Health and Wellness
Website: www.alaisb.com
Email: alaisb.heathandwellness@gmail.com

Chapter 4

Listen to Your Gut

By: Anna K. Rubano

Those who have felt called to a specific field or career can recall a defining moment that changed the course of their path. Whether it came from a negative or positive circumstance, that moment brought them to where they are in the present.

As Holistic Health coaches, we were taught that our work could create for those we serve defining decisive moments that function as part of a healing process. But just as there exists a positive ripple effect, I believe certain choices and actions can create a negative ripple effect. I also believe there is always time to change the course of the ripple.

For me, that defining ripple-effect moment would affect not only my health but how I lived my life for years to come. A month before my twentieth birthday, I made a decision that would change my life, my health, and my opinion of myself. It would leave an imprint that I would spend years working to remove or as I would later realize, accept on some level.

Meant to Be

I was born two months premature, in Athens, Greece. My parents told me I was the size of a rabbit with two big eyes [thankfully, I grew into my eyes]. Looking down at her beloved child in the incubator, my mom instinctively knew that I would live. The attending nurse reassured her saying, "This one is a fighter." Indeed, the nurse was prescient. It wasn't at first evident, however, that I had a fiery spirit and determination.

Growing up, I was a sensitive child. I had a strong reaction to people and situations. I couldn't explain why I would feel uncomfortable when meeting someone new, or if something felt wrong in my environment, but being able to pick up the energy of people in a room, I often felt very anxious. My inability to express the strong feelings that I didn't quite understand brought frustration and fear. Overwhelmed, I turned inward. My imagination fueled a constant stream of never-ending ideas, hopes, and aspirations. It was clear to me that I was created for more than just existing.

But despite such affirmation, I never really felt like I belonged anywhere. Try as I might, I never honestly thought I fit in. Though I would be expressive when I didn't like something, or something made me uncomfortable, I was so only in the comfort of those I knew. Yes, I had a fiery, strong personality that could be bold, confident, and passionate, but I struggled with deep insecurities that stemmed from a need for perfectionism. I was an all-or-nothing type of person. If I didn't believe it or want it, I didn't do it, and if forced to do it, I was miserable and would make others around me that way too.

This insecure, perfectionist doubt soon found a place of comfort and strength. I was drawn to the creative arts. I was my happiest when in dance class or playing the piano. By ten years of age, I started to experiment with composing piano pieces. My composing improved as I grew up, and I knew that I wanted and needed to do this. Music gave me a voice to express the depth of all the emotions I came across, not just my own but of others that I would perceive. The music spoke to me in a way that nothing else could. I could be stilled with a melody, moved to motion with the right rhythm, and plunged deep into the furthest corners of my soul with the right song.

I felt that music had chosen me. I could never have imagined anyone or thing holding such power over me as did music.

Reign Over Me

At seventeen, my life was forever changed when I came to faith in Jesus Christ. I was raised Greek-Orthodox, but this wasn't about religion; this was about relationship. It changed everything for me, including my viewpoints on the world, life, and relationships. I could see my path becoming clearer, despite the fears of stepping out into this new life and faith.

Our Transformative Journey

At nineteen, I had a core of friends that were supportive both spiritually and emotionally, and I was in a loving relationship with someone who shared my beliefs and supported the dreams I had for my music career. I was majoring in music at college, writing songs, working on my first recording and pursuing vocal studies. Everything seemed like it was going in a forward, positive direction.

However, despite all these affirmations, I was still searching for something and searching for someone to make sense of me, to make my life complete. I now understand that no one human being can give you all that you need, that to be complete as a human we must own who we are, claim our journey and connect with something bigger than ourselves. Lacking such perspective then, I was vulnerable.

I will never forget the first time I saw him. Everything about him seemed dynamic, exciting and magnetic and something inside me stirred that was unfamiliar. He was recording at the same studio I was at the time, and as we got to talking about all thing's music, I discovered he knew so much more than I. He seemed well-connected and knowledgeable. I absorbed every word, every compliment, and critique and after a while realized I cared a lot about his opinion, not just of my music but about all of me.

Unknowingly, I gave him power over me and how I saw my worth. What also intrigued me was his confidence; nothing and no one seemed to shake him. He lived out-loud without caring what anyone thought. I would realize much later that his self-confidence was unbalanced and egotistical. My strong attraction to him intimidated and confused me for it was clear that we were not in alignment when it came to spiritual beliefs or worldviews. He was the opposite of everything I was.

Despite knowing that truth, I allowed myself to be drawn to him. Knowing what was right but wanting what was wrong tortured me! A "rule-following" personality, I had pretty much tried to do the "right thing" most of my life, but this? This was challenging me in a way that felt dangerous and exciting, not at all playing by the rules. As a young woman of faith, I grappled with this difficult pull that I didn't understand. Soon, I disabled my God-given intuition pulling at me to run the other way and fell for the lie that the life I had wasn't enough, that I could only discover and be my true self with him.

Despite warnings from close friends, I refused to see that the green grass was fertilized with manure. Despite the turmoil, despite the deep aching that felt like a warning deep in my soul, I chose to run towards him, like a stubborn child that must touch the hot stove. I dove head first into a relationship that would end up burning me beyond recognition.

Of my own free will, I abandoned the world I knew. My friends, my loving, devoted boyfriend and a community that had embraced me were all left by the curbside. I broke hearts and shattered my reputation.

At first, it was enthralling that I dared do such a thing. I felt alive, and the doubting torment no longer seemed to be there. Everything seemed great. I was having fun, and I believed I was with someone who understood and loved me in a way that I hadn't experienced before. A few weeks later, my body would give me a hint of how untrue that indeed was.

Beneath the Veil

Before this, I never had a panic attack, but a few weeks into the relationship, while at college, what I thought was an asthma attack became a crippling panic attack. It came on suddenly and without warning.

That was the first time my body tried to get my attention in this way. Despite my telling myself I was happy; my body knew that deep inside I wasn't. The torment I thought was over, never left. This life wasn't freedom; this was self-inflicted imprisonment. Still being someone that felt torn most of her life, I ignored the voice of reason, as I tried to make everyone around me happy, including him. I would never admit to him that something felt off. When the cloud of temporary happiness wore off, I realized that I had thrown away a life for someone I understood I couldn't fully trust, not that I was myself with him either, far from it.

Soon enough, the relationship started to show its faults. Being in a healthy relationship is hard enough, but when two people who inherently don't believe in the same things, no matter how attracted they are to each other, it isn't going to work out in the end. The cracks were beginning to emerge. Nevertheless, I stayed. But why?

I stayed because I had convinced myself I was meant to be there. I stayed because of fear. I stayed because of pride and not wanting to admit I had made a terrible mistake. I stayed because I felt such guilt about what I had done to my life, and thought I had nothing for which to go back. Despite it all, I did love him or maybe the idea of him. And I loved the idea that somehow, I would bring something good to his life. Looking back, the arrogance of that belief makes my stomach turn what was worse though was that I had come to the warped conclusion that I had to accept the consequences of wherever this relationship went. In my darkest moments, many times, in the depth of my despair I prayed for death.

I suffered from more frequent panic attacks. After about ten months, they were so bad I never knew when they would hit. They would occur even on my commute to university. I was the reason the train had to be stopped on a couple of occasions. It was awful and humiliating. I was a prisoner in my own body. Out of control, I began experiencing depressive episodes.

Finally, before my 21st birthday, he ended the relationship. He blamed my health. How ironic I thought. Admittedly, I was angry at myself for not being the one to end it, for letting it get that far. The coldness and cruelty of how he ended it ripped through my heart, but in the stillness of that moment, I felt like a bird flying freely out of its cage. I felt calm despite the searing pain.

A few months after the relationship ended, the panic attacks dissipated. However, the damage was done. I would spend years trying to repair the physical and emotional harm.

After a couple of years, my brokenhearted boyfriend and I found our way back to each other, and a few years later we married. My friends would eventually welcome me back into the fold. I felt hurt at their judgment, but I hoped time would heal their hearts and mine, for I hadn't forgiven myself.

Out of Tune!

Time passed. From the outside, I looked like the person everyone knew and loved. But I was miserable. I wasn't doing what I loved and felt disconnected to myself. I hadn't realized how one person's opinions, voice, presence could linger so long. Without realizing it, my confidence and sense-of-self had eroded. I could no longer trust myself, my voice, my talent, my calling. Would I ever drum up enough courage and passion for living how I wanted? The girl that once believed she was made for a purpose, always fighting against her insecurities to live-out-loud, felt like nothing more than a body taking up space. Though I struggled to keep my music aspirations alive, my attempts were half-hearted. I had convinced myself that maybe following your dreams, your belief in what you are meant to do, just wasn't that important. I was broken.

For years, I worked jobs to pay bills. One of these jobs was so stressful to me that it quickened and perpetuated my declining physical health. By age twenty-seven, I was sicker than ever, suffering from chronic sinus infections and diagnosed with IBS (Irritable Bowel Syndrome). I could barely stand without feeling extreme fatigue. It was traumatizing to go out places or socialize because I never knew when the IBS would be triggered, and I would have to run to a bathroom frantically. I gained weight without trying, despite not keeping many in foods. I was diagnosed with allergies that I never had growing up.

One of the weirdest symptoms I experienced was when my skin felt like bugs were crawling all over me. My poor husband and I were at a loss and desperate for answers. Doctors prescribed antibiotics repeatedly for the sinus infections and told me to stay away from caffeine and chocolate for the IBS. They said what I was feeling was psychological and that I was depressed, to which I retorted that I was getting depressed because I didn't know what the heck was wrong with me, and nothing was helping.

Thankfully, my co-worker at the time recommended I see a holistic doctor, who almost immediately diagnosed a severe overgrowth of yeast (Candidiasis) as the cause of all these physical symptoms. He suggested a protocol that included significant diet changes. The improvement was unbelievable. But the road to health would prove to be a journey and not a destination. It was filled with setbacks and revelations as my decisions both in diet and lifestyle directly affected my health.

Holistic Health Coaches are taught to look at the whole person and the entire picture. Stress and unresolved past situations whether chosen or not leave an imprint on the body which will manifest physically, spiritually and emotionally. When not dealt with healthily, one becomes stuck. Years may pass by, and from the outside, you may function in a "normal" way, but lack of acknowledging and connecting situations with how they affect you prolongs the suffering and the deterioration of your health.

But here is what is so magnificent about our bodies! Our bodies let us know when things aren't working right. Sometimes the clues are subtle. Sometimes they are megaphone loud.

Holistic health coaches make a distinction between what is feeding you both on and off the plate. What feeds you off the plate includes our relationships, career, exercise, and spirituality. Even if I had been eating as clean and organically as possible, it would not have made up for the fact that what was feeding me off the plate was completely off-balance. The present turmoil didn't happen all at once; it was a ripple effect of one decision which led to other choices that prolonged and even prevented healing. I was living a life that wasn't aligned with my beliefs; in fact, I wasn't even living my life, I was tolerating it.

Despite my faith, I saw myself as someone unable to contribute to others. Were there moments or glimmers of hope? Yes! But the profound truths remained uncovered. My impatience and my unwillingness to surrender to, understand and accept the responsibility of what was causing the waves of instability in my life hid my joy and my faith. I needed to realize that my loving and forgiving God had a plan for my life, despite my propensity to derail it all. I was too stuck in my mire to release that faith. I had to own my past, forgive myself, and move on.

Relationships are hard enough. If you are in one that doesn't serve your needs in a genuinely emotional and spiritual way, and you aren't walking in alignment with who you are, it cannot work. If your partner doesn't share the same core beliefs with you, eventually that will be problematic for both individuals involved. I am not talking about whether one prefers Italian food over Chinese, or whether the toilet paper should be put over or under (it's over in case you weren't sure). No matter how magical and euphoric it may seem in the beginning, time will reveal the cracks in the shaky foundation. Of course, in my case, the relational foundation was never stable, to begin with.

Being with the wrong person changes you. I lost myself trying to fit into a world I didn't belong. The faith that I had about my calling wavered. My life's plan felt uncertain, a burden that was too heavy to carry. I had a voice without sound, overshadowed by the voice of the past which continued to poison my opinions of myself. Simultaneously, my faith weakened the longer I wandered away. When I realized that by nature, I was prone to stray from the God I loved, I became fully aware of how I needed to cling and center myself in my faith. Such centering required daily attention. One decision then caused a ripple effect of self-doubt, inability to trust others or stand up for myself in making the right decisions. Instead of getting closer to what I envisioned being, I was further from it.

The Story Isn't Over Yet!

Healing came slowly. At some point, my passion for music reignited, and I began writing songs again. They told my story in a way I hadn't written before. I would eventually find my voice, in a powerful, raw way. In between all of this, there was a season of loss. Both my husband and I experienced the trauma of losing the people we loved. I lost my dad to cancer, my husband lost his childhood best friend, and I lost a dear friend who meant so much to me. Her name was Maria, and she was a woman of God I greatly admired. When I struggled through this path of finding my way back, my beautiful friend Maria had reminded me to be patient in the longings of my heart. As she put it, "The story isn't over yet." That simple statement was an encouragement to hold onto my faith and hope. It would bring me to a place of surrender. Surrendering the past, I was no longer afraid to step into the light.

And indeed, my story wasn't done yet! While all of this was taking place, a new passion emerged. I fell in love with holistic nutrition. After years of dieting and tormenting myself with various methods of weight-loss that in the end left me deflated and emotionally constipated, I discovered how food could heal. For years, I thought healthy meant skinny, and that you had to eat a particular way to feel good, inside and out.

After my first child was born, I wanted to lose weight, so I went to a nutritionist who put me on 1,000 calories a day. Yes, I lost weight, but I was miserable, happier for the short-term results, but still without energy. I never thought the foods I thought that were healthy could be hurting me until a friend introduced me to my first elimination diet. This was my first taste of how food could heal you by revealing the foods that triggered reactions. I loved how my body felt when I removed my trigger foods. I bounded with energy. I didn't count anything. I lost weight, but most of all, I felt good. I re-kindled my love for cooking and started to get creative in the kitchen. For the next few years, I would experiment with this type of eating, testing or re-testing certain foods to see how I felt after consuming them. I would read whatever I could get my hands on about nutrition and started to get plugged into the holistic health field. I overcame hypothyroidism through changing how I ate. By this point, I knew that what we ate mattered; it wasn't just about calories.

At the end of 2015, my husband, two children and I moved from our home in New York to Florida. Like many who have moved away from family and friends, I dealt with the emotions of leaving my family behind, let alone the stress of moving. I once again noticed that my body wasn't feeling so great. Admittedly, I had started to stray from the way I had been eating while discovering new and exciting places to dine in my new location. I noticed a change in my moods, and there seemed a perpetual feeling of tiredness and discomfort after eating. Almost instinctively, I modified the way I ate. Driven by my recognition of the connection between food and body, my thinking was changing. I realized that over the past seven years I had gone from a diet mentality to a mentality of eating to live. No counting calories, no fad diets. Nutrition was key.

I was so excited about my profound understanding that I wanted to tell everybody. I tried to help anyone who wanted to make a difference in how they felt. Of course, I didn't know what I wanted to do was an actual occupation. At that time, I hadn't heard of Health Coaches. Then I met this fantastic practitioner in my community who was a Holistic Health Coach. She was impressed at how much I already knew about nutrition and holistic health in general. I will never forget the moment she looked me in the eyes and said, "You should consider becoming a Holistic Health Coach." After she explained what that was, something inside me lit up. After a year of praying, questioning whether the move was sound and feasible financially, I was granted the opportunity by way of scholarship to attend the Institute for Integrative Nutrition. My education opened my eyes and answered a lot of questions that seemed to have been stirring in me all along.

I now knew that this was a path that I was called to. It wasn't so much about having more knowledge, even though there was so much more to learn. I had lived through all sorts of health and life challenges. I had familiarized myself with gut-health and as many diet theories that were taught. What was more profound than the education I would receive, was that a transformation had taken place, a way of connecting all of it. I knew that I could help someone else experience the same thing. I accepted that purpose and believed that I could have more than one passion and more than one calling.

I have come to fully recognize how stress, anxiety, anger, all these things and more, can trigger symptoms in the gut, most of these physical manifestations of not listening to my "gut" and thereby destroying my digestive system. I was failing to address the chronic stressors and imbalances in my life. These can come in many forms: a bad relationship, a job or career you don't love or have passion about, not listening to your intuition when it comes to people, saying yes when you should say no, not having healthy boundaries, low-grade stress or high peaks of stress. The result is that we fall out of tune with ourselves, disconnecting spiritually. Healing the gut with nutrition is vital and shouldn't be taken for granted but treating what causes the disconnect is just as significant.

My Gut Tells Me

In an article entitled "The Gut-Brain Connection," Anthony L. Komaroff, M.D., Editor-in-Chief, Harvard Health Letter, says this:

"Given how closely the gut and brain interact, it becomes easier to understand why you might feel nauseated before giving a presentation or feel abdominal pain during times of stress. That doesn't mean, however, that gastrointestinal conditions are imagined or "all in your head." Psychology combines with physical factors to cause pain and other bowel symptoms. Psychosocial factors influence the actual physiology of the gut, as well as symptoms. In other words, stress (or depression or other psychological factors) can affect movement and contractions of the GI tract, make inflammation worse, or perhaps make you more susceptible to infection."

No doubt, it is important to address what we eat for good "gut-health." Perhaps equally, if not more important, is paying attention to the spiritual, emotional factors that affect us daily, and recognizing those defining moments that impact our lives. Only then can we address the gut in a genuinely holistic way, body, mind, and spirit.

It feels like I've spent a lifetime trying to undo the adverse ripple effect of my past. I used to look at my past with disdain but have come to accept that it prepared me to help others with their health journey. Fortunately, now I realize that everything we do has a ripple effect for good or bad. My hope, my intention, my prayer is to be someone who has a positive ripple effect in helping others. I regret that I didn't meet a health coach back in my twenties, or even my thirties for that matter, or I would have soon realized that there will never be perfection; Perfection isn't possible. What is possible is to accept imperfections with grace and love, trust the process of growth, and trust the journey.

How many times have we heard or used the expression, "My gut tells me"? The popular phrase recognizes that within us we all have this God-given intuition, a gut-feeling. We can sense when something isn't right, when we are in danger, or when something is good, and it's a clear path for us to follow. Perhaps you had moments when you ignored your gut feeling and made choices and decisions that were anything but good for you in the long run. The story I have told has many such moments. When we ignore that and make decisions against our alignment, beliefs, core values, we can affect our bodies in such a way that physical manifestations present themselves. Our digestive system, our gut-brain connection is brilliantly connected to help us know when we are in unalignment with our eating and our lifestyle.

I know that staying in tune is a daily practice. What I eat, having healthy relationships and spiritually connecting creates a more harmonious balance. I have a renewed sense of self where I am embracing my God-given uniqueness. I accept that I don't need to fit in. I can celebrate who I am with full gratitude in my heart. The transformation came when I forgave myself, released the past and accepted who I was. That my beliefs, talents, all facets of me were what made me, me, and I permitted myself to celebrate that! Transformation comes when the old stories about us are released. When we do, we forgive and begin to tune into who we are meant to be and accept where we are now. We realize that our story isn't over yet.

About Anna K Rubano

Anna K. Rubano is the creator/founder of "In-Tune with Anna K.," a holistic health and lifestyle coaching service whose mission is to inspire and motivate transformation through education and support. Her passion is to help those who feel stuck and get them to connect or reconnect with their health. To be in-tune with themselves for optimal wellness.

Anna herself has overcome several health challenges including Candidiasis, Hypothyroidism and Gut Dysbiosis, to name a few. Through her own experience of gut health ailments, she saw how they directly affected her physical health as well as her emotional and mental health.

A passionate cook and foodie who loves to cook for others as well as show that eating healthy doesn't have to be bland or boring. Anna shows how you don't need fancy tools or kitchen gadgets (even though they can be fun) to create delicious, healthy meals. If cooking were a love language, it would be one of Anna's! To cook for oneself or others is the ultimate expression of love.

Anna received her Bachelor of Music from New York University in 2000 and is a recording artist, singer/songwriter, pianist, and music performer. She has performed in NYC, Long Island, NY, New Jersey, and Los Angeles. She is a dynamic speaker and performer who captivates her audience with her story. Her creativity expands into all that she does including her coaching, cooking, and living. Her unassuming style is focused and direct bringing a refreshing presence to whatever project she is involved.

After years of struggling to find a connection and understanding of food and how it can heal, Anna's excitement for the holistic health field grew exponentially. Anna is very knowledgeable about gut health and the effect it has on overall health and well-being.

She graduated from the Institute for Integrative Nutrition® in March 2019 as a Certified Integrative Health Coach who is passionate about helping others achieve balance and good health through addressing symptoms to uncover their root causes. As a Holistic Health Coach, she uses a warm yet direct approach with clients to help them connect with themselves, empowering them to own their journey, and realize the power they have as the narrator and author of their story.

As a speaker, she shares her insights, journey, and knowledge with a real and raw passion for inspiring others to look further and deeper to the root cause of imbalances in both food and lifestyle. Anna provides a direct yet compassionate space with motivating and encouraging support to help others realize that health is a journey, and you can start from any place, even at the bottom as she once did.

Anna's faith and spirituality are crucial parts of her wellness journey. She is transparent about her growth and struggles over the years. She believes that true faith isn't wrapped up with a perfect bow that sits in a pew with life seeming perfect and all-altogether. True faith is seeing the beauty of the broken, imperfect mess that is life and accepting it.

After living in NY for almost 30 years, she currently lives in Sarasota, FL with her husband and two children. When she is not coaching, she can be found writing music, singing, cooking, exercising or spending time with her family and friends.

Contact Information

Anna K. Rubano
In Tune with Anna K
Website: www.intunewithannak.com
Email: info@intunewithannak.com

Chapter 5

A Life Evolving- Growing, Changing, Living

By: Rachel Fitzgibbon

Life is a fascinating process, while the passage of time ebbs and flows each phase takes on a persona of its own. The psyche bears the task of guiding an individual through each stage whether turbulent or tranquil. As I reminisce my thoughts settle on a quiet, curly-haired girl with big blue eyes. It was a happy childhood filled with loving experiences. Growing up in a middle-class home in which the mother stayed home and the father went to work was common in the small pipeline town where we grew up. My brothers and I were fortunate to be raised with loving parents and a supportive community.

Even in the most favorable circumstance, the perception of one's self does not always replicate the observations of others. The power of our thoughts is tremendous. Much mental and emotional suffering can come from how we speak to ourselves in our mind, and it has the potential to affect us in some very damaging ways. It often leads to higher levels of stress, lower levels of self-esteem, decreased motivation, and greater feelings of helplessness. This has rung true for me throughout my life. Maybe you relate to this habit of self-defeating behavior which has so many times prevented me from doing what I wanted or getting where I needed to be. The process of transforming my thoughts has been a daunting, introspective journey.

Just as most stories progress, my childhood years passed, and the teenage years began. Over time shyness dissipated and a more outgoing personality emerged, however, outgoing did not translate to confident. It was wonderful to have many friends as it provided many shields to hide behind and I hid behind them often. It was much easier to permit another to speak on my behalf. Doing so, I would not have to initiate conversation.

Other times I would overcompensate, being louder than life to disguise my self-doubt.

Now I realize that all teens are concerned with the way they come across to peers, but at that time this was not how I saw it. I often felt silly, inferior, and anxious never realizing this was only my perception. Many opportunities, experiences, and relationships were sabotaged due to this pattern of self-defeating thoughts. Even so, the high school years eventually ended, and the next chapter was college. College life proved challenging for a variety of reasons and circumstances. I made a bold move to attend a small out of state college, several hours from family and friends. Alone in a new place, I was forced out of my comfort zone into an unfamiliar realm.

Independence

Eager for independence yet still unsure of myself, off I went. As a new college student, I was intimidated by the demand. I made friends easily within my dorm yet felt out of place among the students at the small Christian school I had chosen to attend. The students I knew all seemed to have it together, a solid plan. I, on the other hand, had no clue what I wanted out of college much less beyond. They were also deeply religious, and I was not at the same place spiritually as them.

Working as a waitress, I found my solace at the restaurant. I felt much less intimidated and overwhelmed with my friends there. I didn't feel like I needed to have it all together, it was comforting, and I could relax and be myself. My confidence relating to my schooling was poor. The voice inside my head told me I was not smart enough and without a plan what was the point. My class attendance began to slip as I preferred to stay out late with my friends at the restaurant and slept through classes often. Thoughts become choices, choices become actions, and actions become habits. It became easier and easier to skip classes. My grades plummeted, and eventually, I landed myself on academic probation, losing the scholarship monies I had been granted. It was easy to let it go as I genuinely believed I didn't deserve it anyway.

Rather than take a break, I bounced right into another university, and I was certain a new location and the comfort of old friends would improve how I felt. It never occurred to me that the problem was within me, that it was necessary to make changes in me and not my surroundings to succeed. It was all fun and games initially. Reunited with friends from high school, I was enjoying myself. Overall, things felt pretty good. I was even doing better academically, attending classes and completing assignments. As college students do, I found myself dating and began a relationship. Things seemed great in the beginning, he told me I was pretty, sent flowers, all the little things that make a girl feel special. Slowly things began to change but so subtly that I didn't seem to notice until I was in too deep.

Losing My Voice

As is often the case with "young love," there were many red flags I failed to notice. Initially, it was comments and small conflicts which occurred between him and my friends when I wasn't around. Then he became controlling, jealous, and demanding of my time. Over time, I found myself alienated as longtime friends slowly drifted away. He did an outstanding job convincing me he was there for me and would provide the support and safety I craved. This made me feel closer to him but also reliant. I feared that without him I would be alone as I did not understand what had occurred and why my friendships had dissipated.

As time went on the relationship grew more controlling. He wanted me at his place within a short time of leaving work and made comments that invoked fear and dread. Because of the statements he often made regarding his emotional state, I truly believed that his emotional well-being depended upon me doing and saying the right thing at all times. I always rushed over to see him after school or work because he expected it. When I was there, however, it was quite the opposite. I often felt isolated and afraid, unsafe due to his hostile temper. He was easily angered and often agitated.

One experience, however, shook me to the core. On this night I arrived later than expected from work. It was dark inside, so I quietly entered, afraid to disturb him yet knowing that I had to let him know I was there. As I closed the door, I noticed a shadow across the room. It was him. He stood there, silent. In his hand, he held a pistol which was pointed directly at me. I honestly thought he was so angry I had arrived late that I was about to pay a devastating price for my mistake. Noticing my fear, which I realized later was the desired response, he then began to comfort me. His explanation felt less than genuine as he tried to convince me he believed someone was breaking into the home. I was riveted with fear and many sleepless nights followed.

Our Transformative Journey

Even so, embarrassed and afraid, I kept the emotions, fears, and incidences buried. I felt trapped, alone, and unsure of how to get out of the situation without being harmed. Officially, we did not live together as I had a dorm room at the time, but because friendships had faded, and my relationship obligations had prevented new relationships from developing, I felt there was nowhere to go. I could always go home to my family but wasn't ready to admit I was in over my head. He had even convinced me to let him move several of my furniture items into his place claiming the need for furniture and the inability to afford it for himself. I felt obligated to help as I thought he needed me but was also fearful of what may happen if I chose not to.

A mother can always sense when something isn't quite right which is probably very lucky for me. My family saved my life because I am confident that I was in for a long life of fear and pain if I allowed the relationship to move to the next step as he was working hard to convince me it should. Fearful they may lose me forever to this young man, my parents managed to convince me that moving home was my only option.

My anxiety and stress level was high, and my confidence was shaken, it did not take much to convince me. I wanted out, but if I broke it off, I would never feel safe living in the same community. I told him that my parents were forcing me to move home because I was too afraid to give him any other reason. It was so difficult to admit to him I couldn't move in with him which was what he was pushing. Finally giving in to the fact that I was indeed moving home, he swore we would stay together and bought a small "promise ring" insisting that we would make a long-distance relationship work. I played along because I was emotionally weak and had nowhere to go if things got ugly.

When the day arrived for my parents to take me home, emotions were high, the air charged with tension. All my belongings were placed on a trailer to be taken home. Amid all the stress I also felt some relief. My parent's presence provided an immense feeling of safety. My dad had always been my silent protector, the gentlest man I knew. Although I had never seen him harm a soul, I knew without hesitation, he would protect me fiercely. At that moment I realized that I was blessed to have a strong, supportive family with love so strong they would always protect me. Without this support system, I would certainly be sharing a much different story today.

After some time in the safety of my parent's home, surrounded by them and my brothers, I gained the confidence to break off the relationship. He wasn't happy about me leaving. I had been so weak that I think he thought he could convince me to stay with him. He surprised us on a few occasions after that by showing up unexpectedly at our home. My dad made it powerfully clear that he was unwelcome without uttering a word. The next few times he would appear was more frightening as he was able to obtain my location by just asking questions in the small community where we lived which shattered my sense of safety.

On one occasion he stalked me at my workplace. Making phone calls from the gas station across the street, he described my activities as he watched from afar. On another occasion, he appeared in my office unannounced striking fear to the depths of my being. I had however gained some confidence while living at home and within our small community which helped me resist getting in a car with him or giving in to his demands. When I didn't give in, he eventually grew tired of the situation and moved on leaving me to live my life without fear. Over time, I regained some sense of confidence, but the negative self-talk remained. I still didn't deem myself worthy of success and continued to feel inferior in most situations.

New Life

As luck would have it, I met a young man who sparked my interest. With him, I felt safe and protected in much the same way my father made me feel safe and protected. He was a gentle soul and a fierce protector. We connected at a level that I had not connected with another before. He was gentle, playful, spiritual, and artistic. He was a musician and we both valued music, time in nature, and living with a sense of adventure. We dated only briefly, but our connection was deep. After a short time, we became pregnant. This was sudden and unplanned, yet we were happy and determined to create a life full of adventure, tenderness, and stability.

We married, and our beautiful little girl was born, full of light and life, she lit up our world. We took her home and began life as a young family. As we were settling into our new reality, our little one turned a month old. Two days later we kissed our hard-working husband and daddy goodbye as he headed out to a favorite spot in the country for a quick hunting trip. He deserved some time to relax and enjoy nature as this was his solace. I waited for him to come home and as daylight turned to darkness, many scenarios began to run through my mind.

Our Transformative Journey

At first, I dreamt up a story that he was with friends. But finally, although I didn't want to allow my thoughts to go there, I was riveted with fear and dread. I pondered the worst-case scenarios as I wondered why he still hadn't arrived home to us. My brother was my hero that night as I called him to help me look for my missing husband. He and his roommate drove the dark country road to the hunting spot and arrived at a dark, overgrown intersection to find the unimaginable. As my husband and our precious baby girl's daddy headed home that evening at dusk, his truck met another in the center of an overgrown intersection and the man who had rescued my soul never returned home.

I have never felt such despair. The pain was unbearable. Sleep eluded me, my appetite vanished, and my desire to escape was inescapable. I wanted desperately to run far away from my shattering reality. Somehow, I made the necessary decisions and arrangements for a situation that I never dreamed possible. This is something that one should experience decades down the line. So many times, I wanted to jump ship and run, anywhere. Each time I felt this way I looked at the beautiful child we had created. She kept me grounded, responsible, and sane.

As is the nature of grief, it comes and goes, is manageable one moment and unbearable the next. The healing process is slow while the pain shows no mercy time and time again. Once again, my family came to my rescue with their unconditional love and protection. I know how fortunate and blessed I have been throughout my journey to have been supported so tremendously. I am certain this was the key to my survival and why I had the strength and courage to grow emotionally over the years. Family and friends were patient and kind, gently walking the path alongside me.

As I spent time with family and friends, healing occurred. I had a wonderful friend and workout partner, and we worked out several nights a week and spent countless hours talking, laughing, and just being. Journal writing served as an outlet for expressing my darkest emotions. I connected with others who had experienced similar circumstances, and we communicated through letters and occasional phone calls. These relationships were very comforting as we were each experiencing grief in our ways yet able to help each other process the emotions we were going through using our unique experiences.

Slowly, I worked through my grief and continued to grow, gaining strength and confidence every day. Life as a young mother also allowed me to grow in many ways as the responsibility required me to make decisions that I would have normally allowed others to make for me. Realizing my financial resources limited my ability to provide for my daughter, I returned to school. Often, I had felt pitied in the small town where I lived and because of this was driven to show the world that I could do it all and take care of this sweet little one on my own.

I returned to college with renewed self-confidence and performed quite well in school, receiving high grades even being chosen to participate in a practicum for my major that few undergraduate students were selected for at that time. Things were starting to look up for us, and I was feeling successful and had grown in confidence. My thoughts and feelings of inadequacy had shifted, and instead of questioning my ability to succeed in school and professionally, I allowed the negative self-talk to direct itself toward my parenting abilities. I often felt that I was not providing a worthwhile experience for her and was less than adequate. Even with many steps forward, I could not shake the self-defeating thought processes that I had spent my life creating.

Dreams Come True

As I was nearing my last year of college, once more I met a young man. This time a young professional who could provide a good life for my daughter and me. This was a promising scenario. He was kind and treated me with love and respect. More admirable, he loved my daughter from day one and spent time playing and demonstrating his willingness to love and care for her. After graduating, we were married and shortly afterward chose to make a big move far from the comfort of family and friends. This was an exciting adventure for us. We spent long hours as a new family, hiking in the mountains and sightseeing. It was a time of tremendous growth as we had to rely on each other when money was tight, and there was no extra help nearby. We made amazing memories together.

The day that my new husband adopted my precious daughter is forever etched into my mind. It was a mighty act that solidified our future as a true family unit. As the years progressed, we experienced countless challenges and changes. We moved three more times over the years, added a second child, navigated an autism diagnosis, anxiety, the teen years, relationship ups and downs, and much more. Through it all, we have come out stronger although there were times that I know we both questioned whether our relationship would withstand the challenges set before us.

I know that I am not alone when I say that being a wife and a mother is one of the most challenging pursuits to undertake. During these years I lost a piece of my identity, spending the majority of my waking hours caring for the needs and desires of my family. Taking care of my family was my dream, so it was difficult to understand when I experienced feelings of isolation, irritability, and found fault in other's actions. The result was guilt, guilt became shame, and both resulted in more negative feelings of self-worth and lack of confidence in the ability to do what I desired to be the best at, wife and mother.

Rather than care for me too, I deprived myself of my needs and wants. All the while, believing this made me better at my most important job. I no longer exercised or even headed out for a short walk. I convinced myself that to be inaccessible for even a few minutes made me a bad mother. The thought of meeting friends for coffee or drinks was terrifying because one of my children may have needed something while I was away. It was utterly irrational, and not once did I consider that only living to meet the needs of others could lead to some low moments of despair and guilt.

There are many moments I would love to take back, but with much emotional work and progress, I have come to know that at every stage of my children's life I made decisions based on the knowledge I had and if I had known more I would have done more. I loved my children with every cell of my body, and I have done the best I know how. They know I love them, and they are amazing humans, so I have had to learn how to let the "should have, could have, would have" go for good.

Losing Control

In addition to being a wife and mother, I am a teacher. Over the years I have spent time working with many students, some who have experienced significant trauma, challenges with behavior, mental health concerns, autism, cognitive deficits and much more. My experiences as a teacher have been inspiring, astonishing, and, at times, unbelievable. The rewards, however, were colossal.

I gained relevant knowledge about the inner workings of the brain as well as the great effects trauma can have on one's brain development. I have been taught methods and skills designed to encourage both emotional healing and healing of the brain. I have utilized these strategies time, and again while working with students through the pain, they were experiencing. I obtained training from and consulted with experts in the field and achieved much success in working with my students. The feelings of pride were indescribable when students use learned coping skills and begin attaining academic growth. My students, the adults who worked alongside us, and I experienced everything together. We laughed together, cried together, and learned together.

Unfortunately, for me, teaching is not a profession that was conducive to leaving the work at work as I felt their pain deeply. Many of my students endured circumstances and events that affected me immensely and, over time, I too began to struggle with my own emotions. Feelings of shock, sadness, guilt, and grief started to become overwhelming. All the while I was able to teach others about trauma and guide my students to utilize strategies and tools aimed to help heal and cope with strong emotions but failed to apply them myself.

There is a term that I had heard and used often, vicarious trauma, which is one's response to an accumulation of exposure to the pain of others. These children trusted me to keep them safe and often confided in me. They lashed out at me verbally and physically. They cried, shouted, and acted out the anger and fear they experienced.

The toxic stress I was experiencing began to overpower me without my noticing. I lost sleep, awoke from frightening dreams, and was moody. My body started to feel the effects as well. I craved junk food, gained weight, experienced joint pain, headaches, and upset stomach. Emotionally, I lost interest in activities that previously brought joy and helped relieve stress. Relationships were no longer fulfilling, and I was generally disinterested in most things. I felt isolated and unable to fend for myself.

Any negative experience I had personally experienced paled in comparison to some of the horrendous experiences of which I knew. The result was tremendous feelings of guilt and anguish. Additionally, for a variety of reasons, I had begun to feel very unsafe in my work environment and woke each morning with inexplicable feelings of fear and dread. As things continued to spiral downward, the mental anguish became more than I could have imagined. There was a point I realized I could not continue this path much longer. I was slowly losing the pieces that I liked about myself and my world felt as if it were beginning to fall apart.

As much as I loved my students, I could no longer help them unless I found a way to help myself. I plead with my team lead to allow me to change settings and the following year I began working with a new population. There was such a feeling of guilt as I felt as though I was giving up on something at which I had worked so hard to do well. However, I knew I could no longer be effective in my current state.

Coming Back

Removing myself from the stresses and pressure allowed me time to process and reflect. I knew many more changes would have to be made, so I embarked on an elimination diet, cutting grain, dairy, and sugar while adding in some essential supplements and nutrients. This had a tremendous outcome on both my physical and emotional health. I had more energy, was less sluggish, and my mind was clearer. The intense pain I was experiencing in my joints also began to subside. I still felt significant stress and desperately needed to learn to manage it better, so I began using guided meditation and journaling as tools to help reduce stress.

Over time I began sleeping better, no longer waking in the night and the frightening dreams dissipated. Yoga and breathing provided my body and mind with soothing abilities and released tension allowing relaxation to occur. The positive results were astounding, but I still had much more healing to do. I became more intentional with my taekwondo practice and training, which allowed me to focus my thoughts and understand my weaknesses more clearly.

Well over a year later the process continued. My relationships had improved and were continuing to grow. Hobbies and interests were beginning to feed my spirit once more. Throughout my life, I have been blessed with strong family bonds, and these are my lifeline. My parents, my children, my husband, extended family, and close friends have never left my side. Because of this, I am stronger. I realize that even when I have felt isolated and alone, it was only in my mind because they have been with me along the entire journey.

I gained a lot from my experiences, and it left me with an even deeper desire to be a lifelong learner and continue to find new ways to give back. My biggest hurdle throughout my 45 years has been overcoming negative self-talk and its power over my confidence and self-worth. I will continue to learn and put in the work to change these habitual, self-defeating ways of thinking. I have learned to be mindful and pay attention to what I say to myself and how I say it.

I have also learned that it is helpful to ask myself direct and goal-oriented questions about my thoughts and to be reflective without passing judgment on myself. By being mindful, practicing regular self-care, and learning to love myself exactly as I am my journey toward transformation has been far-reaching. I have deliberately transformed my thoughts, making way for confidence and power to grow within me. I now have the confidence and am willing to step up to begin building what has for years been merely a dream.

You can gain control of your thoughts and lead yourself to confidence, but it requires significant effort. You cannot just flip a switch and change what you say to yourself. You must be mindful of every thought and intentional when redirecting yourself. One of my most trusted mentors told me many times, "anyone can overcome anything." I believe this wholeheartedly, and you can overcome your hurdles, just as I have.

You can possess the power to change lives, but you must start with your own if you truly want to live your dream.

About Rachel Fitzgibbon

Rachel Fitzgibbon is the founder and CEO of Evolution Wellness, providing holistic health and wellness coaching. Rachel is passionate about the concept of balanced living which is achieved by utilizing a holistic approach that blends mind, body, and spirit. Healthy relationships, a fulfilling career, regular physical activity, and spiritual awareness are just a few essential elements of wellness. Rachel also understands the importance of providing simple, practical steps to achieve optimal wellness over time. Her mission is to walk alongside you as you seek the pinnacle of your health and wellness. Collaboratively, you will discuss your desires and develop attainable goals. As your guide, Rachel will provide education, motivation, guidance, and accountability throughout the process. Assessing how all areas of your life are connected is vital to attaining and sustaining health and wellness goals. Rachel's gentle, unassuming approach provides a safe space to examine and explore one's struggles, dreams, and goals resulting in a true transformation.

Rachel embarked on her wellness journey when realizing that lifestyle choices were impacting both her physical and emotional health negatively. Armed with the knowledge of the mind-body connection, she experimented with food by adding in and eliminating foods to find the right balance to decrease inflammation and pain within her own body. Plagued her entire life by self-doubt, she recognizes the power of thoughts and the connection of negative self-talk to higher levels of stress, lower levels of self-esteem, decreased motivation, and feelings of helplessness. She discovered how this was hindering her ability to move forward and resolved to transform her self-talk by being mindful of her thoughts, ensuring they are purposeful and lead to a positive result. This has affirmed her belief in herself and given her the opportunity to realize her life's purpose.

Rachel has also had a fulfilling career in education, as a special education teacher. She has had the opportunity to be inspired by countless students of various ages, abilities, and backgrounds. For several years she worked exclusively with students who experienced trauma and has witnessed firsthand the healing power of positive relationships. She has been inspired by the growth and resilience of her students over the years. The effects of trauma are far-reaching and can continue to affect both emotional and physical health into adulthood. This is one of the reasons she is expanding her work to provide adults the opportunity to take control of their health and wellness to lead healthy, happy lives.

Rachel is a certified Integrative Nutrition Health Coach and recent graduate of the Institute for Integrative Nutrition ®. She resides in Saint Louis, Missouri with her husband, Michael. Their daughter, Kennedy, is a spirited, hard-working young woman. They also have a son, Riley, who will be headed to high school soon. Rachel enjoys spending time outdoors, practicing yoga and martial arts, as well as traveling and spending time with her family. Rachel's future includes becoming certified in Usui/Holy Fire Reiki, a Japanese technique for stress reduction and relaxation which promotes healing.

Contact Information

Rachel Fitzgibbon
Evolution Wellness
Website: www.evolutionhealthcoach.com
Email: info@evolutionhealthcoach.com

Chapter 6

Coming Full Circle and Finding True North

By: Caren Logan

If someone had told me when I was ten that I would someday be co-authoring a book and living on the East Coast as a single mom–and loving it–I would have told them they were crazy! Back then, I was a California girl through and through. Growing up in Newport Beach, California, was the opposite of the tsunami of technology we are experiencing today. Getting exercise while riding my bike to school, inhaling the fresh ocean air, and having time to reflect and think about my day in the quiet of the morning was, and still is, the definition of a healthy lifestyle. In the summer, I would go to the Sierra Mountains with my cousins and ride horses, jump streams, and catch trout with my bare hands.

My cousins and I would sleep on cots in a small cabin with no door, and our shower consisted of dumping a bucket of cold water over our heads every few days. I realize now that my life then just might have been the definition of wellness in action and one that I strive to return to as an adult. My life has been an amazing journey and continues to unfold and get better. Not that I was always aware that it was getting better. There were times that I didn't think I could endure the heartache and anguish that life sometimes brought, and yet now, I can see that even those times brought blessings and helped me find my true north.

Wellness is an all-encompassing journey that includes healthy food, lifestyle, and emotional health. I love how Andrew Weil, M.D. describes the best position on the mood spectrum is neutral, what he calls emotional sea level – it's not happiness but rather peaceful contentment and the calm acceptance that is the goal of many kinds of spiritual practice. The notion that a human being should be consistently happy is a uniquely modern destructive idea. The concept where the middle life will take you to the peaks of the mountains with joy, the depths of the ocean in despair, but you will have comfort in knowing that you will return to your sea level and live a happy, healthy life.

Throughout my life's many unexpected twists and turns, including my father's suicide, infertility, and a painful divorce, health and wellness have been my compass always guiding me back to my true north. I hope that my story will encourage you and that no matter what unexpected twists and turns your life throws at you, that you will have faith that there is a life of joy waiting for you as you journey toward your true north.

Spa Evolution

Many of the lessons I have learned happened over the past 30 plus years that I have worked in the spa industry creating holistic experiences for hotels, fitness centers, wellness centers, and spas. I still remember my first real job in the industry. I had to keep blinking to make sure this experience was real, is this my job? I am at a welcome reception at a beautiful destination spa in California situated on 250 acres. Thirteen guests are arriving to start their week of transformation. The program is designed to provide a wellness experience to improve their health and well-being. This is the start of an experience that will change their lives and health forever.

A typical spa day starts by meeting for a morning smoothie before heading off for a peaceful and invigorating hike. Upon returning, a delicious and healthy breakfast prepared by the spa's chef is served. Guests then partake in exercise and wellness testing so that individualized program can be developed. At lunchtime, everyone comes together again to enjoy another sumptuous meal prepared by the spa's chef and to hear an educational discussion on wellness. The afternoon is reserved for quiet time and includes journaling, walks, and spa treatments. In the evening after a delicious dinner, everyone gathers for a wellness presentation. The most popular presentation being the cooking demonstration by the famous spa chef and where everyone gets to participate and learn how to prepare and cook healthy meals in a delicious, satisfying way.

My role was to provide personalized customer service for the guests and make sure their experience was beyond exceptional. In talking, hiking and sharing meals with them and scheduling all their services and supporting them through their week, I had the pleasure of seeing every person transform their health and share the joy of their newfound wellness. It was astonishing how they started to look physically different around day three as their facial muscles began to relax, and their eyes began to shine. By the end of the week, most looked as if they had left a few years behind and appeared younger. This became an annual event for most of the guests. The consistent feedback was that when the guests returned home, they did well for a while but as the days and weeks went by it became more and more of a challenge to battle the stresses and challenges of everyday demands. So, to them, the return visit was necessary to refresh and revive and add years to their lives.

To back up a bit, I was passionate about health and wellness for as long as I could remember, and four years before my new job at a destination spa I remember going on a walk with my dad. I recall telling him that as much as I loved horticulture and design, my major in college, I didn't think that they were my true passion. My real passion was to support people in the transformation of their health and help them to be the best person they could be. I didn't know what that looked like, but I was determined to investigate my options in making this come true. My dad's wise words were, "I know that if you set your mind to something, there is no doubt in my mind you will achieve it. Remember, the definition of luck is opportunity meeting preparedness." I kept the vision, studied, learned, and never gave up. It's amazing how encouragement and love can help us achieve our dreams.

As the climate of the spa concept and wellness began to attract the attention of the most beautiful hotels in the world, I was contacted by The Ritz Carlton to help them add this concept to a new hotel they were building. With the elegance of the hotel, the exceptional standard of customer service, and the clientele who were looking for this spa experience throughout a long weekend, it was a wonderful fit. This was a new concept for the hotel industry, but as we know now, it wouldn't be a luxury hotel without a spa.

With luxury hotels adding spas there was a new concept developing as well. Destination hotels where starting to add spas to appeal to attendees of corporate groups as one of the amenities from which to choose. The spa was now in competition with the golf and tennis functions trying to lure attendees and their spouses into using their services during their free time. I stepped into a new role of Marketing Manager for a Marriott Destination Resort and got to work creating marketing strategies. This was an excellent opportunity for people to exercise and get treatments while attending a meeting or conference for their job or while on vacation. As the resort and hotel spa industry grew, the familiarity with spas expanded and the desire to go to a spa to rejuvenate and get restored grew in popularity.

Spas were in high demand and were being added to existing hotels and fitness centers, as well as being developed as stand-alone day spas. Soon, however, the industry began to see challenges with rapid expansion. One of the most significant problems was having enough knowledgeable and qualified people to fill the number of job openings being created, especially since job burnout is relatively high in the industry. In 1996, I launched my spa consulting company, Virtual Spa to help address these evolving challenges. I created the first online job placement and training website. Today there are specialized recruitment companies who help identify qualified employees.

As the spa industry was growing in leaps and bounds, my company was hired to be a part of a project that developed a wellness facility associated with a health care system. It was a concept to test and measure individuals' wellness and provide support in improving their health and well-being. The facility had a state-of-the-art fitness center, exercise classes, a nutritionist, a healthy café, and of course a fantastic spa. The concept rolled out in many different states. Further reinforcing that holistic wellness is critical to our long-term health.

One of the projects I am most proud of involved working with a well-known cosmetic company to develop the "Ultimate Spa Treatment" for its customers. I was responsible for designing the Ultimate Experience from beginning to end. We started with the treatment room, designing it to address all the five senses. The light that came on as the treatment started was set at a specific frequency to heal the body, the product line was , so we had a large aquarium with tropical fish built in the wall, the music was the sound of waves at the sea, and the smell of a fresh beach was filling the room. We then designed the treatment with the goal of removing any connection with the outside world. It started at the feet and continued to flow up the body and then to the face to completely relax you. The consistent feedback we heard from clients was, "I feel like a new person." The project was a huge success and written up by the top magazines that highlighted its healing and therapeutic intention. It launched in four countries and touched people from around the world. This project reinforced my belief that treatments need to be designed with the intention to heal and address the true nature of someone so true healing and wellness can take place. The power of human touch, whether it be from bodywork, massage, or facials should be included in everyone's wellness routine to maximize whole health.

Just as the spa industry has evolved, so have I. In my youth, everything was more straightforward and easier, but as I grew and evolved, my challenges have become more significant. If I didn't face them with the same creativity and vigor that I put into creating my spa consulting company, then I fear I would have stayed small never adventuring outside the safe cocoon of my California youth. When you are faced with an opportunity to grow, grab it. Don't just move outside your comfort zone, leap outside. And, most importantly, don't neglect the importance of incorporating human touch in your wellness routine.

The New Luxury

Spas in the past have been thought of as a luxury. If you think of luxury what comes to mind? Is it a lavish vacation? The dictionary defines luxury as "the state of great comfort and extravagant living." Traditionally, luxury denotes something that is enjoyed by certain people and not by others. It speaks to the privilege and exclusivity enjoyed by the elite. However, there is a new approach to the idea of luxury specifically within the new generation, that puts the subject in an entirely different light. It's not that we don't want nice things; instead, we realize that the existing definition is only describing one part of life. The shift seems to be from acquiring things to acquiring experiences. There is more focus on the quality of life than the quality of goods. Luxury in its new context is enjoying the best in life, the experience of beauty and humanity at their deepest and most inspiring. With this new insight, great health is the ultimate in luxury.

My evolving meaning of luxury is to have a well-balanced life and a healthy mind and spirit so that I can enjoy the people I love to be healthy and contribute back to the world. I believe the reason the circle of life is a circle is, so it can always be turning and balancing as we go. In my coaching practice, we address items in the circle of life to achieve a healthy balance and optimal health. If one area of your life requires attention, it can affect your overall health. At this point in my life, spending time with my girls is a luxury. However, I will never give up my love for the spa industry, and so I have "downsized" this to fit what matters most. I have a mini spa in my home providing specialty facials and educational seminars on wellness topics, and coaching. I have come full circle in my wellness and spa life.

This more intimate setting is a small sampling of the first destination spa where I started. Doing what I love and having a mini destination spa while being able to spend quality time with my family is my luxury living lifestyle.

I encourage you to look at what luxury means to you and start taking steps, even small ones, to shift your focus to what matters most. The happier we are, the healthier we are. When faced with a challenge, or choice, step back and think creatively about how you might be able to achieve both. Perhaps it won't be to the scale you would like, but you might find a way to have a smaller piece of cake and eat it, too.

Cloudy with a Chance of Challenges

Throughout my life I have always been motivated to be the best I could be, always striving to reach my next goal. I loved everything about the spa industry and had a plan to grow my spa consulting business. The spa industry satisfied my nurturing personality, and I enjoyed creating relaxing experiences for people. Another goal I had for myself was to have children someday. I loved children and always knew I would get married and have at least one child, hopefully, more. However, I was so focused on my career that the years went by and I thought I had passed the time in which I could have children.

In 1995 I moved from California to the East Coast and opened two spas and planned to go back to California. However, after being on the East Coast for five years, I met the man who would become my husband and father of my children. We both wanted to have children, but it was taking much longer for me to get pregnant than we expected. After many disappointments, and surgeries we got the news that our dream of having children was finally becoming a reality.

In 2005, my beautiful twin daughters entered this world. I knew the first minute I looked into their newborn eyes that my life was changed forever. I didn't know my heart could expand so much with love.

My struggles with infertility felt insurmountable. I would go through what seemed like daily peaks and valleys of hope and despair. To help me get through this time and make the decisions that were right for me, I enlisted the help of a wellness coach. After feeling so alone, scare and hopeless, it was a very supportive, educational process. Life is full of roadblocks on our path to fulfilling our dreams. Don't try to go it alone. Surround yourself with people who will provide you with love and emotional support.

The End of a Season

It was early fall 2010, and as I worked in the garden cleaning up the leftover harvest from the summer bounty of flowers and vegetables, I fought the feeling of wanting to freeze time in place. I couldn't bear the thought of fall ending and winter coming. It had only been six months since my father had taken his life and I feared that as the seasons passed, I would lose his memory with it. How could I possibly go on and leave him in the summer season and not take him with me into the winter? As I sat in the garden, not able to move, I realized that the man I adored, my best friend, and my strength had committed suicide and left me forever.

Over the past nine years, I have had moments where I didn't miss him, but they have been brief. With each milestone in my life, I pause and wonder, "How could he have missed the opportunity to look into his sweet granddaughters' eyes and see their sweet spirit and love? How could he choose not to be here for this milestone!"

My dad was a strong, positive, kind, charismatic man and everyone who came into contact with him left feeling like a better person. When he committed suicide, it was a shock to everyone who knew him. We were all in disbelieve that he, of all people, would take his own life.

At the time of his death, I had never known anyone who had committed suicide. So, the journey to understand, grieve and try to make sense of why anyone would make that decision has brought me extreme pain and compassion. After experiencing, and seeing others lose someone to suicide, I believe that the devastating impact it has on those left behind is far more significant than the person committing suicide could have ever comprehended.

While all loss is devastating, I have learned that dealing with the death by suicide of a loved one is much different and, in many ways, harder than losing a loved one in any other way. It is never easy to talk about death, and no one is comfortable talking about death by suicide. Due to the stigma and lack of education that exists with suicide, mental health, and depression, people have no idea what to say to comfort those left behind. Since they don't know what to say, they often say nothing, leaving the survivor feeling even more devastated and isolated. There is also the awkward silence in conversations when the topic comes up. By not talking and expressing the feelings and emotions, the healing process can take longer and for many never even happens.

For me, being authentic and talking about my dad's suicide feels the most respectful in honoring his memory. I may never understand or fully heal, but I can honor my father by helping others and providing advocacy and support for others who must endure this journey. Doing so has helped me to heal on my journey of loss. Living a healthy life is about finding meaning or purpose even when the meaning may be hard to find.

Journey to Joy

In 2013, I thought my biggest challenges were behind me. I was enjoying my children, home, and husband. Unfortunately, I uncovered information that my perfect life wasn't so perfect after all. I filed for divorce and left the home that I had poured so much time and love into.

One of the challenges with marriages and society in general today is that we only listen to be heard and aren't listening to hear. When you are first falling in love, the other person tends to listen deeply. Deep listening means listening with compassion. Even if the other person is full of wrong perceptions, discrimination, blaming, judging, and criticizing, you are still capable of sitting quietly and listening, without interrupting, without reacting. You know that if you can listen like that, the other person will feel heard, respected, and loved. You are listening with only one purpose in mind: to give the other person a chance to express himself or herself.

Unfortunately, as time goes by, our capacity to listen in this way is impacted by our willingness to do so. When another person has hurt us, it is natural to have hostile thoughts, feelings of anger or hatred, and even a desire to take revenge. All of the feelings often happen without much inner thought or control. We simply find ourselves brooding about what we are going to say or do to pay back the person who has hurt us. To choose blessings instead of curses in such a situation requires awareness and willingness to let go of our internal dialogue. It calls for a willingness rally against all our urges to get even and instead to choose a better response. Sometimes this seems impossible. Still, whenever we move beyond hurt, we give life not just to ourselves but also to the ones who have offended us.

Our Transformative Journey

At this point in my journey, I realize one thing that has remained consistent and true through all of the challenges and surprises in my life. What matters most is the size of your heart and the strength of your character. When love ends, especially when it is abrupt, it takes time and effort to trust again, but you have the power and ability to begin anew by creating an intention of what you want to build going forward.

Creating a new home and new traditions for my daughters and myself has brought a new level of joy and love to our lives that I never thought possible. We all have the power to create a life of love, whether we are single or married, alone or in a partnership. Love, joy, and peace are about how we choose to deal with the hand that life has dealt us. The primary foods (everything other than the food on your plate) will nourish you and allow room for gratitude and vitality.

A loving heart is the beginning of all knowledge.

~ Thomas Carlyle

Life is better than what I expected

Reflecting on my first destination spa job in California, where 13 guests at a time checked in and stayed a week to rejuvenate themselves, I realize how valuable this is to do for ourselves. They were able to step away from the stresses of their lives, eat well, exercise, receive body treatments and facials, educate themselves on new ways to improve their health, share community support, and most importantly rest. The transformation in one week was amazing, as their faces relaxed from the absence of stress and everything about them glowed with vibrant health. That's when the spa industry was in its infancy and was designed to be holistic encompassing all areas of wellness.

As the industry changed and grew, the holistic concept started to recede, and a more a la carte approach became the norm. It is now commonplace to get a massage here and a facial there. Destination spas led to hotel spas, then day spas, followed by medical spas. Given the easy access and affordability of hotel and day spas, destination spas are now considered a luxury as many people feel they can't take the time or afford the cost of such places.

But, what if, you could create a destination type experience without the high-end cost? This was a thought that stayed with me throughout the evolution of the spa industry. As I was creating spa experiences, training employees, and designing treatments to keep up with the rapid growth of the industry, I kept this thought in mind. Surely my love and talent for creating wonderful treatments and experiences that foster health and wellness could be a luxury everyone, not just the elite, could afford. Twenty years later, I am bringing that thought to life. I have incorporated the destination concept of holistic health and wellness in a place where my local clients can come and get a facial, wellness coaching, and connect with the wellness community. Clients who are not close can take advantage of support and coaching online and learn ways to do for themselves if they can't come in for regular appointments.

When I look back at my first destination spa experience, it reminds me we have come full circle. There are so many healthy lifestyle choices, and one size does not fit all. The challenge is to navigate the best options for you and incorporate them into your busy lifestyle. Whatever approach you take, I encourage you to not look at your health and wellness as a luxury but instead to nurture and care for yourself daily. This doesn't mean you have to go to a destination spa, but it does mean investing the time and energy in taking care of your whole self. Wherever you are in your journey of life, reaching out to others is a great way to get started. I have found that having a coach helps give you clarity and guide you to your unique true north.

Life is fragile, and it goes by quickly. Pick what is important to you, cherish it, and choose love as you go. When you sore to the highest peaks of joy enjoy every moment, and when you dip down to the depths of despair, have faith, hold on tight, and know that it won't last. You will return to your sea level and continue to experience the joy of life. One thing is certain that life doesn't stand still. I was a hospice volunteer for a while, and it was one of the most enlightening experiences. I found that people at the end of their lives would look you in the eyes and speak honestly from the heart. They were so authentic and loving. A lifetime of love and loss humbled them. All the pain and suffering, as well the love and joy they had experienced, were transparent and real.

If you haven't yet started your journey toward health and wellness, my recommendation is for you to start with gratitude. I start each day with gratitude and approach it with the attitude that says, "This is a wonderful new day. I've never seen this one before, and I am going to make it the best day ever." I suggest you invest 5 minutes each morning to reflect on and then write down three things you are grateful for and one thing you will do for someone in need. It's a life-changing experience. Never give up and get ready for the next blessing.

Everyone has a story. If you would like to share your story about your journey to health and wellness, I would love to hear from you. If you have found my story helpful, I would love to hear from you. You can email me or check out my website for upcoming webcasts and lectures.

About Caren Logan

Caren Logan is the founder and president of the holistic coaching firm True North Integrative Wellness. Coaching clients towards lifestyle strategies that contribute to optimal wellness, Logan provides knowledge, nurturing and support to help clients reach peak health and longevity. Her specialty is navigating difficult transitions—from divorce to death or illness of a loved one, to children leaving or returning home.

Logan worked for 30 years in the hospitality industry, creating spas and treatments for the world to come to relax, get treatments, and rejuvenate. She developed numerous resort and medical spa projects in London, Vienna, Zurich, Russia, and Malaysia. She also launched the spa industry's first online resource — VirtualSpa.com. Next came a successful career in luxury residential sales with Sotheby's International Realty.

As Global Training Director for top skincare brands, she educated the staff at prestigious properties such as Canyon Ranch, Hilton, Marriott, and Ritz Carlton on spa products, treatments, and retail strategies.

Logan is a graduate of The Institute for Integrative Nutrition health coach training program, and a licensed esthetician. Working at a destination spa in California, she saw the transformation that happened after watching guests begin to glow and improve their vitality with healthy eating habits, exercise, and receiving massage and skin care treatments, as well as addressing personal growth.

True North Coaching helps clients embody the destination spa lifestyle through integrated, results-oriented and flexible programs. Developing a deeper understanding of nutrition and lifestyle choices that work best for each individual lead to definitive results, such as improved energy, balance, health, and happiness. Be customized to fit your life, your schedule, and your goals. Every person has individual needs and lifestyles. Logan believes in a bio-individual approach to coaching –clients are offered individual coaching programs as well as group coaching.

Our Transformative Journey

True North's standard and customized programs for groups and individuals provide an intimate and individualized approach to wellness. **The Integrative Nutrition Plate** emphasizes the importance of local and organic produce, whole grains, high-quality proteins, plant-based fats, and water. **Integrative Whole Health** is a 6-month program that incorporates lifestyle factors that create optimal health, including relationships, career, physical activity, and spirituality. The program identifies achievable goals to accomplish a well-rounded, healthy lifestyle and optimal health.

The Corporate Wellness Program is a two-day wellness training program for management to set healthy lifestyle goals and learn strategies to start and maintain a daily practice that produces results. Contact us to discuss a Corporate Wellness Program designed just for your company, or to design a Wellness Package to offer to your guests.

True North's Aesthetics Program provides useful and practical knowledge to inspire you to execute an optimal skin care program for truly natural beauty. Groundbreaking research shows the interconnectedness of your body's systems and your skin. The skin's health reflects diet, sleep, schedule, stress level, exercise regime and the state of the microbiome. We have created a comprehensive package to test your body's biome and make an in-depth assessment of the products you are using on your skin. Personalized recommendations are provided for optimal skin and body care. In-person skincare treatments that will restore healthy skin and renew your appearance are available by appointment.

On-Demand Wellness is a membership service which provides personal access for ongoing support and education, resources, webinars, and inspiring guest speakers. Connect with others who support each other with energy, enthusiasm, and commitment via a private Facebook page. Participants learn, gain support, share your challenges and celebrate your triumphs within a real community.

Contact Information

Caren Logan
True North Integrative Wellness
Website: www.truenorthintegrativewellness.com
Email: caren@truenorthintegrativewellness.com

Chapter 7

Journey to The Other Side of Fear

By: Lana Shapiro

Every time I talk about my transformation, I am asked about what my defining moment was, that moment when I knew that a change was needed. I have yet to be able to pinpoint one defining moment, and I don't think I ever will. The truth is, for me, it feels more like a series of defining moments, one building on top of the next.

The Early Years

My life started at a small military town in Russia, where my family is originally from. My dad was an officer in the Russian military, and most of my childhood was spent moving from one small town to the next. I was the younger of my parents two children, seven years younger than my sister. When I think about this time of my life, I realize that I have very few early childhood memories.

What I do remember, however, is that there was a general sense of secrecy and fear. As children, we were told that we could not let anyone know that we were Jewish. Later in life, I found out that my father changed his first name to ensure that he would be able to serve in the military without anyone finding out that he was Jewish.

As I grew up, I began to understand more about anti-Semitism and how common it was in communist Russia. As young as ten years old, I remember hearing stories from my parents about Jewish people being attacked in their homes and taken things from them by the authorities. Were those stories true or were they told to us to ensure we kept quiet about our heritage? Honestly, I am still not sure about it, and at this point in my life, it doesn't matter. What I do know though, is that living in that secrecy and fear for my safety was the start of a fearful mindset that I adopted as the norm and took with me into adulthood.

First Major Transition

My father eventually retired from the military, and in 1993 my family was able to emigrate safely to the United States. Talk about a culture shock! For the first twelve years of life, all I knew was scarcity. I experienced things like no running water, shortage of groceries and other essentials, hand me down everything from my older sister or neighbor kids. I have this faint memory of being young and waiting for the water truck to show up and my mom standing there with large water pails waiting to fill them. When I was a little older, I remember a time where there was a national shortage of eggs and standing in line with my mother for several hours waiting to buy fresh eggs.

Those scenarios may seem shocking to you as you are reading this, but to me that was normalcy, it was all I knew. The real shock for me was going from that to having everything readily available. As a young twelve-year-old, it seems like we went from having nothing to having everything! I remember going to a supermarket and seeing shelves stocked fully with products I had previously only seen on TV. I tried foods that I had never tried before, and it all tasted so amazing.

Initial Struggles

This significant change brought much confusion to my young and developing mind. My environment drastically changed, but it took years for my mindset to catch up. Even at that young of an age, I had already developed a curious and over-analyzing thought process. I didn't just accept things for what they were, and I questioned everything. For a long time, internally, I lived with this "all or nothing" mentality, that underlying fear that things are too good to be true, that eventually, that abundance would disappear.

This has led to my initial struggles with food. When you grow up always being told "don't waste your food," "you have to finish everything on your plate," "it's a sin to throw food away," that sticks with you. I understood as I grew up that there was a reason for those messages in the situation, but I still could not break the habit of not finishing everything on my plate.

Even if I wasn't hungry, there was this obsession with never wasting food, not throwing anything away, the fear of scarcity stuck with me for years.

As difficult as this cultural transition was for my sister and I, it was rough on my parents as well. Not only did they have to leave everything and everyone they ever knew behind to take a leap of faith at a new and better life, but they also had to learn how to acclimate to a brand-new country, foreign language, inability to use the vocational skills that they knew and managing two teenage girls.

They continued to raise us the only way they knew how, in an extremely strict household, with lots of rules that could not be broken. Although my dad was retired from the army, his military manner of speaking to people never really left him, there was never any physical abuse from my parents, but there was this constant feeling of tension, fear of breaking the rules, of getting into trouble, of doing something or saying something that was out of line.

Even though we were away from the environment where we had to fear for our safety anymore, my parents continued to raise us as if we had to be cautious of everyone and everything. I didn't experience a typical American teenager upbringing, while all my friends were spending their weekends at sleepovers, parties, going to the mall, movies, etc. - I led a very loner life because I was never allowed to do those things. I buried myself in books, spending most of my time reading everything I could get my hands on, it was my way of escaping, identifying with different characters and living out my wildest dreams and imaginations.

Seeking Independence

I know my parents had the best of intentions and were only looking out for our safety and that they didn't know any different. I am not angry with them, and there are no more resentments against them for doing what they felt was the best thing to ensure their children's safety. However, at the time I graduated from high school, all I wanted was to get as far away from that strict environment as I could, I felt so suffocated, I wanted and needed a sense of freedom and independence.

I applied to several state Universities and was accepted to all four that I applied. University at Buffalo called to me, and I picked it even before I went to visit it. I think that was the first time I used my intuition to make a decision. That July, before my school semester started, I took a brave step of getting on a bus for an eight-hour bus ride with about twenty other total strangers to attend my college orientation. Spending those first three days in Buffalo, I fell in love, with the city and its people. I remember thinking at one point "I never want to leave here." This felt like my opportunity to leave the old me behind, and I didn't have to be that quiet, shy girl anymore.

Things aren't ever that easy though. Change doesn't just happen when you change your environment, and I was about to learn my first harsh life lesson. I was completely unprepared for all the independence I was about to get. I wanted so desperately to change who I was, I wanted to have lots of friends, I wanted to go out and socialize and do all those things I never had a chance to do in high school, or so I thought. Being an introvert, socializing proved to be a lot harder than I anticipated. I had no difficulties with introducing myself and meeting new people, but when it came time to further developing a friendship and opening up, I couldn't do it.

It was at that point that alcohol entered my life. I discovered that when I drank, something magical happened and I turned into the person I thought I wanted to be. Going out and drinking became a daily routine- parties, bars, there were always places to go, it didn't matter if it was a Saturday night or a Wednesday night, every night was party night in college.

I felt high on life, and I felt like I was finally able to talk to people about myself and my life without feeling like I wanted to crawl into a shell and hide. This was all I cared about, the wildlife, the party life. I was putting myself in so many dangerous situations, getting into cars with people who would drive drunk, going home with people I had just met, not knowing anything about them, drinking to the point of blacking out and having no recollection of the events from the night before. School and education took a back seat, I rarely went to classes anymore, and when I did, I was usually either still drunk from the night before or completely hung over. That whole first year and a half of college turned into one big blur. I gained so much weight that year, almost doubling that infamous freshman fifteen. When I wasn't drinking and partying, I was trying to eat my emotions away.

That summer I went back to New York City and stayed with my parents, got a job for the summer to earn some money. I wanted and needed to clear my mind and start taking care of my body. I felt like I needed to lose all the extra weight that I'd gained over the past year. I started walking every morning before work. I'd put my headphones on, listen to music and walk around my neighborhood and I aimed to walk at least two miles every day. But the weight wasn't coming off as quickly as I wanted, so I started looking into diet pills. I worked as a cashier at a pharmacy, so over the counter diet pills were readily available. I got the result I wanted, but I remember these feelings of extreme shame for taking the pills, it felt like my dark little secret, no one knew I was taking them.

On top of that, I was back in that strict environment of living at my parents' house and I couldn't re-adjust back to that. After getting a taste of freedom to be able to come and go as I please, do whatever I wanted when I wanted it, being back at a place where I was told when to be home by, reporting when and where I was going and with whom - it felt unmanageable. I couldn't wait for that summer to end so I could go back to college.

Time of Major Wake Up Calls

When that second year of college started, I was in rough shape, physically, mentally, emotionally. I kept taking the diet pills and kept losing weight. If you know anything about those pills though, you know they can wreak havoc on your body and mind. My anxiety started going through the roof. I felt like my heart was constantly beating fast and my mind was all over the place so I couldn't focus on anything. As I neared the end of my third semester of college, I received a letter that at the time felt like it was the end of the road for me, but in the long run, ended up being what I needed, academic probation due to grade point average is below 2.0. I had two choices: get my act together or get kicked out of school and be forced to go back to living with my parents.

My initial reaction was not good. I felt completely hopeless and lost. I had no idea what to do, how to even start turning things around. I remember laying on the couch in the college house that I rented with a few of my friends, in tears, with a bottle of beer in my hand in the middle of the day, staring at that letter and trying to process the words that were written on it. For the first time in my life, I had to admit that I needed help, I needed to reach out to someone, I couldn't figure this out on my own.

The next day I made an appointment with my academic advisor. I felt so anxious about going into that appointment. I felt like I was a little kid who got into trouble at school and going to see the principal. She ended up being very understanding and supportive, and we met for a while trying to figure out how I can dig myself out of the hole I was in. We talked about things that I liked and what I was interested in doing with my life and how my current major of pre-med was not the right fit for me.

I changed my college major over to psychology and picked my courses for the following semester. I felt excited about it. I finally felt excited about the school aspect and was looking forward to starting a new major. I've always been interested in learning more about human behaviors, my own included. I've always been a good listener, the one all my friends came to when they needed to vent, I was always very good at advising other people - but never very good at listening to my own advice.

That semester my priorities started to change, the drinking significantly reduced, much less partying and going out. But I still had so much trouble with focusing. I was still taking those diet pills, and my sleep was all over the place. I wasn't eating very well, often skipping meals altogether. But I wanted to succeed so badly. I did not want to be a failure. So, instead of doing the obvious thing and stopping those diet pills, I started searching for what else I could take to help me focus. That's when Adderall and Ritalin came into my life. Both were readily available through friends who had scripts for them. Any time I needed to study for a test or take a test, those were my magic pills. My grades went up significantly, and I enjoyed going to classes. I loved everything I was learning about human behavior, and it was all so fascinating. I was connecting with other students who had similar interests to me.

I was participating in a group project for one of my courses, and in conversation, the topic of diet pills came up. One of the girls in my group was talking about all the dangers of it and shared that a close friend of hers had a heart attack and died at the age of eighteen, everything she described how he was feeling leading up to it: heart palpitations, anxiety, moods swings, all the things that I had been experiencing myself. I was nineteen at the time, hearing that story scared the heck out of me! That day I went home and tossed all the pills out. It felt so liberating, and I don't think I realized how much of a hold they had on me, how dependent I had become on them. The following year, I remember hearing that one of the main ingredients from over the counter diet pills had been banned, due to being linked to heart attacks and deaths.

Looking back at this time of my life, I would say that it was the beginning stage of my overall transformation. I began to understand the true meaning of independence and being on my own. I learned that all actions have consequences and I started to accept taking responsibility for the choices that I was making. I guess you could say I finally grew up during that period, finally understood what it meant to be an adult. That school year, I ended up raising my grade point average to 3.5 and met a guy who would later become my husband.

Relationship Struggles

I'd love to tell you that it was all rainbows and butterflies from there on, but if that were the case, I wouldn't be writing this story. The relationship started great, for the first time in my life I felt like I was with someone who genuinely cared about me and loved me. But here was the problem - he loved me, but I did not love myself. I never made myself or my feelings a priority. I was so desperate to hold on to this relationship that I completely ignored all my feelings. I never spoke up when I didn't like something, and I made excuses for everything he ever did or said that did not sit well with me. I became completely emotionally dependent on this relationship.

About a year into dating each other, we moved in together, and that's when things started to feel disconnected. Within a few months of living together our communication became almost non-existent, basically felt like we were two roommates living in the same apartment being cordial with each other. I was still trying to hold on though, I wasn't sure what I was trying to hold on to, but I did not want this relationship to end, I completely defined myself by being in this relationship, I felt like I needed it, needed him to be happy. But I wasn't happy, I felt worse and worse about myself every day, once again feeling like I failed at something, feeling like I was doing something wrong. When it was time to renew our lease for the apartment - that dreaded "we need to talk" time came. Hearing those words of "this is not working out" felt like a knife cutting through me, it was such a strong emotion that I literally could not handle it. I remember going from feeling so emotional about the situation to feeling completely numb and going through the motions of finding my own apartment, packing, moving out and being alone.

That first month after moving out, I was going through the motions, still feeling numb to everything. I'd go to work during the day, usually go out to bars with friends in the evening and weekends. Then one night, I saw him out at a bar. I remember us just looking at each other and not saying a word. I got in my car that night and completely broke down crying as I drove home. All these emotions that have been stuffed down started to come out - so much anger and sadness. Anger at him and me, sadness that the relationship didn't work out, admitting to myself how much I missed him and then forcing myself to accept that it was over, and I needed to learn how to be alone.

As difficult as that process was, it ended up being the best thing to happen to us. Living alone was what I needed to start figuring out who I was, to learn how to become comfortable with me, to start making everyday decisions by myself and for myself, not to make anyone else happy, but to make myself happy. I thought I'd learned about independence when I moved away from my parents' house to go to college. But it wasn't until I was on my own - no family, no roommates, no boyfriend, just me and my thoughts, that I really learned, not only how to be on my own, but how to be comfortable being on my own. Learning how to be able to rely on myself, learning how to trust myself and my intuitions.

This time apart and away from each other showed each one of us what we were missing. It gave us time to appreciate the little things and stop taking each other for granted. We ended up talking about a month after that encounter and giving the relationship another chance.

Losing Myself in a New Role

Within a year of getting back together, we bought our first house, then got engaged and eventually got married. I was doing well emotionally during this time, felt happy, things were going well, and we started planning for a baby. A few months passed, and pregnancy wasn't happening. Every passing month it didn't happen felt like a failure. I became completely obsessed with tracking everything. I knew when I was ovulating, I knew exactly when it was time to take a test, and yet, they kept coming back negative.

I was so focused on trying to have a baby. I made this process stressful for myself. Other changes were happening at that time - promotion at work. We were in the process of purchasing our new home. At that point, it's been about eight months since we first started trying to conceive. With everything else that was going on, my focus shifted a bit and then it happened, right when I least expected. I will never forget that Friday at work. I felt awful: nauseous, headache. I knew it then, before even taking that pregnancy test, I knew it had finally happened.

I was probably the happiest pregnant person you'd ever meet after the initial first trimester morning sickness passed, I felt amazing the rest of my pregnancy, emotionally I felt like pregnancy hormones evened me out. Our little girl came in March 2012, via c-section because she was stubborn from the very beginning and decided to be in a breech position. I felt like everything with her was easy, easy surgery and recovery, she was a perfect baby, and I loved being a mom.

Two years later we decided to try for another baby, this time it took about four months to get pregnant. I was a little less obsessed about the process, plus having an active toddler takes your focus away a bit. The second pregnancy was a lot different. The morning sickness lasted longer, and I had very little energy, emotionally I felt like I was all over the place. I turned into this irritable person with no patience that I did not recognize. I thought it was all related to pregnancy hormones, and things would get better after my son came, but they did not. He was not an easy baby, it was very difficult to console him, he cried most of the time that he was awake, the only thing that made him happy was breastfeeding, and I felt attached to him all the time. I felt like I was failing at this mom thing.

I didn't want to admit it to myself, but I started to experience symptoms of postpartum anxiety, the irritability became so much worse than during pregnancy. I felt like I was losing my patience at the drop of a hat and I was either yelling or on the verge of tears. My sleep was terrible, by eating was terrible, and I felt like I lost myself. But I tried so hard to keep it all together, felt like admitting that I was struggling and how I really felt was a sign of weakness, a sign of failure. I went to my doctor and asked to be put on medication for anxiety. A few months into taking the medication, nothing has changed, other than now having side effects from the medication.

Internally I felt so unhappy and uncomfortable in my own skin, externally I pretended like everything was fine and I was adjusting to having two small children. Then I noticed that any time I took my son out for a walk outside, I would come back feeling so much better mentally, it became a daily habit. Every day after dinner, I'd put him in the stroller and go for a 2-3-mile walk. Once the weather changed and it started getting dark early, I had to stop doing the walks, but I wanted to continue experiencing the benefits. So, I started going down to my basement every night after putting the kids to bed, turn on an exercise DVD and workout for 30-45 minutes. It's so true what they say, "exercise is the most under-utilized anti-depressant." I gradually went off my medications, and daily exercise became my therapy. It was my "me" time, time to clear my thoughts and focus on myself.

The Final Transformation and Re-discovering Myself

I joined an online community of like-minded people and then created an online support group for all my friends who liked to exercise. That's when this whole idea of becoming a coach was born. This was what I loved doing, sharing my passion with other people for fitness and health, advocating for natural ways of improving health, not just physical health, but mental health. I started researching mind and body connections, and this path eventually led me to attend a nutrition school to become certified as an integrated health and nutrition coach. I took my passion for fitness a step further and became certified as a fitness instructor - leading group fitness classes. Making these changes helped me find my identity again, helped me re-ignite my passion for helping people.

As I reflect on all the changes I've had to make, I recognize how each difficult life circumstance led to discovering who I truly was as a person, not who other people wanted me to be, but who I wanted to become. From that shy twelve-year-old who moved to a new country, to a newly independent college student, to a young woman discovering the value of self-confidence in a relationship, to a new mom, feeling so lost during all those transitions. There was a theme that kept coming back throughout my life, this theme of irrational fears which often led to feeling stuck, almost paralyzed and unable to move forward, numbing my emotions along the way.

My message to you, my reader, is that fear is a liar. That voice inside your head that keeps saying "you can't do this" is a liar. You can make incredible changes in your life, and you can achieve so much more than you think you can. You will hit roadblocks, and you will sometimes hit brick walls, you will get close to accomplishing your goals and get scared - this time not from fear of failure, but fear of success. You will start to doubt yourself, start to feel like you don't deserve to succeed. I leave you with this quote by Marianne Williamson that has been guiding me for the last several years: "Our deepest fear is not that we are inadequate. Our deepest fear is that we are powerful beyond measure. It is our light, not our darkness that most frightens us. We ask ourselves, Who am I to be brilliant, gorgeous, talented, fabulous? Who are you not to be? As we let our light shine, we unconsciously permit other people to do the same. As we are liberated from our fear, our presence automatically liberates others."

Remember that life is a journey, not a destination. As you embark on your transformation adventure, don't look for an end goal. Set a goal, reach it and then set a new one. My transformation story is far from over, and I will continue to work on improving myself every single day and keep spreading my light to empower all others around me.

About Lana Shapiro

Lana Shapiro is the founder of Shapiro Holistic Health - a health and wellness coaching service that incorporates a holistic approach to helping people improve their physical, mental and emotional health.

Lana is a licensed mental health counselor in the state of New York with nine years of experience providing direct clinical services to individuals with mental health conditions, specializing in the treatment of trauma-related disorders. Lana focused the last six years of her career in the mental health and addiction field on training new clinicians at a non-profit agency where she's been working for the past 15 years.

Lana began her health and fitness journey in 2013, shortly after the birth of her daughter. After struggling with emotional eating, yo-yo dieting and lack of physical activity for most of her life - she decided to take control of her overall health and wellness finally. Lana joined an online community where she began to educate herself on proper nutrition and how to eat clean and use food as fuel. She began to exercise regularly with in-home workout programs and developed a passion for physical fitness

Lana became a certified fitness instructor in 2017 and began teaching group fitness classes, expanding her certifications to teaching three different group fitness class formats. Lana enrolled in Institute for Integrative Nutrition Health Coaching program in 2018 - receiving her certification in March 2019 as an Integrated Health and Nutrition Coach.

Lana currently resides in the suburbs of Buffalo, New York with her husband Michael and their two young children Elissa and Joshua.

Lana is a firm believer in the mind-body connection and teaches her clients to find a balance between the two areas. She uses a gentle and empathetic approach to help her clients connect the dots and figure out how every area of their lives has an impact on overall health and wellness.

Contact Information

Lana Shapiro
Shapiro Holistic Health
Website: www.shapiroholistichealth.com
Email: shapiroholistichealth@gmail.com

Chapter 8

In the Garden, He Met Me

By: Rebekah S. Hockley

I don't remember any part of my childhood or adult life in which my brother hasn't verbally assaulted me in some way or every way. Twenty years later into what I can remember of my childhood, he cannot still speak to or treat me with dignity, respect, kindness or love. I recollect too many instances of his verbal violence that colored so much of my life. I'll be honest, up until the last several years of my life, I have tried to change our story on my own. I've thought, "If I make the change, then he'll inevitably follow." Wrong. See, every abusive relationship consists of – a victim who desires to change the relationship so that circumstances will be different, but the fact is, only the abuser can change their behavior, and no amount of love, forgiveness or healing will make that change for them.

There was never a "first instance" of my brother bullying me. He had often called me names; my favorite has always been "Fat." Now that I look back, I laugh, as I maintained a 90-95lb frame until I was 17 years old. At seventeen, I hit a growth spurt that only sent me to a max of 105lb. It wasn't until I was pregnant that I ever reached over 110lbs on my worst day.

It didn't even matter what my friends said, every time I looked in the mirror, I saw an ugly, pimple-faced, fat, and flat-chested girl. I knew that every time I tried to make myself more than those names he called me, I would never measure up. This is what is called, "Memory Field," "Image Energy," and "Post-Hypnotic Suggestion." Sentences, experiences, and phrases that we or someone else create that become ingrained in our subconscious mind, and until we identify and release these energies, we will continue to seek to fulfill them – no matter how true or untrue they are.

My brothers' verbal abuse is impeccable, which should be when you've trained with it for twenty years or more. To this day, he continues to use his fear tactics and physical aggression to assert his authority in his relationships with his immediate family, including his spouse (which she happily applies in return). The last statement he made, which was the reason I would choose to never allow myself alone with him in the same house again was, "I could kill you, and no one would even care." If he wasn't throwing TV cables at me to get his way or threatening me with some physical violence or verbal assault, like "How stupid are you?" or "Why do you have to be so dumb?". He was ensuring that I didn't leave his presence with dry eyes. His statements were broad, and even now, I struggle with hearing those same words echo through my mind.

It was all his verbal aggression and threats of physical violence that grew the garden of self-hatred and depression that I lived with for a large part of my life. Having this for groundwork led me to the lifestyle I would lead for a long time. By the time I reached sixteen/seventeen years old, I had not only tried to kill myself three times, but I had spiraled far enough in my depression that my vice became an addiction.

Liberation Day

When you are taught to despise everything about yourself daily, you develop a lack of self-love that can lead you to anything and everything degrading and destructive – physically, mentally, emotionally, and spiritually. You believe you are worth nothing, and therefore disposable.

The first time I remember trying to cut myself, I was alone in a public bathroom. I worked through all the emotions – fear, doubt, self-hatred, denial – virtually every emotion that I could fight against before committing to the decision I did. I didn't succeed on this particular occasion, but eventually, that wouldn't matter, because I would follow-through soon enough.

When I finally did cut myself, it felt so good. It was as if every time the blade would slide between the thin, minute layers of skin I could feel the rush of anxiety and darkness slip away, allowing me the opportunity to breathe; to exist without the endless chatter that took place inside my mind. Every single slide of the knife, every single minute spent pressing the blades of scissors against my skin, every single moment I spent time on myself, I experienced liberation from the personal assault and the oppression of outside relationships pressing, baring down against my psyche.

There was an entire year of wearing long-sleeves to cover up scars that looked healed but wouldn't fully until years later. On the one hand, I didn't want anyone to see what I inflicted upon myself nightly, but on the other hand, I secretly hoped all my secrets would be seen, and someone would finally reach out to find me the help I desperately wanted.

I continued the physical assault against myself for an entire year before I decided that one addiction was enough, so I took up smoking cigarettes. I didn't have the energy for self-harm in more than one way, so I had to choose. It also helped that I had two best friends who helped keep me accountable in my endeavor to stay clean. I will say that if it weren't for both of them, I would have continued my self-harm addiction for much longer than I did.

Without A Fence

When you're raised in an environment where unhealthy relationships are allowed to flourish without being curbed or boundaries set into place, you are bound to subconsciously make the same choices throughout your life by choosing equally unhealthy relationships – romantically and personally. At sixteen, I would find myself in yet one more boundary-less relationship; another relationship filled to overflowing with manipulation, selfishness, and constant psychological assault. I would end up dating him on and off, for the next five years.

I was broken from the years leading up to sixteen, so adding another abusive relationship to my repertoire wasn't blindsiding or unpredictable. He was perfect. He was tall, dark and handsome, minus the tall part. I thought he was meant to be my savior and so we built a life together.

It was all very hush-hush since we were both from good Christian households which didn't condone dating much less sex, especially outside of marriage but we carried on, with or without the approval of family or friends. Late nights of sweat and virgin love would go off and on, as we debated back and forth between what was "right" or "wrong"; every decision depending on how it would look to his parents or how others would view him.

Every time he would go back and forth about whether we should be together, I was always to blame, and it was never his fault, just mine. When his mother found out, years later, she blamed me for the entire affair too. This is how I spent the on and off relationship – taking the blame, stripped of my dignity, and never once being viewed or thought of with love. It was always onto the next high, the next thing that would gratify him or bring him attention. He made damn sure I knew that as his side-piece, not a soul could ever know about me.

I'd spend countless days imagining every detail of the life we had and even more so the life we would have, always believing that these days of moral wrong-doing would be behind us and we could start anew. It never did. Instead, days turned into nights, which turned into weeks and months and finally, after all the deception, fakes façades and insincere gestures and remarks - he was gone.

Every sin we had committed together and apart was wasted. The trust I had built in another person was once again destroyed. We were engaged for about a year before he decided it was time to go, and he told me, "You're manipulative, and I'm not ready for marriage yet." Less than two months later he was dating someone else, someone with a child. How ironic, he wasn't ready for marriage with me but was ready to parent someone else' kid.

Some of our darkest experiences can often serve as our most tender memories, and this is what the summer of sixteen brought me. If I wasn't confused or neglected enough while being thrown back and forth between his, "I love you" and "We can't be together," I found out I was pregnant. So, there I was alone, young, struggling with a severely misconstrued sense of sexuality, and pregnant in a strictly Christian household. If there was ever a time I felt terrified, desperate, and completely abandoned, I can comfortably say it was the three months of this pregnancy.

At first, I chalked it up to being stressed with all the fear of being found out, fear of being left by the only man I was convinced would ever love me, and fear of disappointing my Christian family. I remember sitting in the bathroom, praying desperately that it wasn't happening to me, and that if "it" would go away, I swore to God I would never sleep with him or anyone else ever again until I was married. I never told him I was pregnant since I knew he'd immediately tell me it was my fault, wonder how "it" had happened, and then blame me for having not made sure "it" didn't occur. Instead, I kept the pregnancy to myself, yet another secret to hide.

Then one sunny summer afternoon, in a small town in the middle of Pennsylvania, I sat alone in the bathroom, in the house I can still smell the scent of as these words fall from my fingertips. I prayed, asking for my salvation from this situation. They say be careful what you wish for, and no truer words have been spoken because I lost the baby that afternoon, and I'd never be the same. I didn't realize it until the baby was gone, but that baby was my world, and I had wished it away.

I carried this secret until I was nineteen and then I told him. He was angry, told me that it wasn't my secret to keep and that he deserved to know. He told me he would have done right by me. I realized the culmination of events that added up to the insanity that was our relationship, and it was then I said, "I never told you because I knew you'd marry me, because we had to, and I wanted you to choose to marry me because you wanted me." He denied nothing, and his silence spoke more than any words could ever hope to say. It affirmed that everything we were was a figment of our childhood imaginations, our desire for normality in an insane environment of upbringing.

During the five years we were together, there was a lot of emotional and psychological upheaval. There was so much that should have been left unsaid that passed the lips of regretful children. There were many red flags and reasons I should have walked away. There were even more times I wish I could take back adolescent for Rebekah. I lost so much of myself to someone who had no idea how to treat himself much less a woman, and if all the other abuse wasn't enough, his infidelities should have been.

From the very beginning, I should have known. I just let myself be the abused girl my brother taught me how to be, and his psychological torture would present itself in this relationship too. It was indeed a dark time in my life and would later pave the way for all the disrespect I'd offer myself for years to come.

Once A Marine, Always A Marine

A couple of months later, I found myself trying a dating app after a friend told me to "get back on the horse" since I had sworn off ever dating again; that decision would change my entire life. There was a decent human being in the world, and he'd somehow found his way to me. We ended up becoming good friends. He was stationed overseas so our conversation would tend to take place on his time, which would end up meaning me skipping class just to Skype with him. It was truly the first time I had a man treat me like a lady with love and kindness and no ulterior motives. By the time he chose to leave the military, he had flown home, and I picked him up at the airport. We ended up dating for almost a year, got engaged that December, and I left him a few months after. Somewhere in my psyche, I realized he wasn't my best friend, and though we had a good friendship, it would never go any deeper. Until he faced his demons, a barrier would always keep me at arm's length.

Prince Eric

Within a few months of having left my second fiancé, I spent the summer living with my grandfather, assisting him with his wife who was dying of cancer. After she passed away, I stayed, and the bond I never had with a male figure was exemplified. He embodied what I hadn't had in a male role-model and taught me what true love was and the real meaning of marriage.

One night, I was working when a couple of friends called, texted, and direct messaged me about a mutual friend, Daniel, they were worried was going to hurt himself. Where my grandfather and I lived, we were only fifteen minutes away, so I assured everyone I'd check on him when he got off work. Daniel and I, our families, have known each other for almost twenty-seven years. In between my insanity, I had pieces of normality, and Daniel, his sister, and my second-oldest brother were the fragments I enjoy recollecting from those slivers of a good life. We were like the four amigos. We stayed out late, listened to music too loud, ate bad food, and had genuine, innocent memories together.

When I was asked to check on Daniel, it wasn't weird, and there was nothing sexual perceived by anyone because we had been raised so close as friends. There was this one time we tried to date when my first fiancé and I were on one of our "breaks" but what we tried creating, ended badly in my zeal for ensuring I didn't end up in any healthy or loving relationship. Daniel held a grudge about that, rightfully so, but that grudge wouldn't stop me from checking on him.

I remember waiting outside his door and how confused he was to see me standing there. He let me in, I'm sure begrudgingly, and I proceeded to sit down on his futon while he fixed himself a drink. He stood against the hallway wall, and we talked. I'm not entirely sure about what we discussed that night, but I remember the vodka bringing him liquid courage to eventually probe the question he had long struggled against, "Why didn't it work between us?"

At that moment, I remember hearing the entire universe telling me that he was it, and this conversation would be the most significant turning point of my life.

Over the next month, we would spend so much time together, making up for lost time.

Less than a month later, we took a trip to Las Vegas, Nevada for a three-day music festival, which was a pastime we enjoyed with our families as kids together. We got married on a whim and came home sailing on cloud nine. We've been married for almost eight years this year. He filled the gaps a normal, healthy relationship should have and has been the friendship and equally loving and nurturing partner I had always dreamed of. Daniel is the one who restored my soul to hope for something better than what the past had offered; he is what has restored my heart to love and shown me how to heal the holes I punctured in myself for so long.

Believer of Mercy

We had just celebrated our fourth anniversary when we found out we were expecting our first little bundle. As far as health was concerned, I carried a very healthy baby girl for 9+ months with no issues and excellent lifestyle. I had become obsessed with the proper nutrition, lifestyle, and mental health once I found out I was expecting. It seemed as though I was finally making a turn-around in acknowledging the healing and changes that needed to take place in my mind, my heart, and my soul. I engrossed myself in excellent nutrition, ensuring I was providing my baby with the essential nutrients she needed for all fetal development. I also took every step I could to put a boundary between me and every negative person I came in contact with, knowing that even their energy-output could affect my growing human.

Our Transformative Journey

I ensured my diet was the best it had been in my entire life up until that point, and aside from being swollen, I felt the best during that pregnancy, too. Food had been my medicine, and I enjoyed how the medicine made me feel and how it positively affected my tiny human.

While waiting for this tiny human to make its entrance, I became increasingly frustrated, overwhelmed, and very uncomfortable. I was past my due date, and my intuition told me something was keeping her there – I did many meditations to release the block I felt held her prisoner.

My mom, who was staying and waiting with us, suggested I reach out to a friend who was training in an emotional release and energy healing technique called EmotionCode. At this point, I was willing to try anything, so I reached out to her, and within the hour I was sitting at my computer engaging in a session that would be the pinnacle of what would change my entire life.

It was a Saturday, during the early afternoon on July 4th to be exact, as the woman began identifying and releasing trapped emotional energies. I could sense it with every wave of release I experienced as she worked. As she identified the energies and found the age associated with them, I would have vivid images of exactly what that energy was attached to; I could see the moments that caused it to harbor itself in my body. Amidst the removal process, she had identified that my tiny human was frustrated, rooted in the womb something had occurred (probably sensing my frustration) that was causing her to resonate with that energetic frequency.

By the time our session was complete, I was sobbing uncontrollably. I left the session feeling like I had released a tidal wave of pent-up energy. I laid down for a nap once we finished. I took four days to process and tried to relax, and on the third day, we took a trip to the beach.

Day four of my processing came, and I went into labor having a 100% natural birth with my hefty 8.4oz baby at 10:51 am. It was in that revelation that I realized that emotional baggage isn't just something we carry to attend counseling then to release. It's the reality for so many of us, holding us back from pursuing our passions, loving ourselves, and bringing healing to the generations – past, present, and future. By the time I delivered my baby, I had learned that I had to implement what I would later come to learn is called "Elimination Diet" – I nixed dairy and coffee. Miraculously, the whole-body rash I had struggled with the entire nine months vanished quickly, and my daughter's constant spitting up also disappeared. The correlation between learning how to eat better, treat myself better, and live better was very clear once she arrived. It was as if the entire universe had conspired to allow my life to begin to heal and true transformation to begin.

Baggage: Yours, Mine, Ours

Offering oneself as a gateway for generational healing is a step forward from victim to survivor, a true act of ultimate forgiveness. Looking back, I'm proud of myself, because despite choosing that first step for my healing, I never stopped to realize that I'd learn how to let go, forgive, and allow healing to take root where death once held me down.

Over the next year I would attend countless sessions, and with every meeting as I unearthed the damage of twenty-six years, I revealed generations of similar damage throughout my familial lineage.

I was able to experience the healing within myself, for with every therapy session I let go of my hatred, pain, bitterness and every ounce of misery I had held so tightly. Wounds that I had buried for decades were released, forgiveness started seeping in and eventually began pouring the more I chose to release. I let go of soul-ties to those who had abused me, abandoned me, and I repaired the healthy ties that had been damaged over time leading up to this renewing.

Childhood Reboot

Unfortunately, the following year, we ended up moving back to our home state of Pennsylvania and in with family. Within a month, my older brother and his family also moved in. I got pregnant, and my brother's wife did, too. After all those years, my brother was still the same abusive person with whom I had grown up. He went back to pushing and shoving, threatening and name-calling, and of course, throwing TV cables and screaming.

To top off his behavior, he also had an older daughter, close in age to our Cortana. His daughters' behavior mimics his own, and she would manipulate and physically abuse my daughter. My brother and his wife would brush her actions and reactions off as that of a typical small child, and so, just like my brother his daughter, too, was not held responsible for her actions either.

Coming back to my parents' home made me feel as if I had taken five million steps backward. As I had made headway with my healing over the first year of my daughters' life, I felt as if the following two years of unearthed pain, despair, abandonment, and lack of support. I never dreamt that I hadn't released what I needed to from the broken relationships I had within my family. Suddenly, I was swept up in every realization and recognition of the work I had ahead of me to do; work I never thought I'd struggle so hard to attain nor would bring me deeper healing than I had already experienced.

The cycle hadn't ended it had merely been in hibernation.

By the time my brother and his family had moved out (two years later), Daniel and I were adamant about boundaries being implemented and strictly kept. When my brother and his family would come over, I would remove our two girls and myself from the house. Any time they would show for a family event, we would ensure we weren't around. If no one else in my family believed in creating boundaries, we would be the first to start. For healing to occur within and between broken and abused relationships, boundaries are crucial for the ultimate healing – forgiveness, for the abused and the abuser.

Food for the Soul

The Spring my brother and his family moved out, and I enrolled in the Institute for Integrative Nutrition (IIN). My education through IIN continued the journey I had begun when I was pregnant with Cortana, and while I was learning boundaries, limits, and soul-healing, I was learning how to love my body from the outside-in.

It was as if the healing, which had started while pregnant with Cortana, was only the tip of the iceberg that was my transformative story. I didn't know it then, but I would learn more about my own heart, soul, and testimony than I ever imagined. With every dietary implementation, I tweaked and changed not only my eating habits, but I began to truly feel as if my soul and mind were also being transformed – simply by what I was putting into my body.

The second summer we were with my parents. I was diagnosed with Diverticulosis, Colitis, and hypothyroid. It was as if every correlation between what was going on in my outward life was a direct mirror image of what was being communicated on the inside.

Once diagnosed I began to eat differently and with more intention. I got a taste for Kombucha and loaded up on it for the next six months. I focused on trying to eat less sugar too. By the next summer, I was engrossed in IIN, and I went back to my doctor for a reevaluation. I was thrilled to say that while lessening my animal product, sugar, and processed foods intake, along with everything else I was learning at IIN, I had healed my Diverticulosis, and severely reduced my Colitis and "tired" Thyroid.

It was as if through choosing to heal from my soul-wounds, my choices in food and drink were also healed and in turn began to heal my physical self. It made me realize that to heal my physical ailments I needed to begin with my choices of not only what and who I surrounded myself with, but also how I think and talk to myself in my mind. If I lived with depression and anger in mind, I would manifest depression and anger into my heart which would translate to garbage and dis-ease in my gut and throughout the rest of my body.

It was as if through boundaries and living with the same abuse I had grown up with that I needed to revisit that place of pain and despair to find the deepest of healings, beyond the body, mind or soul. Choosing to heal, forgive and transform myself led me to begin true restoration of unhealthy relationships that I had long-suffered, and break the habits that had held me captive my entire life.

If there is nothing else you would take away from my story, I wish you would read the transformation that came about through letting go. It's not about how difficult your journey has been or how many people have disabled and abused you, it's about the lessons you pull from the experiences you endure. Where in your life do you deserve healing? Is there forgiveness you're withholding, because you have wounds that are left unrecognized?

Until you're ready to let go of whatever life you've led until now, your access to deep healing and restoration will be denied. You, alone, are the key-holder to your transformative journey. You are the keystone to your health, restoration, healing, and ultimate life transformation.

About Rebekah S. Hockley

Rebekah S. Hockley, co-owner of Restore, Family Health & Wholeness, LLC, operating alongside her feline-obsessed business partner and favorite sister (and only sister), Victoria, has been in and around the healthcare industry for twenty years. Providing care in the company of nurses, doctors, and other modern and alternative healthcare professionals, she educates and supports individuals and families towards healing and wholeness using products, coaching services, and teaching events.

As a child, Rebekah spent most of her time in healthcare facilities, playing BINGO or cards and talking and sitting with residents. By age 18, she began working as an Activities Assistant and found she enjoyed running the Dementia/Memory Care Unit. Over time, she progressed from Activities Assistant to Caregiver to Dietary Aide and eventually certified as a Nursing Assistant (CNA) where she began to specialize in Mental Impairments and Disorders.

As a CNA of over ten years, Rebekah administered care to private clients and facility affiliated patients throughout the Central Pennsylvania and Central Florida areas. She has also taught as an Aromatherapist for the past two years and conducts teaching events in healthcare facilities as well as one-on-one with individuals & families. Rebekah is also a Certified Emotion Code Practitioner and a Holistic Health Coach, providing training and support through emotional release techniques, and personal empowerment. She encourages the implementation of life-long health and wellness.

An addiction and domestic violence survivor, recovering from years of depression, generalized anxiety, emotional and psychological abuse, Rebekah uses her story of healing to shine an example of hope and possibility for individuals and families to discover their healing through mental and emotional transformation. She assists those suffering from mental anguish and generational affliction in identifying, releasing, and implementing lifestyle changes through healing techniques and other therapies.

Having overcome these traumas allows Rebekah to comprehendingly understand the pain and suffering of persons in these situations and thus she offers a unique approach to mental health and generational healing using empathetic and holistic health tools. She empowers individuals and families struggling with mental disorders, impairments, and injuries by providing them the space to rewrite their stories and testimonies, restore their health, and assist in returning them to wholeness.

Recently, Rebekah resigned from speaking in healthcare facilities, where she would educate and instruct clients, families, and staff towards integrating holistic healthcare practices in efforts to reduce patient medication use within facilities. She now serves as Vice President of Susquehanna Valley Home-school Diploma Program, a non-profit organization which assists individuals and families in graduating with state-issued diplomas through home school education supervision.

She has enjoyed volunteering for a local non-profit food pantry, Love Covers, which transports and provides food and dry goods for a sustainable family living. Rebekah has also volunteered for Tibetan Mastiff Rescue, Inc in re-homing and transportation, and has spent a considerable amount of time rescuing strays and re-homing cats and kittens from local farms.

Rebekah received her certification in Neurological Care in Central Florida in 2012. She received her Certification in Emotion Code for emotional release and energy healing through Dr. Bradley Nelson in 2016 and has an Associate Degree in Theatrical & Performing Arts from Harrisburg Area Community College (2011), which she utilized for eleven years performing and working with local theaters. Rebekah is a recent March 2019 graduate of the Institute of Integrative Nutrition wherein she obtained her certification in Holistic Health Coaching.

Rebekah and her husband Daniel, currently reside in Harrisburg, PA. They have two daughters, Cortana Christine, and Iris Nyx, as well as four cats, Moo, Neebs, Gir, and Mordecai (Morty). She hopes to pursue her education of energy healing in Body Code and T3 in 2019 and 2020. She enjoys exploring new holistic tools with which to experiment on her family, continuing her education in alternative health, spending weekends at her sister-in-law's family home in Chambersburg, PA, inter-state traveling, and infrequently working independently and in conjunction with animal rescues to rehome cats and dogs alike. It is her mission to continue serving her community and healing the world one mental transformation at a time.

Contact Information

Rebekah S. Hockley
Restore, Family Health & Wholeness, LLC
Website: www.restorefhw.wordpress.com
Email: restorefhw@gmail.com

Chapter 9

From the Darkest of Nights, Emerged a Shining Star
My Journey Through A 'Mystery Illness'

By: Donna Marie Costarella

Things are not always the way they seem. Perception can be distorted, for what we see through our eyes in actuality maybe just an illusion. You never know what other people are going through unless you go through it yourself.

Hindsight is 20/20, and as I write this story, my life's picture becomes clear, feelings of hopelessness, helplessness, fear, and despair all emerged. I never realized how all of life's challenges and years of stress and toxic exposure would, in the end, cause me to get sick. I hope my story will inspire others to realize that no matter what they are going through, there "IS" a light even in the darkest of nights.

When we fear the unknown, or are terrified of situations, a protective mechanism in our brain takes charge and tries to help us get through those trying times. The brain can suppress many of these horrifying memories to protect us so that we can move forward with our life, never realizing how we were affected. These subconscious thoughts may not be known to us, but the still play a role in how we live. When under stress, our bodies move into fight or flight mode. This can be a good thing when we need to act quickly in dangerous situations, but sometimes this stress response can become a default mechanism that can turn against us.

When our bodies are consistently in "fight or flight" mode, our bodies can mistake situations as a 'danger' when in actuality, they are not. When we are always in this state of high anxiety, it will do more harm than good, robbing us of our energy and exposing our bodies to inflammation and disease. I believe this is what happened to me.

I was born in 1956 the third child of an Italian mother and father. My mom and dad were 43 and 46 years old when I was born, and my brother and sister were 21 and 18. I can only imagine how my parents felt bringing a new life into the world after they had already raised two children.

As a young child, I knew something was different, my nieces and nephews were my age, and I became an 'aunt' at the ripe old age of 2. It was clear to me that my parents were older than the other parents at school and as a young child, it worried me so much so that many a night I cried myself to sleep thinking they would die. Little did I realize that one day I would be right.

Growing up I was a very picky eater, and my mom would do anything to get me to eat. As I grew older I developed a taste for food. Growing up in an Italian family, carbs were the norm. Eventually, gaining weight came easy and my pre-teen years were a nightmare for I was teased and called names due to my weight and always felt like I didn't belong. This played a very big part in my adult life since I was already insecure and developed a poor body image which was reinforced by some loving relatives when I was constantly told "I had such a pretty face," I just needed to lose weight. Of course, this added to my insecurities.

Life's reality hit me hard the night I was told that my mom had terminal cancer and only had a few months to live. I was only 16 years old the night I found out, and on my way out with my boyfriend. My mom was not told about her prognosis, so I had to pretend all was ok as I walked out the door. Walking out for the night was the hardest thing I ever had to do holding secret to the devastating news I had just heard a few minutes earlier, kissing her goodnight without crying as I left just killed me inside when all I wanted to do was stay home and hold her and tell her "PLEASE DON'T DIE, I'M TOO YOUNG FOR YOU TO DIE ON ME, I NEED YOU.

Every day was a struggle for me as I had to be strong for my mom's sake but who was going to be strong for me? I was living a lie going about business as usual when in fact it was anything but. In the end, watching my mom's health declined rapidly helped me accept her death as a blessing for she was in pain and on heavy medication.

Our Transformative Journey

After mom passed, my dad wanted me to help around the house, at 17, I had no clue how to cook, nor do anything household related for my mom did everything. Dad and I had many arguments over this when all I wanted to do was hang out with my boyfriend and friends. Being a headstrong teen, I rebelled and left home to marry a young man who I was dating and loved me very much. We were only 19 and 20 years of age, how could we possibly have a clue as to what married life would be like? I thought I knew everything.

My first "real" job was at a bank where I held a clerical position and a week before I was to go on maternity leave there was a robbery at our bank. I was seven months pregnant at the time when I heard a lot yelling coming from the front of the bank, and as I attempted to walk toward the commotion, I heard the sounds of gunfire erupt which stopped me right in my tracks. I ran back to my desk and squeezed my big pregnant body under the small space underneath; more shots were fired as I cringed. Many thoughts ran through my head, who were they shooting?

Would my baby and I be next? I was too terrified to utter a sound, I hovered in silence as I tried to be quiet as I sobbed uncontrollably. This terrifying event only surfaced as I wrote this chapter for I realized I had suppressed this devastating memory for over 40 years. Thankfully nobody was hurt.

I was 20 years old when my son was born and knew very little about life, babies or anything for that matter. I was in for a rude awakening the day I left the hospital for I had gained 70lbs and none of the clothes I brought to wear home fit me. Desperate, to lose weight, "Bulimia" was also born. At that time, I had no clue that eating and purging even had a name. I thought I had found a new way to have "my cake and eat it too." Before I knew it, I was in a vicious cycle of eating and purging, and before long my hair started to fall out in clumps, and I experienced my first of many panic attacks. Of course, this scared me, but not enough to stop. I was told by a doctor that losing my hair was related to my hormones after having my baby.

As I reflect, I'm sure my hormones played a role, but the bigger sister "BULIMIA' was robbing me of all essential nutrients needed to fully thrive. Of course, I didn't discuss my "dirty little secret" with anyone (well until now). This led to bigger problems and eventually affected my stomach, and at 21 I had my first endoscopy, one of many through the years. I tried my hardest to stop purging, but it only lasted a little while, sadly the vicious cycle of binge/purging continued to deplete my body, even more, compromising all of the nutrients needed to sustain a healthy mind, body and immune system.

The anxiety I experienced through all of this scared me too, little did I realize that I was doing all of this to myself. Now I was thin, but not healthy. I entertained bulimia through my second pregnancy four years later, and I gained only 11 pounds. Happy to stay thin, but the anxiety and panic attacks continued, determined to get "healthier" and manage my weight. I joined the gym, sadly my eating and purging continued.

Joining the gym was a new beginning for me. I loved it so much that I became addicted and eventually went on and became a certified fitness instructor and personal trainer. For once I was happy to accomplish something and loved leading my classes and helping others get fit. Too bad I couldn't help 'myself.'

During these years I went through a long, difficult separation, and the stress started to build up even more. With no child support, I had to figure out a better way to support myself and my family, so I enrolled in night school full time to further my education. Trying to juggle two part-time jobs, attend night school, homework, take care of my boys, along with trying to hang on to a relationship was getting tougher. Even though I was working at the gym, I still didn't have enough money to support my family. Thank God for financial aid, my dad, and my boyfriend.

Eventually, my relationship with my boys started to suffer as I tried to better my life. My only outlet was going out with my boyfriend on the weekend to escape my home life; in reality, all I escaped was my two precious sons. (Little did I realize the damage I would cause to our relationship would be a huge price that I'm still paying for today). The guilt continued to consume me, and I didn't know how to fix any of it. For many years I silently cried myself to sleep, unaware that all the stress was taking a huge toll on my health.

Eventually, my boyfriend moved in with us, and we enjoyed a great relationship until our household became a war zone when his teenage daughter moved in with us. I was living in a two-bedroom apartment, so our living room became her bedroom. The tension in the home escalated from there, and I could not handle the stress of my situation in a way that would benefit us all. I made many mistakes, but I did the best with what I knew at the time, and I had no way of knowing how I could fix any of it. My life was in shambles, and we all suffered.

It was July 4th, 1991 that one of my biggest fears came to life. Every year we would take the kids away for the 4th of July holiday, but this one year we stayed home because of all the fighting. Against my better judgment, I allowed my boys to go with their father who was having a big party. It was at this party that tragedy stuck. My 11-year-old son was left alone to play with a sparkler, being a curious young boy, he was letting the drippings of the sparkler fall into a pipe used earlier for the bigger explosives, something went wrong, and there was an explosion, and my son was injured.

As I went to pick up my boys unaware of what happened, I was told that my son was hurt and taken to the hospital, but nobody would tell me what happened to him. As I approached the entrance to the hospital, I saw my ex outside crying. Hey, wait! Why was my ex outside the hospital? WAS MY SON OK? As my body trembled too afraid to hear the worst, I was relieved to learn that my son was alive.

We were told that my son's finger was badly damaged and that they would have to amputate. WHAT? Can't you fix it? They did not do reconstructive surgery at this hospital, and in a desperate attempt to save my sons finger we signed him out and at midnight drove to a hospital that did reconstruction. Upon examination, we were told us that the nerves might be too frayed to reattach, but they would try, in the end, they had to amputate. My heart broke as I had to tell my son that they could not save his finger. My son just took his arm and covered his eyes, I died inside as I saw a single tear stream down his face. He was only 11.

During this time my work life was going well until terrorists attacked New York City on September 11th, 2001. Working downtown NYC, I felt the impact as I watched on live TV as the planes hit the WTC Towers a few blocks away. When I realized NYC was under attack all I could think of was "WHERE IS MY SON"? (My older son worked directly across from the WTC). Since the phone lines were down, there was no way to reach him.

As a mother, I wanted to run and to look for him, but the common sense inside me knew that trying to find him would be impossible. This added to the guilt I was already carrying around inside of me.

Living through the terror attacks was terrifying. Not knowing if my son was ok was even worse. I tried to stay focused and not panic as I directed a few of my coworkers to take the ferry out of NYC. There was no way of knowing if the ferry was even running, but it was the only way I could think of to escape the nightmare that was unfolding right in front of our eyes.

As we walked through the streets of downtown Manhattan, I'll never forget the look on people's faces as we walked the few blocks to the ferry. The blank stares, the fear of uncertainty, disbelief, and shock was written on everyone's face. I felt like I was in a horror movie and the big monster was coming to kill us all never knowing where the next plane would land. As the second tower fell and the choking dust started to enter the ferry, we were lucky to catch the last ferry out of NYC.

Fear of the unknown consumed everyone. There are no words to describe the intense feeling of helplessness as we prayed to leave the dock before the dust would choke us even more. I tried to stay calm, as my thoughts were with my son, it seemed like an eternity before I was able to reach him but a welcome relief to know he was ok.

It was in April 2003, when I saw a major decline in my health while working in an old building undergoing major renovations. Just trying to function became a huge challenge, but eventually, I had to take a leave of absence, I just couldn't function. I was exhausted (not the normal tired; it was a nervous tired). Taking a shower would cause me to have to rest for hours as it took away the little energy I did have.

What was even worse was not knowing what was going on with me. Getting out of bed was a chore. I could not even hold a conversation without getting exhausted. Many times, I wanted to cry out of frustration, but I didn't have the energy. I experienced extreme brain fog and functioning became a daily challenge all while dealing with debilitating nausea.

Just when I thought things couldn't get any worse, they did, I didn't know what was going on with me, and I was scared. While I did see many different specialists and went through many tests nothing significant was found to explain my symptoms and many times I was told "It was in my head" just because 'I looked healthy."

High Blood Pressure Spikes (Hypertensive Crisis)

As I gained back some energy and my nausea subsided, I was able to eat again when another symptom surfaced. One day while eating, I felt a weird sensation in my upper stomach, and when I touched the area I felt a huge lump. I tried to feel around it, and as I explored the sensation, I could not have imagined what I would experience next. I felt as if something inside me had burst open which sent this feeling of fluid running up and down my entire body. It ran up and down my insides like a faucet running out of control.

I could feel the pressure in my head, and behind my eyes, I thought my eyeballs would pop right out of their sockets. What was going on with me now? This was it "I WAS DYING." As I drove myself to the ER, terrified I would die on the way, I was glad to arrive alive. While at the ER they tried to take my blood pressure, but it would not register, as the rush kept running up and down inside my body I remember saying "IM DYING, I'M DYING HELP ME." I was given some blood pressure medication, and when they were finally able to get a reading, it was 186/120.

God only knows how high my blood pressure was when I first got to the ER. I now know that what I experienced was a "hypertensive crisis" and I experienced a few of these life-threatening episodes for a while until we found the right medications to control them. Side by side along with my high blood pressure spikes I was also experiencing tachycardia. My heart rate would zoom up to over 200 beats per minute many times with the slightest bit of exertion. This included just getting out of bed, walking up a few stairs, using the bathroom, anything I did would cause my heart rate to skyrocket. Along with everything else I was experiencing, extreme anxiety, major fatigue, none of these left my side. My symptoms continued to mount.

My life now consisted of one specialist appointment after another. If I didn't have a doctor's appointment, I had a test scheduled. My calendar was booked for months. My symptoms continued to wax and wane, and I was terrified. I didn't know what was going on with me and eventually, severe depression set in. Again, I didn't care if I lived or died, as a matter of fact 'dying' would have been a relief.

I accepted death as a way to escape my own body. I was scared and tired of all the tests, the hospital stays, including ER visits, angiograms, MRI's &

Our Transformative Journey

Cat Scans, sonograms, echocardiograms, EKG's, tilt table tests, brain scans, colonoscopies & endoscopies, capsule studies, nerve testing, halter monitors, Octreotide Scans, blood tests, and two trips to The Mayo Clinic. I saw every kind of specialist, and I still didn't have any answers for my "mystery illness."

My body had turned against me, and I didn't know why, and neither did any of my doctors as I lost all hope of ever finding an answer. Even though I was diagnosed with many different things, they didn't add up. Another puzzling symptom was my reaction to foods, smells, light, sound, medications, dyes, cold, heat, season changes and so much more.

As I look back, I realized that my symptoms came in clusters, and there were times that I would be able to "function," but after a short period my symptoms would return many times with a vengeance, this went on for 14 years. I also noticed that I would get worse during the spring and the fall. During the good times, I was able to go away on vacations and not entertain one symptom. Now, this doesn't make any sense whatsoever. RIGHT? Through all of this and as this mysterious illness took over my body and my life, Doctor Google became both my friend and my enemy. Time and time again, the anxiety of looking up things would bring an immediate panic attack. I was sure I had many of the horrifying disorders I read about. The good thing is I did rule out many disorders, and learned about so many others. "Would I ever find an answer?

In 2015 my symptoms escalated to a new high again, my nervous system was shot. I thought I saw my low point many times through the years, but this time it took on a new meaning of "LOW." I experienced too many symptoms at the same time and digesting food was impossible. Anything I ate would sit in my stomach and not move. Debilitating nausea that came with it was relentless. What made things even harder was that I was unable to 'relax my body, as I try to lay down to rest my body would stiffen up unable to feel the bed underneath me as I lay like a stiff board.

This not only took a huge toll on me. It also affected my husband. "Joe" felt helpless and didn't know how to help me. Every time I had an 'attack' **(and there were many),** I'd call him for support, and after many years of this, he too started to feel the stress of it all.

There were many nights that I was unable to rest, my body would shake uncontrollably, and my anxiety level was through the roof, Joe would be right there by my side holding me until my body calmed down so that we both could go to sleep. Many days he went to work with very little sleep and life as he knew changed drastically. Joe has been by my side through thick and thin, through every doctor visit, test hospital stays and more. As you can imagine, this started to wear him down, and he suffered too. I was desperate, and nobody was able to help me.

Again, the idea of death was my only escape. I wanted to run away from myself as I sat sobbing and shaking uncontrollably on the floor curled up in a ball like a crazy person. I prayed that God would take me that night as I lost all hope, welcoming death would be a relief, and I was at peace with that.

Desperate, I made an appointment at the Mayo Clinic and sent them all my records along with a list of my symptoms and diagnosis. I suspected "Mast Cell Activation Syndrome" I made two trips to The Mayo Clinic and I was diagnosed with Ehlers Danlos syndrome Type 3 Hypermobility. This diagnosis led me again to Mast Cell Activation Syndrome (MCAS), and by chance, I found a correlation between MCAS and EDS of which I had many of the "Red Flags" mentioned. This explained the reaction I would get after eating or being exposed to toxic chemicals. I didn't realize that the palpitations, stomach distress/bloat, extreme anxiety I was experiencing through the years were also considered an allergic reaction. I was diagnosed with Mast Cell Activation Syndrome.

My Turning Point to a Healthier, Happier Life

After years of searching, I realized that doctors were NOT able to help me and that it would be up to me to "TAKE BACK MY BODY." I made an appointment with a nutritionist/kinesiologist Dr. May who explained to me that my body was working overtime and in a constant state of 'fight or flight'. She also went on to explain that when our bodies are used to responding in this way it becomes a default mechanism and it would be up to me to 'retrain my body.' I also learned that many of my disorders were related to inflammation, she put on an anti-inflammatory diet, and within a week I saw a huge difference in my stomach issues and my body pain was gone too.

I then incorporated guided meditation, rhythmic breathing, and visualization techniques and to my surprise, I finally was able to see "a light at the end of the tunnel." This became part of my daily routine, and finally, I was able to relax my body, and my extreme anxiety was now minimal.

Now I'm on a roll. I belonged to many support groups and was referred to a program that was known to have many positive results. Hay, since I already saw progress with my research what did I have to lose? I diligently practiced the exercises as instructed, and within a few months, my symptoms and outlook on life continued to improve. My attitude was positive, and I was happy to be functioning again.

I learned when a part of our brain (our Limbic System) receives mixed signals and perceives stimuli as a threat it could cause our bodies to overreact. When our brains don't function properly due to certain stressors or toxins etc., the messages our brain receives becomes distorted, and our bodies respond. Maybe everything I was experiencing was "All in my head"?

I now know that my stressful, toxic life had caused a breakdown in my limbic system causing my body to go haywire for I was a perfect candidate for this due to my long-term exposure to mold and other toxic chemicals along with the mental and physical stressors that I endured through the years.

I learned that if I 'rewired' my brain to build new pathways, build new experiences and to think in a new way than I would heal. I became aware of old limiting beliefs and knew by changing the way I perceived my illness would be a major factor in my recovery. If my brain was ruling my body and trained to 'attack' me, then I could reverse it. To my excitement and joy, I made major improvements to my symptoms, my happiness and finally my life.

Road to Health and Happiness

I now have a new lease on life, "a purpose." I now look at things in a positive way and have become an inspiration to those around me. I can honestly say there is no stopping me now. I learned to forgive those who had hurt me in the past, and that 'forgiveness' is not for the other person: it was for me to heal, for me to let go, and **most importantly I learned to forgive myself**. I realized that I had been punishing myself all along through the years with self-doubt, insecurities and not loving "me." I now realize that I did the best could with what I knew.

I am a loving person who made some bad choices and had some pretty bad things happen in my life that affected my health. I refuse to let any of this define who I am. I stopped living in the past, and I felt the freedom of letting go, the power was now inside of me to choose how I wanted to live the rest of my life.

My Life's Purpose and Commitment

My passion for helping others through nutrition, and awareness of the mind-body connection, lead me to enroll in The Institute of Integrative Nutrition, with a title of a certified "Integrative Nutritional Health Coach. I am now able to help others who are ready to turn their life around. We "DO" have choices. (I will talk more about this in my upcoming book to be released in 2020). If you or someone you know can relate to my story and want to know how you too can enjoy life through its hard times, let me help you find the way. I know what it's like, I've been there and you're NOT ALONE.

About Donna Marie Costarella

Donna Marie is the Founder and CEO of Think Healthy Live Healthy. As an Integrative Nutritional Health Coach, Donna inspires and guides her clients to achieve happier healthier lives through diet, mindfulness and lifestyle changes. She brings awareness to her clients so that they can take the necessary steps to achieve their ultimate goals. Donna's dedicated to helping educate her clients through her Health Coaching Practice, offering personal and group "Discovery Sessions."

Before Donna's "Health Crisis" in 2003, she was a certified group fitness instructor and personal trainer for over 25 years with several certifications under her belt. She enjoyed helping her clients get into shape with her extensive knowledge in the fitness world, always keeping up with the latest trends & certifications.

In 2003, Donna's health took a turn for the worse, and she faced many debilitating and chronic health issues. Donna endured 14 years of countless doctor visits, diagnostic tests, hospital stays, which also included two trips to the Mayo Clinic in her quest to find answers, sadly not one of her many specialists was able to help her.

Only recently Donna realized that her debilitating symptoms were caused by her stressful lifestyle and her longtime exposure to mold and other toxins throughout her life. What Donna believes happened to her is that her body just went haywire. Her immune system was mistaken everything as a 'danger' and was 'malfunctioning and attacking all of her bodies systems. Also affecting Donna was her heightened sensitivity to smells, light, sounds, heat, cold, and more which she now knows as Multiple Chemical Sensitivity. Her autonomic nervous system was unbalanced, and she experienced allergic reactions to many things that we take for granted even food. (For a whole list of symptoms, please refer to her website) www.thinkhealthylivehealthy.com.

Donna's passion for living a better quality of life began when she became desperate and she decided she had to take charge of her failing health to recover from "Her Mysterious Illness", for there were many times Donna wanted to give up, for dying would have been a relief, but the natural fighter in her kept her going. She realized it would be up to her to take charge of her health and "TAKE BACK HER BODY."

Through Donna's determination and extensive research on diet and the mind/body connection she finally was able to attain her mission to live a happier healthier and productive quality life. Through her success, Donna uses a holistic approach to bring awareness to her clients and brings attention to the fact that it's not only about the food they eat that affects their health but how happy they are in many other aspects of our life. She is committed to helping others attain the knowledge necessary to move forward in their life implementing individualized tools to help her clients attain their health goals. Her compassion for others is unsurpassable.

In March of 2018, Donna decided it was time to get her certification and enrolled in The Institute of Integrative Nutrition® and is excited to be certified as an "Integrative Nutrition Health Coach" which she holds that title proudly. Through her darkest hour, Donna has reaped the rewards of her efforts and now can see daylight. She loves speaking to local groups sharing her impeccable knowledge and is dedicated to her mission of helping others. One of her favorite quotes is "Life isn't about waiting for the storm to pass…. It's about learning to dance in the rain".

Donna's is married to Joe, her best friend and soul mate for over 30 years. She has two married sons and two married stepdaughters, and between them, they are blessed with seven beautiful grandchildren. In her spare time, Donna enjoys hosting and planning game days for her grandchildren. She loves introducing them to the old games she played as a childlike bobbing for apples, jacks, pick up sticks, hopscotch and so much more. Donna also enjoys doing the same for her family and friends for she truly believes that laughter is the best medicine. She also enjoys working out, reading, traveling and is committed to furthering her education and has a continued interested in the mind-body connection. Donna truly believes that our minds rule our bodies and play a huge part in our health and happiness. Donna is a committed professional who continues to educate and inspire others in their quest to live happier and healthier quality lives.

Contact Information

Donna Marie Costarella
Think Healthy Live Healthy
Website: www.thinkhealthylivehealthy.com
Email: info@thinkhealthylivehealthy.com

Chapter 10

Don't Like Your Story? Change It!

By: Lynn Friebel

Each of us has a story to tell about our lives, but how many of us are truly satisfied with its content? If it includes struggle, does it also include triumph? If it includes poor choices and brokenness, does it also include love and forgiveness? For over five decades, I struggled with my own story. Not only did I realize that it was extremely unbalanced, I realized that I let the negative sections of it— chronic pain, emptiness, relationship failures, self-doubt, and fear—define me. My story kept me from living the life I truly deserved to live.

It was during the process of discovering this ugly truth, however, that I experienced one of the most powerful and healing moments of my life! I realized that not only did I have the ability to change my story; but also, sharing it with others could fulfill my purpose, making my own story even better.

Take a step back; listen

Helping others has always been part of my desired life. I have worked in the fitness field for over 35 years. I am certified to teach, coach and empower women in a variety of ways from yoga to Zumba®. What I teach others is from the heart, and a result of education, research, and training that I wholly believe makes a difference in people's lives. For many years, I was not living the life I was teaching others to live. On the outside, I looked and sounded great—perfect at times. On the inside, I suffered greatly.

People would tell me I was powerful and beautiful, but all I felt was a pain– physical and emotional. I was fearful of the future, of what it may, or may not bring– personally and professionally. I ignored all of the signs my body was sending. *How dare I slow down?* Some women depend on me– need me. Who would help them navigate through *their* insecurities, poor habits, shame, and stress? Who would build up *their* confidence? All of this began to weigh on me.

Sometimes we forget who we are and become who we think others want us to be. So many of us are lying to ourselves— putting on an identity we want others to see, hiding who we are from ourselves and others. For decades, I hoped that some magic would reveal my true purpose.

Now I realize, of course, that the answers have always been in me, I just needed to be quiet, and listen.

Become *friends* with the pain

Just after I turned 53, I felt something inside of me shift. Daily, for years, I was keeping up the act of being healthy to help others become healthy. But, suddenly, I started to feel like every part of my physical and spiritual being was fading; like I was suddenly wired differently. I began questioning and doubting myself. I began to blame myself for not doing the things I thought I wanted, and not being where I thought I wanted to be in my life. I became confused, which led to intense loneliness and isolation. Eventually, I could no longer embody the peace of the present moment.

One cold, January morning in 2018, I awakened with what I thought was an *explosion* inside of my head. The pain was so intense that I had to hold my head up in my hands. My husband carried me to the car and drove me to the emergency room. Multiple tests provided a few answers, and I was sent to another hospital for further evaluation. Those results revealed that something inside me did shift— the C2 in my cervical spine. It shifted to the left, creating the intense pain in the back of my head and neck. At that time, the suggested treatment was to go home and rest. It was hoped that the problem would resolve itself in time, with physical therapy and pain management.

My days were consumed with doctor appointments, physical therapy, acupuncture, massages, and IV treatments. As if dealing with my neck issue was not enough. I also learned that I had a leaky gut and celiac disease. I changed my diet, applied manual cervical traction, did physical therapy exercises, and used a ball rolling method, three times a day. I tried to stay active with yoga, but even forward-bending resulted in nauseating pain. *Nothing* made the pain subside.

Medication barely helped. I was on Gabapentin, Vicodin, and steroids, which took away some of the pain, but left me in a sedated state, living in a dark place. I was disconnected and praying to be released from this hell. The fear of addiction was real, and I sank into depression. There were many times I just wanted to give up and asked God to please let me fall asleep and wake up in Heaven. I would often tell people, that if I overdosed, it was surely an accident. I even left a note one day beside me in bed saying, "I am sorry— it just happened," because I could not remember if I had taken my meds already or not. The pain was severe.

Somehow, through the fog, it occurred to me how badly my mother fought to stay alive despite her many health issues. How dare I treat my life so casually? It was time to find a way to re-design my life—figure out how to live with chronic pain and make the best out of the terrible hand I was dealt.

I was finally ready to face the pain, forgive it and even *make friends with it*. I started to embrace my suffering and reframe it as a path to spiritual maturity. I believe God put me on this path to recover, restore and to draw near to His word. I'm not going to lie; my flesh struggled with this—there was a fierce battle between my flesh and spirit. I committed to daily scripture-reading and prayers, which helped significantly.

Find a new path

Sometimes it is necessary to stop what you're doing, what you've always known, and look for a new path. While I was recovering from cervical spine disorder, I couldn't exercise. This was especially difficult for me because I relied heavily on exercise as a way of avoiding the emotional and mental pain I had. I played exercise videos on my laptop, while in bed, in hopes of soothing my restless spirit. I tried to visualize my body doing the different postures and movements. At one point, a restorative yoga video popped up. I watched in awe and thought: *this is something I can do!* I propped myself up with pillows and blankets and followed along with the video. I did it, and I loved it! Restorative yoga lit me up inside, gave me a sense of triumph, and it gave me hope.

This new path to a better me, a better life, revealed itself to me and I knew I had to follow it. I wanted to expand my knowledge and gain the tools needed to deepen my practice. I called local yoga studios hoping to find classes, but no one offered restorative yoga. When all else failed, I asked Google. It brought me to a studio in Dayton, Ohio.

I attended the training and soaked up as much information as I could. One of the owners, Barb, created positive change and influenced my life. She was beautiful, kind, and brilliant. She shared her knowledge, passion, and love with her students. I experienced such spiritual awakenings while in her presence. My meditations led me on journeys where I experienced beautiful color bursts and explosions of crystal-like fireworks. My body felt like it was floating at times. I could feel energy and warmth flowing through my body from head-to-toe. The entire experience resonated with my soul and I finally felt alive again!

I did not want to leave, but I returned home so I could share what I learned with others. I ordered bolsters, blankets, blocks, sandbags, eye pillows—everything I needed to hold a class.

Fight the doubt and fear

As soon as I became excited about this new way to turn things around, a familiar flood of self-doubt reared its ugly head: How can you teach a class when you never know how you will feel from day to day? How can you show up for others when you can't show up for yourself?

Sadly, despite my recent surge of purpose and my strong desire to help people, I wasn't strong enough in that moment, and the voice won. I put a hold on adding the restorative class at the studio, and the props stayed in boxes in my garage for over a month. But why? I knew this practice was important, magical, and healing. I knew others would benefit as I did.

Then, on a morning just like all of the others, while reading my daily devotional, a voice spoke to me that was not full of doubt. I heard it loud, and clear: *Do not fear change, for I am making a new creation, with old things passing away and new things continually on the horizon. When you cling to old ways and sameness, you resist My work within you.*

I knew what I had to do! I went out to the garage. I felt like a little girl on Christmas morning peeking in packages to re-discover my restorative yoga props.

My head still felt like it was going to explode from physical pain, but I was determined to push through it, and fight the doubt and fear. I set up a station with a chair, put on my favorite Christian music, and I did not stop until each bag had 7 pounds of sand in it. It took me longer than most to complete this task, but at that point, just finishing the task was a huge accomplishment. I added restorative yoga to the schedule, and the first class sold out quickly, with a waiting list! The clients loved it and signed up for more.

I still suffered from terrible pain, but sharing this practice was my gift to others, and myself. I felt I owed it to myself to show up– for them, and me. Eventually, I became strong enough to overpower that voice and looked for ways to advance my training. I felt like I had more to give and more to gain.

Trust the journey, the process

Self-awakening is not an easy journey, but it has infiltrated my life, and I am all in. I now meditate, breath, pray and serve. Everyone's journey is unique—I want my clients to know it's okay if they can't touch their toes or throw a "Bird of Paradise." It's okay if they never throw an arm balance because, what they will learn, is to balance their body, mind, and spirit. Our journey may not be without struggle, but if we trust the process, we will eventually find our way.

Sometimes, to move forward, it is necessary to look back:

Who am I?

What is my purpose?

What fills me with joy and laughter?

These questions took me over five decades to understand. To find the answers, I needed to understand what led me to this point in my life. I needed to revisit my past.

At the age of three, I was found in my bed suffocating on my blood and was rushed to the hospital. I had emergency surgery for a post-tonsillectomy hemorrhage. The doctor told my mother that I would always be a sickly child; that the odds were simply against me.

Throughout the years, I took on the identity of a sick and frail child. I carried my childhood emotional wounds with me into adulthood. I created a false self—the person I presented to the world. I was perfect so others would not see what a mess I thought I was. I pretended everything was good when it wasn't, I pretended to be happy when I was miserable, and I pretended to love when I did not. I lived most of my life wearing a mask to hide the pain and protect myself.

At the age of 29, I had a job I enjoyed and great friends, but it still felt like something was missing. I had everything I thought was important in life so why wasn't I happy? Was I too selfish? I struggled to understand it, but the huge void I felt bothered me. Looking back, I realize I didn't know who I was yet, or what made me happy. I kept expecting something or someone to make me happy. Unfortunately, I applied that to love and thought marriage would make me happy. Eventually, that naivety led to divorce, a career change and another illness— chronic fatigue syndrome.

I didn't realize it then, but this was just another example of holding myself back. The doubt that I would ever be well kept me from seeking true wellness.

Keep fighting

At the age of 40, I tried, once again, to rise above the label—of being sickly and weak—created during my childhood. I incorporated my love of fitness back into my daily routine and changed careers. Life was good again! It wasn't long before another injury tried to knock me down. This time, a cervical spine disorder required surgery to fuse my cervical spine from C4-C6. After weeks of therapy, I was released to resume "normal activities." I had no idea what normalcy was anymore. I decided it was time to put my life in order—I deserved happiness! I carved out time to practice meditations and self-love and focused on what was important to me, not others. I wanted someone to share my life with, so I invested time and energy into dating. I met a man with similar beliefs and values. He lived out of state, but we hit it off and, eventually, the whirlwind romance turned into a beautiful commitment. We were talking about marriage, but it would mean me leaving Ohio. Unfortunately, around that time, my mother's health started to decline rapidly, and I felt pressured to stay close in case she needed me. Much of that pressure and guilt was self-induced, but she made her feelings about me "leaving her" clear.

Reluctantly, I ended the relationship and remained in Ohio. I ended up resenting my mother for it, but I didn't want to let it hold me back. I went back to my workouts and running. I meditated in the middle of my living room daily and found God as my comforting source of love. I went back to my roots and found a charismatic church that I attended every Wednesday night and Sunday morning for services. I fought past the emotional pain and helped care for my mother.

Setbacks

I never really had a good relationship with my mother. The years leading up to her death were especially hard on the relationship we did have, but they color my story quite a bit. When rewriting it to fit the story I want to tell about my life, the sections about my mother were the most difficult to reframe. Perhaps hearing it the way I remember it can shed some perspective.

When planning my second wedding, I tried to convince my mother that she didn't have to be there. I didn't think she was well enough. She just had a kidney transplant and needed to stay home and rest! But, she was a stubborn Italian lady, and she was not going to miss her baby getting married. She bought a beautiful green dress, attended the wedding, and then my aunt and uncle escorted her out early from the reception. What she did not tell us is that her surgical incision had a small opening and she kept that a secret. My mother was very good about keeping secrets. While on my honeymoon, she was life-flighted to the hospital because the wound that she kept a secret was infected with gangrene. Her abdomen looked as though a shark had taken a huge bite out of her.

This was a front-seat rollercoaster ride for my family for years to come and was a huge setback for me as well. But you only get one mother, so I put her first, and don't regret that. Mom was in and out of multiple hospitals and bedridden in skilled nursing facilities. For days at a time, my sister and I would sit by her bedside holding her hand and moistening her lips with ice chips. She stopped eating and slipped in and out of consciousness. It was awful to watch my mother slowly fade away, but one thing that amazed me, and her doctors, was how hard she fought to stay alive. Eventually, my mother went home but needed 24-hour care. I offered to rotate my time and help take care of her. By that time, however, my marriage had become dreadful, so caring for her allowed me to avoid dealing with it. On the inside, I was suffering, but like always, I put on a happy face.

When I announced that I was filing for divorce, it came as a surprise to everyone. Mom was not happy that I ended that marriage. I got the, *"Oh! Lynnie, life isn't always a bed of roses,"* speech. On top of that, she made it sound like her recovery and her life were jeopardized because she attended my wedding, and for what: so, it could end up in the divorce court? She told me she would never attend another wedding of mine and would often say she wanted to be buried in the dress she wore to that wedding. I told her as long as I was alive, that was NOT going to happen. I would put her in pajamas before I would put her in that dress. I tried explaining it to her— I did not want to see her for the last time in a dress that brought back so many unpleasant memories for me.

Having the last word, so-to-speak, my mother died on April 15, the date of my second wedding. I buried her in the green dress. And, she was right, she would never attend another wedding of mine.

And more setbacks

Just five months after wedding number three, better known as Edward, I learned I had malignant melanoma in my left thigh. I will never forget how I felt that day. I drove home from the doctor's office, grabbed a beer and took a bubble bath. I sat in the bath for a long time just staring at my leg. I had no clue what to expect, but I hid my emotions because I had an event to attend that evening. I got dressed up, put on my party face and went without missing a beat. A few days later, the cancer was surgically removed from my leg, and I was cancer free. I should've been thankful, but the doctor said I could no longer run. That was almost harder to hear than "cancer"—running is how I usually escaped my emotional pain.

I was still grieving for my mother and adjusting to a new marriage when I found out about cancer. Even though it quickly left my body, it left an emotional hole to match the physical one. Since I couldn't physically run from it, I threw myself back into work. I opened a fitness center for women– Adeva Fit. I stayed busy to avoid dealing with the darkness inside of me. Of course, the physical demand took a huge toll on my body and my newly cancer-free leg.

But I began to realize that the way I deal with stress and pain—whether emotional or physical—had become a pattern. ... I always had an excuse and was always ill. When I planned a certification or training, I would become ill or be injured right before it. Was I sabotaging myself? If I didn't perform the way I expected, I played out the same childhood story in my head. I made up excuses for my actions or blamed others.

Desperation

I realized that if I didn't learn how to deal with stress and pain in a healthy way, it would destroy all of the positive things I valued in my life.

I was sick and tired, of being sick and tired. I needed to take my health and my life back! I wanted to feel joy and happiness again. I made an appointment with an integrative physician and started working on my gut health and hormonal balance. My hormones were so low that they didn't even register on the lab results. Enduring this hormonal imbalance was very challenging for me—I'm a redhead for God's sake.

As I strived to heal myself, using food as medicine, I found IIN Integrated Nutrition. I looked into IIN years ago, but I was too busy and thought–really? A health coach? Who would want me to help them? Now, I realize that all of that fear, and guilt, and negativity was keeping me from living my true life! Holding resentment for decades took away my voice; I let my mother's reference to being sick and frail define and confine me. If I could only fight that fear, I would be able to beat it—once and for all.

I began training to become a yoga teacher. Right before the final unit– you guessed it, I became ill. I started having stomach issues. My stomach bloated like I was nine months pregnant. Was the childhood fear-based belief taking over again? Did I make myself physically ill? Who does that? And why? My life was the way it was because I was telling its stories from my nine-year-old self.

Making a change

I finally realized that to overcome this, I needed to change my story. At the time, that revelation sounded simple, but it was one of the most challenging journeys I've ever taken.

It was easy to see why my story didn't change much over the years. I was in my way.

I no longer listen to the sick and frail little girl—that chapter is now closed. Of course, I still hear the negative questions in my head, but now I don't let them get in the way. I now listen to ME. When I look into the mirror, I see my unmasked, authentic self and it's a beautiful image. I can manage my chronic pain, so it does not control me. I am living my best life! I have learned to embrace happiness and inner peace. I thank God for every day, and I am getting better in every way!

Your turn

What is your story? Does it make you smile and feel good about life? If it does, great! Keep repeating it. If it doesn't, tell a new story about the way you want things to be—not the way they are now. Tell it over, and over, until you feel it, and it's your reality. But don't rush! The process is important. Allow yourself to feel the emotions that come with letting go of the past. Revisit, but don't relive whatever negative emotions might come with memories of your family, spouses, exes, etc.– and release them. One way to do this is to tell a close friend, a health coach, write about them in a journal, or even tell your pet!

Then, shift your thoughts to your new story - a story that serves you and your desired life.

Don't give up; even if it takes years. I've finally done it and am living proof that it works! I took back my power to create a life precisely the way I want it. I changed my story to one that makes me smile, and I am doing my happy dance. If you can't find your way, I will be glad to help!

About Lynn Friebel

Lynn Friebel assists women in exploring their relationship with food, movement, sleep, and stress as a holistic nutrition health coach. She personally and thoughtfully guides her clients to make simple, small changes that transform their lives.

She is also a Reiki practitioner, facilitator, keynote speaker and the founder of Adeva Fit and the Ripple Method. Adeva Fit is a boutique-style wellness studio designed exclusively to empower and inspire women of all ages. The Ripple Method is a non-judgmental platform dedicated to helping guide clients get crystal clear about their goals and breaking down their barriers to living the life they desire.

Lynn attended the Institute for Integrative Nutrition (IIN)® in New York City, studying dietary theories, bio-individuality, current health issues and topics, and Eastern and Western nutrition. At IIN, she had the pleasure of receiving instruction from some of the most influential people in the health and wellness field, such as Dr. Mark Hyman, Deepak Chopra, and Dr. Walter Willett.

Lynn's transformation was not an overnight success. Her path led her on a journey of self-awakening and discovery of personal enlightenment. She experienced victories and setbacks as a survivor of Malignant Melanoma. For years she cycled with migraines, inflammation, chronic pain, and a compromised immune system. She shares her stories to inspire and give hope to others.

Lynn empowers her clients to take action and upgrade their mindset. She supports them to overcome obstacles and limiting beliefs, to focus on the present and how to achieve what they want in their life now and in the future.

Lynn has been in the fitness field for over 35 years. She is certified in personal training, group fitness and has taught in diverse formats with a plethora of certifications including Zumba®, Barre, HIIT, Chair Yoga, Restorative Yoga, Vinyasa Yoga, Yin Yoga, Pilates, and Buti Yoga. She also has extensive experience working with senior populations and is a certified Matter of Balance coach and Silver Sneaker instructor. Lynn is on staff as the physical education teacher of Sacred Heart School. She earned her 200-hour RYT and is registered through Yoga Alliance. Lynn was chosen to participate in the 2019 Urban Zen Integrative Therapy (UZIT) program inspired by Donna Karan and developed by Rodney Yee and Colleen Saidman Yee.

Lynn currently resides in Shelby, Ohio with her husband, Edward and the family dog – Oliver. They have two grown children, Aarika and Bryson. She balances her life with fitness, world traveling, experimenting with recipes, staying healthy, and growing in her faith.

Contact Information

Lynn Friebel
Ripple Method
Website: www.ripple-method.com
Email: ripplemethod@gmail.com

Chapter 11

Let it Happen Organically! You Are Meant to Share Your Gifts and Talents with the World

By: Charmaine Fuller

I have always been driven and ambitious my entire life. As a child, I felt like I was going to have an amazing career and I would do my homework at my desk every day and pretend that was my desk at work with my name on it. I would keep it organized and pretend every day that was my job, and one day I would have a nice office and be successful. I worked towards that success every year. I have had several amazing careers, but there was always something stirring inside me that whispered, "there's something more, you are meant to be on a stage in front of millions of people." I would go on for two decades trying to find that "something."

A Tree Grows

Living in Brooklyn, NY as a young, single, African-American college graduate was an exciting journey. I had the world on a string and as my mom would say, "the heaviest thing you should be carrying, is your purse." I could go anywhere, work anywhere, do anything and enjoy life. I did everything that society said I should do. I went to a private Catholic school all my life and went on to go to a private college. My parents always instilled a strong work ethic in me from day one. They led by example, and I was able to witness hard work and dedication every day. Both my parents had great careers, and they fostered a loving environment for my sister and I. In college I loved being around students of every nationality and culture and being immersed in a place of learning. Learning was always my passion even though I didn't love eight o'clock classes. I knew that my parents made several sacrifices for me to get the best education and I had an obligation to be the best I could be and be successful.

I learned a lot about who I wanted to be and what I wanted to offer the world. Or so at least I thought. At that time, I had a plan, and I was going to execute that plan. I was going to be successful, have a high paying job as an attorney, have a family, a dog, and a big house. The little girl from Brooklyn was going to have it all by any means necessary. At the time I didn't know that my "plan," was not going to be completely authored by me and I had no say so in what God had planned for my life. I just knew I had the blueprint and I was drawing out my life in perfect synchronicity. I did not know that the "blueprint," was going to change and my plan was just that "my plan," and not God's plan. I tell you that guy has a funny sense of humor and sometimes he is the only one laughing and I'm crying.

City Life

I enjoyed New York City and everything it had to offer a young working girl like myself. I would go to after work clubs with my friends and chop it up and have fun. We would plan our elaborate vacations every year and debate about which passport stamp we wanted to get next. We were about passport stamps, fun, and friendship. My work life went in several different directions with each career path I chose. Some riddled with hard lessons to learn but ultimately each job and career I had taught me something about myself and other people. What do they say, "what doesn't kill you makes you stronger!" I can truly attest to that because in my best career moments I was happy and fulfilled and in my worst moments I was distraught and confused.

But through it all, I continued to pursue success and be the best I could be despite what people thought I should be. Then one year I got the infamous call from my supervisor saying you are being downsized. My entire world fell apart in an instant. How could this happen? I was doing an excellent job, and I was doing a job that I loved. I did everything I was supposed to do, and this time it wasn't enough. So, I had to figure out a new path and do it quickly because this NYC rent wasn't going to pay itself. I volunteered, I networked, I sent out resumes and still nothing. Then I landed an amazing opportunity, and for once I felt like this is going to be my best career and I am going to make strides in this world doing what I loved to do.

The Heartbeat

Even though I loved what I was doing, I always heard that little voice inside of me that would say, "you are meant for something big." I didn't know what that larger than life thing would be until the night I was hospitalized. I had worked a long day into the night and was feeling tired and made my journey home on the subway. I felt sick to my stomach and had to get off the train two stops from my home. I vomited on the platform, and in New York City fashion no one came to my aid. I didn't know what was going on, but I just prayed and said: "God, please let me make it home safe."

I walked home with a large pain in my abdomen and could barely walk but I made it upstairs, and I called my parents and told my Dad I need to go to the hospital. He rushed over and went with me in the ambulance to the hospital. When I got there, they rushed me to the emergency room, and the doctors had to run a series of tests. They concluded that I was bleeding internally and 80% of the blood in my body rushed to my stomach, and I was told that they had to do emergency surgery on me to save my life.

I was literally in a state of shock. How could this be happening? I exercise every day, I feel great, but why is this happening to me? My parents told me everything would be fine, and the doctors whisked me away after I signed the papers to save my life. I was not scared because something just told me I would live, and I knew I would make it and survive.

While I was being prepped for surgery a sharp pain hit my body, and I screamed, and then they rushed me into surgery. I was told by the doctor the next morning while I was recuperating that I had an internal rupture and they had to rush me in to save my life. The doctor said we must take you to do a sonogram because we heard a heartbeat and I said a "heartbeat," and she said, "yes we heard a heartbeat, and you are pregnant." As anyone could imagine I was in total shock as they wheeled me to the x-ray room. In that room, I heard my son's heartbeat for the first time, and everything in my life changed from that moment on. The internal rupture that I experienced was the other child that passed away, and my son was a twin, and I was supposed to have two babies. From that moment on I knew that God spared our lives for a reason and we were meant to change the world and do great things.

Some medical experts say that stress is the number one killer in today's society, but I say stress can lead you on a path of greater wellness. I decided that I had to take this situation and turn it into a positive experience that I could share with the world. If I had not been stressed out trying to be successful in my career and live what I thought at the time was my best life in the city that never sleeps I would not have discovered my true life's purpose.

Circle of Life

Healing after the surgery was tough because not only did I mourn the death of one child, but I had to be happy about the new healthy baby growing inside of me. I was determined to make my womb the healthiest vessel it could be for the new baby and me. The doctor would run numerous sonograms sometimes too many to count to see the baby and hear the baby. Each time I was excited to hear the baby, but I was never once worried because I knew the baby was special from the first time I heard his heartbeat. The pregnancy was a great time of eating anything and everything within reason and watching my body grow to accommodate this new life. I continued to exercise at the gym doing strength training and practicing yoga for seven months until I couldn't bend over and tie my sneaker. I was still in the best shape of my life, and I had this awesome glow. Work was great, I was great, and life was great.

The night of the delivery was very intense and scary at times, but again I knew that we would make it. The labor was 31 hours, and I was so exhausted because the baby would flat line during every contraction, and they would turn me on my side to move the baby off the umbilical cord. I thought it would never end until it finally did, and the beautiful baby boy emerged to the world with his eyes wide open. He looked at every pediatric doctor and nurse in the room with his bright eyes before he even cried for the first time as if to say, hi everyone, I made it. He was dubbed the miracle baby. We were so happy that he was healthy.

It's a Lifestyle

We came home from the hospital and then the real work started. Maternity leave was consumed with breastfeeding, cleaning and hovering every day. Then came the endless pumping, cleaning, and hovering. All in all, it was a great time for bonding and self-discovery. Some days I would look in the mirror and say, "who am I." And then the baby would wake up, and it was back to the routine. I was enjoying my new life as a mom-in-chief, but then I wondered how women do this. Yes, the Dad is there to help, but at the end of the day, everyone in the house is relying on me to make every decision, every minute of the day. What are we going to eat? Do we need clean laundry? Feed me? Take me out for a dog walk. I thought you were still my mom, who is this crying baby? He's cute, but I thought I was the only baby. Why are you always so tired? You never listen to me anymore, and we never go out anymore because you are too tired. Somewhere in there, I had forgotten one very important thing, "me." I continued to be everything to everyone, and then it was time to go back to work. There I could be "me," the young, intelligent, African-American woman moving and shaking in the corporate world by day, mom and chief by night. I can do it, I can do anything, so I thought.

I would carry on this ridiculous routine of being super mom, career woman, girlfriend, daughter, friend, volunteer, class mom every single day. I did return to the gym because after all, I had to get "snatched," since I only gained 25 pounds during my pregnancy. Going back to the gym was tough to do with work and my new mom schedule, but I was determined to make it happen. It was the only thing that gave me the confidence and the energy I needed to survive this thing called mom-life. Going out to have fun at lounges and after-work events was a thing of the past. I just wanted to get home after a long hard day at work and spend time with my family and go straight to bed. I managed to carry on this routine for several years with several great memories of my sacrifices. I knew that my son was still the miracle baby, but I also wondered from time to time, "what is my purpose?" I knew it was something big, but I could never figure it out.

I began to read several books on personal development and enrichment. I tuned in to every episode of Oprah Winfrey's "Super Soul Sunday." I was in search of that thing called passion. Every article and every book attempted to help people "find their passion." It was touted as the thing that made you get out of bed every morning with a smile on your face. It was the job that you would work at "for free," if no one paid you. It was the success that everyone wanted to obtain, but no one seemed to tell you how to figure out what it was. I decided to take the Myer's Briggs personal assessment that helps you unlock your personality traits. I was determined to take every assessment I could to understand what my passion was so that I could align that with my current career. I did all of those assessments, read several books and to no avail was still overcome with a feeling of uncertainty. I continued to do what I thought made me happy, and things were status quo, or so I thought.

I remembered the day that we moved into our new apartment. I had this great sense of accomplishment. I looked out the balcony over the horizon, and I could see the hospital that we fought for our lives in and directly next to that was a large church with a huge steeple. I said to myself there is a reason why this apartment was vacant for a year, and several people turned it down. Yes, the layout of the apartment was a designer's nightmare which would now be my design nightmare, but I knew that the hospital and church were symbolic of our journey and each day as we looked out that balcony we would be reminded of why we are here, to serve the world.

I would go on for several years in the secret quest to discover my life's purpose. I would continue to exercise regularly, practice some form of self-care and continue my quest to be super mom with her cape on by day. No one would know my struggle with perfection and the feeling that I had to sacrifice my happiness to make everyone else happy around me. Some would say you can't be selfish, you have to dedicate your entire life to your family, and you can't have it all. Years ago, I heard a lecture at work where a woman said it's impossible to have it all because one part of your life will always be out of balance because life is like a seesaw and rarely is it always balanced. I was so disappointed by that statement because my meticulous perfectionist lifestyle would never be "perfect," again when it was just me and my purse going on a night on the town.

Now it was me and my baby bag, purse, stroller, etc. going out for a day at the park and my little purses were useless vessels for all of the baby gear I had to carry now. But I could always use them for "date nights," yeah right. What "date nights?" Date nights turned into go "nite nite," sessions where I could see nothing but my bed every night. We are fine; our relationship is fine. We communicate like a well-oiled air traffic control station. I blurt out the list of events at our son's school to you, and we sit down with four calendars every week and coordinate schedules. This is normal; this is our new life. Who cares that we never hang out anymore, see a movie that is not PG, or take a solo vacation sans child to reconnect? We don't have time for that. I have to be Super Mom, and you have to Super Dad, and we have to the best family there is even if that means we do not connect anymore.

Then the unthinkable happened again, and I got downsized from my job for the second time in my career. I thought to myself "how could this happen again?" I did my job, and I was well liked in my field, and everything was going well. I was completely baffled, angry and distraught but I decided to use the time off this time to do a deep dive and figure out who the mom in chief was and who she wanted to be. I began to meditate and pray on it and ask God to reveal to me what it is I'm supposed to be doing with my life because obviously, this wasn't it. This was the second time I was downsized so apparently this is designed to me make me stop and take a step back. Up until that very moment I was still living out the dreams that I thought I had, but that was the dream my younger self had before the baby came.

Evolution

I discovered that motherhood makes you evolve into a new person with new dreams and aspirations. I decided to coin the phase Charmaine 2.0. I was a new version of myself on a new path that led me to a new sense of self. I wanted to understand how my body works, and I realized that exercise was something I enjoyed. I continued to exercise, but I knew that all of my interest pointed in the direction of holistic alternative medicine. I decided to try essential oils that were a therapeutic grade, and I began to understand the production process of the oils and how they were grown. It was fascinating to me, and it was also right up my alley because my mom always subscribed to holistic medicine by taking vitamins and trying holistic treatments.

I then realized that natural remedies were always a part of my life and this was something I wanted to pursue. I decided to attend the Institute for Integrative Nutrition to get a better understanding of the mind, body connection and I enjoyed every minute of it. I realized that I was always the person posting pictures of healthy foods and supplements every day that I wanted to share with my followers. I was always reading health articles and fitness magazines. It became apparent to me that I was doing all these things not knowing that it was preparing me for the journey ahead. I began to observe how food connects and disconnects people. I realized that if I had a bad day at work, I would tend to crave something sweet and have a late-night binge when I was unhappy. I always read about late-night cravings, but I never really paid close attention to how your gut health fueled that. Your gut is your primary brain, and it drives all emotions and actions. So, if your gut is off balance, then the rest of your body is off balance. These key connections sparked an interest in me to share what I have learned with my clients and the world at large.

Lotus Flower

I have always liked blue lotus flowers because they are very symbolic. It is the only flower that can grow out of the water in the morning and afternoon and then it closes up at night. It lays dormant every night and experiences a rebirth in the morning. Blue lotus flowers are Egyptian symbols of rebirth, and they have a strong connection to the Sun and creation. I feel like that represents my life because when people always doubted me and challenged me, I was able to show them that no matter where I came from, I deserved a seat at the table. I chose to rise and shine no matter what the circumstances. I was able to go through life with several rebirths and emerge the next day confident and ready to shine. I worked just as hard if not more than other people, and I deserved to be treated equally.

I remember when I first started in the Technology field there were not a lot of African-American women in that field at the time. I would get a request to go to a client's desk to fix a problem, and I would get this puzzled look like I know you can't possibly be here to fix my computer. But I always took that in stride and set a personal goal for myself that I would work to have a personal record of fixing people's computers in less than 10 minutes. And I was able sometimes to fix the problem in less time, but I knew I had to be twice as better or if not fifty times better than my other co-workers.

I remember being so sick and tired of constantly having to prove myself, but I knew that I was paving the way for the next woman and that was my duty. The thing that gave me the strength to endure was knowing that future generations of female African – American women would not get the rude stares and unwavering Q&A sessions about their educational credentials if I continued to dispel the negative stereotypes. Female technology engineers would be the norm in society instead of the exception. I always tried to remember that I stood on the backs of women who were never able to have a seat at the table and they had to serve the guests of the table. That for me is and always will be the thing that brings me the greatest joy. Sometimes I sit in meetings, and I think of my grandparents and great-grandparents and know they are smiling because someone like me is finally being taken seriously and my opinions and thoughts matter. I believe that if you are in-tune with your intuition, you will hear God speak to you in very subtle ways. He will send you messages and reminders of the places he wants you to be in and the people he wants you to surround yourself with even if you don't understand what it all means. One day you will connect the dots, and it will all be in perfect alignment with his plan.

Trust God's Timetable

God sets forth his plan for your life the minute you are conceived, and it is a lifelong process of growth. I feel that if we tap into our spiritual talents early in life, we have the opportunity to understand what our gifts are and what our purpose is in this life and beyond. As a child we are innocent, and our heart is pure and untainted from the negativity of the world and societies expectations of our lives. When you see children play, they are in their essence because they see another child as an equal human being, and they see a friend and not a foe. They do not see color; they see love.

I think that the process of human growth takes you through different ebbs and flows of life and in the end, we all come back to the natural. The natural being the unwavering love we have for our fellow man and the innocent love that dwells in everyone. We strip away all the negative energy and go towards the purity that originated in us from the beginning of our lives. That is precisely why when someone is sick, and near death, we call in the minister or priest to pray with the family and the ill person to prepare their hearts for the journey back to love.

Our transformations catapult us on a lifelong journey back to love and on the way there we get to share our healing gifts with the world. The lotus flower continues to emerge from the dirt at the bottom of the water, and it continues to endure all of the ripples in the water with grace and mercy and endures forever. It is important to remember that everyone's journey is unique, and it is mapped out for us by a higher power. We must learn to release the reigns and look for guidance and cease our desires to control every outcome of our lives. For once your release the reigns of life true healing can begin, and your healing can then transform the lives of others through your unique and auspicious journey. We are all on the journey of life and each one of our lives matters, and we are all connected through the human experience.

Our Transformative Journey

I encourage you to tap into your spiritual essence and discover who you are beneath the veil of everyday existence. I challenge you to decide to be fair to yourself and everyone you meet because we all deserve to be acknowledged as great human beings that God has made. We can choose love over hate and dissolve negative attitudes and feelings starting with our mindset. Mindset shifts happen when we choose to disconnect from social media and worldly things and tap into daily interactions with other people. Our energetic flows encourage positive ions instead of negative ions. Positive ions always cancel out negative ions. In this "cancellation," we can cancel negative thoughts, negative people, and negative energy. I decided to "cancel," negativity and replace it with positivity by reciting daily affirmations and meditation.

I took baby steps in this area and started meditating on one word every week for a month to see what positive thoughts came up for me that week. It was an awesome process that turned into a lifelong practice that I am personally committed to every week. I noticed that certain things started to happen when I shifted the thoughts of my mind and created my own "cancel culture." My awareness of negative conversations with others in my family and my friendships started to shift.

I began to understand that I could no longer surround myself with negative people who were constantly making withdrawals on my energy reserves instead of making positive deposits. I noticed that my solitude was emerging for a reason and it was time to finally get clear on what I was put on this earth to do and what my gift to the world would be. It was a long process, and it is honestly a process that is still evolving every day. I understand that religious mindfulness had to be my foundation and upon that I realize my purpose.

I encourage you to continue your journey learning from your mistakes and acknowledging that perfection is a waste of time and it is important to enjoy your life and live in the moment. We all have the same 24 hours in a day, and you are in total control of how you spend that time. When we are present and engaged with other humans and not caught up in the digital vortex, we can be in tune with the human energy around us. People need people, and electronic devices can never emit the positive energy that human interaction and human touch gives to us every day. God has created humans to interact and enjoy each other's happy, sad, and indifferent times. When a person leaves this earth, they are never eulogized by how many tweets they sent and the instagramable vacations they had.

Their lives are celebrated by the fond memories that their friends and families have of them. We can no longer let the digital vortex pull us out of reality into a subhuman experience. It is up to us to say we can transform and become present with ourselves and one another to get through this thing called life.

About Charmaine Fuller

Charmaine Fuller is the founder and CEO of Charmaine Fuller Holistic Health Coaching, HHC, a holistic health coaching practice that aims to provide comprehensive health and wellness services to clients. Charmaine Fuller, HHC is a lifestyle brand that offers coaching programs, wellness seminars, and a la carte services focused on assisting clients with their individualized self-care needs in a healing and friendly environment.

Charmaine has embarked on several careers in the legal field as well as the technology field. Her attention to details and passion for technology has been an integral part of her life for many years. She has always had a passion for learning new things and never declines the opportunity to hone her skills professionally and personally. She has recently catapulted her career into the health and wellness field and is committed to offering her clients cutting edge knowledge in holistic nutrition and practical lifestyle management techniques. She knows that your body will heal itself given a chance to do so.

Charmaine has also led an extensive life of community volunteering since the age of 15 when she organized summer trips for senior citizens. She has also hosted relationship forums, and seminars helping people in the community understand relationship dynamics and challenges. She has been featured on Blog Talk radio and other social media outlets sharing her thoughts and opinions.

Charmaine is dedicated to helping women realize their full potential and understand that their body is a sacred temple that is constantly evolving and in need of self-care. She encourages her clients to fine-tune their sleeping patterns and develops morning and evening rituals that will give them mental clarity to be all they can be for themselves and their families. Charmaine's struggle with work-life balance has challenged her many times during her life. It was with sheer determination to make self-care a priority through mind, body, and soul connection that has enabled her to shift her priorities and make critical lifestyle changes.

Charmaine currently resides in Brooklyn, NY with her boyfriend, 7-year-old son, and fur baby Remy. Charmaine holds a master's degree in Business Administration, a Bachelor of Arts Degree and recently graduated from the Institute of Integrative Nutrition® in March 2019 as a Holistic Health Coach. She continues to carry her message of determination, self-preservation, and healing to the world through her coaching practice and everyday activities.

She enjoys cooking, gardening, hand lettering, practicing yoga and meditation in her spare time. Her mantra is, "I want everyone to feel happy to have known me after they spend time interacting with me." Her goal is to leave a lasting impression of hope and happiness in everyone that she meets.

Contact Information

Charmaine Fuller
Charmaine Fuller Holistic Health Coaching, HHC
Website: www.charmainefullerhhc.com
Email: charmainefullerhhc@gmail.com

Chapter 12

Me Vs. "FGB (Fat Girl Brain)"

By: Amy Levitt-Knutson

"You're fat, you're ugly, you're stupid!"

"Be quiet, go to your room, don't say that, don't think that."

"Cover your rear end, nobody wants to see that!"

"You eat too much, you're a slob."

"You'll embarrass me!"

For years, I heard these statements over and over again until I believed them. Though most of the people who made me feel this way are no longer in my life, their criticisms and rejections gave rise to that nagging voice inside my head, that says, "You're not good enough." I found myself believing that I wasn't good enough for my family, for society and most importantly, myself.

It took eating myself sick to begin waging war with the voice in my head. The one that said I would never amount to anything. That said, "My dreams weren't worth fighting for, nobody would value anything I had to say." That I didn't belong, I can't say that the voice is gone, simply that I am better at telling it to shut the hell up. I refer to it as my "Fat Girl Brain."

Home

Because I am adopted, it's hard to say what is my nature and what is the result of how I was raised. Certainly, there are parts that I believe to be my nature. I do not physically resemble the members of my family. I tend to be quiet and sedentary. I don't particularly like physical activity and have a bit of social anxiety. I have even been told that I am a little too fond of my own company. In truly sitting down to examine it, I don't have a way to gauge what is my nature, as I have no one to compare to.

My house growing up was filled with anger, a seething rage that sat just underneath anything that was happening. The best way to try to describe what it was like is that it felt like we were in an episode of some TV show or movie that was under attack. Full red alert, the lights flashing red, the alarm going off, everyone running and shouting. I would try to take cover. There was never a time that it felt safe or calm. Between my mother's anxiety, my brother's ADHD, and my father's emotional abuse, I always felt like we were on high alert.

I don't remember many of the details of my childhood. The overt hostility made meal times tense and rushed. I would often eat as quickly as possible before the next blow up that seemed to be lurking around the corner at any given time. I learned to spend most of my time hidden away in my room. I would lose myself in a fantasy world of dolls or books to protect myself. I replaced dolls with food as I got older. I would sneak up to my room with snacks that I hoped wouldn't be missed and once again lose myself in a book.

I shared my mother's struggles with weight and relationships with food. Even as a toddler I would eat myself sick. I learned early that food equals comfort and love. If your hurt, scared, upset or angry a cookie will make you feel better. By the time I was ten years old I was using my allowance to buy food, sneak food and hoard food. I would go to the store before Hebrew School and buy handheld pies, doughnuts, cupcakes, whatever sugary sweet I could shove in my face on the walk over to the Temple. This is really where I began to sneak and hide what I was doing.

At the same time, I had run headfirst into puberty and began menstruating. My physical body became more and more adult and less like my peers. I began to become self-conscious of the way that I looked. I just wanted to look like everyone else. I had a hard time finding clothes that fit and were still appropriate for my age. I prayed to have brown hair and brown eyes instead of being a strawberry blonde with blue eyes. This was when the weight started to pile on. I was trying to hide my body behind fat.

I continued this way well into adulthood. I was the girl that everyone always said, "If only she would lose weight, she has such a pretty face." I always felt judged by my weight and that in turn caused me to turn to the only form of solace I had ever known, food.

Another Fad

There was always some unsolicited advice about the latest and greatest diet. I knew the basics of what I was supposed to do, and for years, I had tried every diet out there trying to lose weight. It would work for a little while, then I would slip up or be "bad," and that would be it, my "Fat Girl Brain" would take over and convince me I couldn't do it anymore. I would eventually put all the weight back on and then some. I was in therapy and support groups. Nothing ever seemed to work. Every time, there was my "Fat Girl Brain," sabotaging me and couldn't to listen to what anyone else had to say. Every failure compounded my feelings of not being good enough. It felt like there was something wrong with me, which only made my "Fat Girl Brain" even louder.

My sense of failure and the feeling that the whole world was judging me lead me to hide what I was doing. I almost always thought about food. What was going to be for the next meal and where was I going to get it from. Especially snacks. I always had a candy bar in my bag, and every day before work I would go to the store to stock up on junk food that I could stuff in my face while my co-workers were on their lunch breaks. There is something about the way that it feels when you take that first bite. The sense of pleasure that washed over me was intoxicating. It took eating myself sick for me to finally begin taking control of my health.

Getting Sick

I had given up on trying to lose weight and get healthy when I got sick for the first time. I had resigned myself to being obese and accepting all the limitations and judgments that came with it. My life and health came to a crashing halt in August 2016.

I was at work and was having a bad heartburn day, and I was feeling worse and worse on my ride home. I took an over the counter antacid and went about my evening but didn't eat much. I was planning to work from home the following day as my daughter had her camp talent show that morning. That evening we were sitting out with our neighbors, outside our kitchen door under an enormous maple tree, chatting and joking. The whole night I was just off. I was smoking, and that only made me feel worse. It felt like I had overeaten to the point that I was full right up to my sternum. Going to bed that night I was so uncomfortable and felt like I had a too tight belt wrapped around me just below my ribcage.

The following morning, I felt like a spear had been shoved through my body, from right under my ribcage straight through to my back. I could barely stand, let alone go to my daughter's talent show. I stayed in bed most of the day. I would sleep fitfully for a little while and then wake up in searing pain. My husband kept trying to get me to go to the doctor or the emergency room. I refused because I was so afraid to find out what was wrong with me. I was hoping that if I just ignored it, it would go away.

By eight o'clock the next morning, I couldn't stand it and allowed myself to be taken to the emergency room. While I put on some clothes and my daughter got dressed, my husband called my mother to come up to watch our daughter. They dropped me off at the emergency room and went back to wait for my mother. I was left sitting in the hallway of the emergency room for several hours as the doctors waited to see if I was just there for opiates. Eventually, after my testing came back negative for opiates, I was given morphine while they ran more tests. It didn't even dull the pain. Soon after, I was diagnosed with Acute Pancreatitis and admitted to the hospital.

I spent the next several days doped out of my mind on massive doses of opiates every two hours. I was in the hospital for five days and was on gut rest for four of the five days. Gut rest is nothing but ice chips. Other than the attending physician and his students, I didn't see any specialist while in the hospital and even though I had ultrasounds, CT scans and tons of blood work done, they could not find a cause for my pancreatitis. I was released from the hospital and only told to follow up with my primary care doctor. Since I didn't have a determined cause, there wasn't much she could tell me other than I shouldn't drink, and I should try to lose weight.

While in the hospital, I had already lost twenty-five pounds. Since I was unable to smoke in the hospital, it gave me the jumpstart I needed to quit for good once I was released. At home, I did my best to remove almost all junk food from my diet and tried the popular diet ideology of a low-carb, high-protein, high-fat diet. I learned the hard way that this way of eating was not going to work for me. Seven months later, I wound up back in the hospital.

Stressed Out

Even though I have learned that a high fat/low carb diet wasn't the correct way of eating for me, I was trying. In between my two attacks, there was also a lot going on in my life. My grandmother had gotten sick right after I got out of the hospital and her health deteriorated steadily through the next five months. She had always been my biggest supporter and my rock. A voice of calm and reason in my high-stress life. There was also a realization at that time that she wasn't going to get better. She had cancer and was ninety-two years old. There wasn't much that could be done for her. It was incredibly hard to watch her body decline and to know she knew what was happening. She passed away at the end of January 2017. My "Fat Girl Brain" reared her ugly head, and I once again reached for food as comfort. The combination of an incorrect eating style and the stress and sadness of losing my Grandmother made for a perfect storm. It was a short time later I was back in the hospital with a second attack.

Sick again

In looking back, I knew the entire day at work that I was having a second attack. I probably even felt it coming on the day before. Again, I tried to convince myself that it was something else and would go away. I had gone to Yoga class on Sunday morning and thought that I had just pulled something. My back was killing me all day, and by the time I got home, I was almost in tears. I tried to take a shower to see if it was a muscle issue. That didn't help, and I tried to sleep it off. Shortly after midnight, I woke up with that spear through me pain again. My husband asked if I could wait to go to the emergency room until the morning. I tearily shook my head no. I hobbled myself upstairs and slowly packed a bag as he woke our daughter. We arrived at the emergency room at around one o'clock in the morning. Once he saw that I was settled in, he took our daughter home. I wanted to be a good mother and send my daughter home to bed, but I couldn't help but feel alone. I was scared and confused. I was losing weight, following a healthy diet, quit smoking, and yet here I was again.

The second time, the emergency room experience was smoother. They were able to pull up my history and start treating me before they had the blood work back to confirm. Again, I spent several days doped out of my mind on opiates. Again, they could not find a cause. I had another ultrasound, another CT scan, they tested me for diabetes and high triglycerides. I didn't have anything they could find. My bloodwork was normal, and I didn't have any issues with my gallbladder.

The main difference the second time around is that they had me see a gastroenterologist and a nutritionist. The nutritionist advised that I should have been on a low-fat diet, not a low carb/high-fat diet. She gave me a basic printout of what a low-fat diet should look like and told me I should stay between twenty-two and forty grams of fat a day. She didn't tell me much else, and I didn't think to ask. The gastroenterologist advised that we would do some additional testing once I was out of my acute attack and he would follow up with me in the few days after I got out of the hospital.

This time I went through all the extensive testing. I was tested for autoimmune diseases and was sent for an endoscopy and an endoscopic ultrasound. I was even sent to see the Pancreatic Specialist at Yale. Again, everything came back negative. I also called the nutritionist that I had seen in the hospital because I needed someone to help me make this transformation. I was told that they were too busy to see me. They didn't even give me a recommendation for an outside nutritionist. I was on my own and had to make a choice. I could either sit there and feel sorry for myself, or I could start fighting for myself. I finally realized that I had a beautiful little girl that was terrified of what was happening to me and a husband who loved me. It was time to fight.

Change! Change! Change!

The very first thing I did was go on my supermarket delivery service website and order anything I could think of that was low in fat or fat-free.

Our Transformative Journey

In the very beginning, I ate a lot of turkey sandwiches with lettuce and mustard and a lot of nonfat yogurt. My diet was uninteresting and uninspired. Most of what I knew how to cook was filled with fat. I was pretty good at things like meatloaf, quiche, and pork chops. I had to rethink what I was cooking.

The first chance I had, I went over to the book store and looked for low-fat cookbooks. I started with two that looked like they would work for me. I got in my kitchen and started cooking and have never looked back. The real trick, in the beginning, was finding those few items that I liked, and that were a safe food for me. Once I had those mastered, I began to experiment more. I began to try different spices to add flavor without adding fat. I explored different cultures and their flavor profiles. I began to move farther and farther away from the standard American Diet. I incorporated more Asian flavors, more Latin flavors, and more Mediterranean flavors.

Because of the severe fat restriction, it was also incredibly difficult to eat out anywhere. There was no grabbing a quick bite while we are out running around. I ate a lot of turkey on wheat and knew that to be a safe option out. I was able to find several other options as I have gone on but for the most part, prefer to eat what I make myself. I had to learn to budget my time and energy to plan, shop and cook all my meals at home. Even at friends' houses who wanted to be helpful, it is easier and safer to prepare and bring my food. Cooking had become the ultimate act of self-care.

I changed my diet for my health, not to lose weight. I also stopped drinking and smoking because of my fears of not knowing which of my vices might send me reeling back into pain and back to the hospital. The stress of giving up my coping mechanisms of wine, nicotine, and cheesecake, honestly, sucked. My "Fat Girl Brain" hounded me but I could not, would not let her win.

Awakenings

It was just under a year later that <ins>Guy's Grocery Games®</ins> factored into this. My daughter and I love cooking competition shows. This is one of our favorites, and I loved the way that it would inspire me to get into the kitchen and experiment. It was a cold February afternoon, and we had the show playing the background. There was an episode featuring chefs whose lives had been saved by food. One chef, in particular, talked about how the only way she had been able to control her illness was with a major dietary change. Her restrictions were different than mine, but the idea resonated with me. The next episode, it was a marathon, featured food bloggers. I could start to feel the bug in my brain and knew that something was brewing. I was not listening to my "Fat Girl Brain."

I got up to get in the shower, and I started forming this idea. A lot of good thinking happens to me in the shower. I could maybe start a blog about what I had been through, about how I had felt so unsupported. I felt like I had a lot to say about what I had learned over the year and a half that I had been going through this. Since I couldn't find any guidance or support during the process that there were perhaps others out there who needed my help, and I started to think that if this wasn't a career, it should be.

I'm not one who likes to talk about things I don't know a lot about. I knew what my experience had been, but I didn't want to be giving incorrect or harmful information. It was standing in that shower that I decided that I needed to study nutrition and make this my career. That maybe there was a way that I could change the industry or at least make others feel like they had a guide and support in those first few months.

It was the first time in my life that I allowed myself to feel passionate about something. So much so that I wasn't going to let anyone including my "Fat Girl Brain" deter me from this path. That was a new experience for me. I was excited and passionate about beginning my studies and getting out there to help.

I started to investigate different degrees to see what I would need to do. I called my mother and said, "I have something to tell you, and you can't laugh at me!" I fully expected her to laugh at me and to get an "I told you so!" I could not have been more wrong. Not only was she supportive, but she was also downright excited. As we talked, she remembered that there was a nutrition program that she had looked into fifteen to twenty years earlier and she was still getting emails from them. It had to be fate. Later that afternoon, she forwarded an email from The Institute for Integrative Nutrition®. Less than a week later I decided to enroll.

The Path

I have had many mini-transformations in my life. Experiences and choices that have changed the course of my life. In my mid-twenties, I chose to remove some toxic people from my life. When I got sick, I took control of my health which transformed not only my diet but my physical body and my mental health. When I decided to take on health and wellness as my vocation that was another transformation, and the final turn came while I was enrolled in The Institute for Integrative Nutrition®.

When diving into the curriculum, I began to think more about the quality of what I was putting in my body. I started to think less about finding replacements for the foods I had lost from my diet and more about eating foods that were healthy and delicious and just happened to be low in fat. Some of the items that were in heavy rotation at the beginning of my journey, I no longer eat. I have eliminated so many processed "diet" foods and have begun eating more whole foods.

That is not to say that I don't have treats now and then, just that the choices I make are healthier and better informed. I also came to realize that my healing needed to be more than just changing the food that I was eating. I needed to think of myself as an entire person. I needed to learn to feed myself off the plate as well. There is so much more to taking care of me than vitamins and minerals, proteins, fats and carbs.

As I began to think more about my overall health, I realized that it is much more than the food I was eating. I was two years out from my first attack when I began school, and I realized that it was time to work on more than just managing my pancreatitis. I took an art class with my friends to celebrate my birthday. I accepted the challenge of writing a chapter for this book. Where I still struggle is with exercise. I don't enjoy it as hard as that is to admit. So, I got a dog and started taking him for walks.

Re-enter my "Fat Girl Brain." It is the part of me that is anxious about walking into a gym or yoga studio, thinking that I am going to be judged by people that are thinner than me, healthier than me, prettier than me. The part of me that has wanted to give up on writing this piece over and over, so I didn't have to face myself. That felt that I didn't have anything of value to say. That felt that my story isn't as important or interesting as some of the others. The part of me that doesn't want to sign up for an art class because I'm not artistic or creative. I have gotten a lot better about telling her to shut up and pushing through anyway. I have begun to realize that the women I judged to be mean or judgmental of me, are just like me. They have their struggles and stories. I allowed my feelings of inadequacy to justify my judgment of other people.

Clarity

Let me be clear, "Fat Girl Brain" is an attitude not a number on the scale or body shape. I call that self-defeating voice in my head Fat because I identify myself that way. No matter the number on the scale or the size of my clothes, I still see that fat little girl every day in the mirror. Though, by labeling it as something other, it is easier for me to see it as not the entirety of me. I am more than that number on the scale or the shape of my body. My story isn't one of weight loss, it is a story of finding self-worth, and the weight loss happens to be a nice side effect. I took a journey to heal illness and am finding that maybe for the first time I am beginning to heal the emotionally broken and battered little girl that I was. I am finding my fight and my worth on a journey I never intended to take. I am a work in progress, and for the first time, I see that as the point, not the destination. I am letting go of the if only and allowing myself to see the value in the here and now.

Right now, it the happiest and the healthiest I have ever been. I don't remember the last time I stepped on a scale. That number no longer defines me or gives me value. I don't mean for this to be a story about if you lose weight you will be happy. I was told that my entire life and hearing only made me more miserable. People always told me what they thought I should be doing as far as eating was concerned, but nobody ever checked in on why. Why was I trying to eat myself to death? Perhaps that is the most important question that needs to be asked. We need to start looking for why.

I don't mean to say that you can't love and respect yourself at any size and that we are made to be all different shapes and sizes. I let outside influences define me and my self-worth instead of finding that within myself. I am just now beginning to try to define what that is for me. I am working towards an inner peace that is accepting of my body's homeostasis. To do all the things that we all know we should do, but don't always do. We all know we should eat more fruits and vegetable, drink more water, exercise and get a good night's sleep. And remember, we all need to forgive ourselves for having a slip-up or an occasional indulgence.

I started this journey to find a way to find a way to help myself and others who were struggling to live with food restrictions. I have found so much more than that. I found me. I found my voice. I found my fight. I found a tribe. I like the me I found a lot more than the person I was when I let my

"Fat Girl Brain" rule my life. She fueled anger and resentment. The woman I am becoming has let go of so much of that and found her way out of the darkness.

About Amy Levitt-Knutson

Amy Levitt-Knutson is the founder of Zebra in the Kitchen. Zebra in the Kitchen is a health and wellness brand committed to helping clients integrate healthy changes into their lives based on their individual needs. Amy believes that just as every zebra has different stripes, we all have different health and nutritional needs, that each person's road to healthy is different.

After two attacks of acute pancreatitis with no determined cause, Amy sought guidance from medical professionals but found very little support and information about her illness. With no determined cause, the only course of treatment available was a radical lifestyle change that included a rigid low-fat diet, losing weight, no alcohol, and no smoking. Armed with limited information she set out to find her way to a healthier happier lifestyle.

Amy's journey to heal her specific illness has led her on an unexpected journey that has resulted in a healthier lifestyle that she believes is worth sharing. She has had a life long struggle with her "Fat Girl Brain." That nagging little voice inside her head that ate away at her self-esteem, resulting in obesity. She found that losing weight was a side effect to improved self-esteem, self-worth, and self-confidence.

Amy is a recent graduate of The Institute for Integrative Nutrition®. She has become the support for others, that she had so desperately wanted, needed to incorporate food restrictions and lifestyle changes.

Amy enjoys spending the time it the kitchen creating new recipes and experimenting with new flavors. She can often be found at the local farmer's markets discovering new local, seasonal vegetables and fruits to make health locally sourced meals for her family. Family favorites can be found on her website www.zebrainthekitchen.com.

Amy has never lost her love of books, and she is still an avid reader and can be found sitting with her dog Parker in her lap with a good book and a cup of tea.

Amy is attending the State University of New York Purchase College and graduated with a Bachelor of Arts in 2000. She also received a Paralegal Certificate from Mercy College in 2005. She spent 14 years as a paralegal in a boutique Real Estate law firm in White Plains, NY before attending The Institute for Integrative Nutrition®.

Amy currently resides in Seymour, CT with her husband of 11 years Ric, her daughter Lilly, a kind and science-loving child, as well as her fur baby Parker.

Contact Information

Amy Levitt-Knutson
Zebra in The Kitchen
Website: www.zebrainthekitchen.com
Email: amy@zebrainthekitchen.com

Chapter 13

Restored-Healed Inside Out

By: Evelyn Hernandez

My transformation was not only about my physique. My journey took me from skinny to fit, sick to healthy, weak to strong, angry to peaceful, depressed to happy. It took years of utter depression, physical pain, and isolation to one day decide to change. I was tired of being tired, and I wanted to live in the now. I no longer wanted the past to define the person I could become if I learned to love myself. I learned that even though I did not grow up in a loving and nourishing household, I was worthy of love. My transformation was a complete mind, soul and body restoration. It all began the day that I met my soulmate, and I knew that I had to heal myself. I wanted a new start and a chance at a happily ever after.

Mind

I have been in the darkest and coldest of places, I have had financial issues, loss of dear ones, and health problems. I have been molested, abused and violated. I was born in New York, and my parents were two teenage high school dropouts who got divorced when I was just six years old. My mother raised me as an absent single parent until she later remarried and that is where the molestation started. This was when I was taught to be quiet, to hide my emotions, to hold on to anger and resentments. Fortunately, this only lasted three years before he was arrested for drug trafficking cocaine in the state of Texas. My mother was heartbroken, and while we went back to poor, I was finally able to sleep without worrying about someone creeping into my bedroom.

During my complete childhood and until today I have always been an overachiever. At school, nobody noticed that I was hungry, broken and unloved because I was an honor student and mostly stayed to myself. I did not have many friends because I feared they would know too much about me. I continued to build walls to protect anyone from knowing what was going on inside my mind. At one point, I contemplated suicide and remember speaking to a friend about it. She told her cousin who was a psychologist, and they came to visit me at my home and told my mom what I had said. I recall my mother inquiring about the incident, but the topic was never discussed again.

At the age of 15, I thought I met the love of my life, and that I had finally found someone to love me and give me the home I never had. I started having unprotected sex at the age of 16 and got pregnant a few months after. Sex nor birth control were a topic in our household. Hispanics did not discuss these things because it was taboo. At the age of 16, I was very naive and was not sure I was even pregnant until I had missed my menstrual cycle for four months and decided to take a pregnancy test. When the test confirmed my pregnancy, I ran away from home. Since my parents were divorced, they each figured I was with the other.

It took them a month to figure out that I ran away with a man. At that time, my father found me and took me to an abortion clinic. Since I was already five months pregnant, the doctor was not able to proceed with the termination. My father did force us to get married, as he was embarrassed by the fact that his unwed daughter was pregnant and worried about what others would say. He planned a beautiful wedding as quickly as possible, and I was married in a Catholic church, with a white wedding dress, and had a beautiful wedding party. Everyone was happy and had a great time, except for the bride. I was so unhappy and felt like I was having an out of body experience. I was now 16, pregnant and married.

My pregnancy with my first son was not easy. I was alone and depressed most of the time. Later during the pregnancy, I developed preeclampsia. Spent most of the time going to doctors or at the hospital. My blood pressure was high, and I developed edema. All my life I had been an honor student, but pregnant and in school was not the norm. I dropped out of high school during my senior year and gave birth to my first son, Jordan. Life did get crazier, and as young teenagers, we did many crazy and regretful things. Jordan's father was killed at the age of 23 by a family member, and I lost myself even more.

At this point, the only thing I do remember is being medicated, drugged or drunk to avoid the intense pain. There are many painful memories that till this day I do not remember. I worked with many therapists and psychiatrist that diagnosed me with PTS and clinical depression and of course prescribed psychotropic medications. This lasted for over ten years. During these ten years, I lost it all. I lost freedom, friends, job, money, home, son, health, and I lived in a dark hole for ten years.

I am not sure how, why, when, or what happened but one day I decided that I no longer wanted to take medication. Against the doctor's orders, who advised me, that I needed to be weaned, I stopped cold turkey. I was tired of being numb for ten years that I welcomed the pain my body was feeling. I couldn't sleep, but I could think again, I was crying all day, but I was feeling again. I had an appetite, and above all, I started having a will to live. I started feeling that maybe, just maybe, I was worth it and should try living.

It was not easy to join the living, after many years. I had to re-learn the basics. I was now scared to drive, so I had to teach myself how to use a computer, I had to make new friends, find a job, re-establish my credit, and learn how to do everything that normal healthy citizens did. Since I was scared to drive while going to catch the public bus, I had a panic attack, and my sciatic nerve started acting up. I was rushed to the emergency room barely able to walk.

I was diagnosed with sciatic nerve pain, given an epidural steroid injection, painkillers, and anti-inflammatory meds and sent home. I had just gotten off my medication and scared to have a set back by numbing myself again with painkillers, but the pain was so intense I had no choice but to take them. This set me back for another three months. I was on painkillers for 60 days and then fell back into a depression for another month. Luckily, I was still eager to live and wanted nothing else than to be happy finally and at least at peace.

SOUL

I often wondered if I had a soul since I was numb and no longer felt pain. I believed in my mind that only people that had emotions was capable of having a soul. I learned that this could not be further from the truth. After I quit my medication and went through a few months of recovery, I slowly went back into the dating scene. I dated a few men that the old me would have chosen because the old me thought I was worthless and full of anger and craved pain and regret. The new me kept reminding me, that I was worth it, that there was somebody out there that would love me and my scars, I had to be patient. In 2003 I met my soulmate. I had placed an ad on a dating site, Match.com.

A week after placing the ad, I received an email from Match.com with a list of guys that matched my criteria. He was on that email. As soon as I saw his smile, he brought joy to my life. I emailed him, and we set up the first date. The very first day I met him, for the first time in my life, I saw sunlight. It was like somebody had let pure sunlight into my dark hole. My heart was so raw, I felt pain, love, regret, and hate, all at once but I knew that I had finally found the man of my dreams. I was still skeptical as this is a guy I just met online, so I played it cool, and we scheduled a second date.

On this second date, I asked if I could pick him up, as I wanted to see where he lived and felt safer having my transportation. He gave me the address, and while the address looked familiar, I did not recognize it until I pulled in the driveway. He happened to be my aunt's tenant and had lived there with his parents for the past 25 years. I started crying as I knew right there, that there was a higher power that was answering my prayers. I knew right then and there that I just met my soulmate, and that I was going to marry him and be happy ever after.

We dated for two years in which I tried to sabotage our relationship many times because old behaviors are hard to change. Luckily for me, even though it seemed like I was the strong one, he was stronger. With his love and patience, he helped me see that I too was worthy of being loved. He accepted me and loved me with all my scars. He claimed many times that I saved his life, but in reality, he saved mine! He finally proposed, and I accepted. This time there was no forced marriage, false wedding or reception. We eloped to Las Vegas, and since we met online, we had a virtual wedding! Happiest day of my life.

In 2006 I became pregnant with our son. This pregnancy was different. I was healthy during most of my pregnancy but did have a lot of weight gain. Due to the baby being ten lbs., I had a C-section. I also had the autoimmune disease return a few weeks after giving birth. I visited my gynecologist regarding a rash I had developed across my stomach. He advised it was a rash, asked me to apply Benadryl and sent me home. This "rash" started spreading to my back. I now see my primary doctor who advised that it was an allergic reaction to something and asked me to continue applying Benadryl. The rash kept appearing in different parts of my body, but I was so busy with the baby that I just ignore it. I was so happy with the birth of my son. I didn't want a rash or my health to interfere with this special moment. I had never in my entire life been so happy. He completed me and only made me want to love harder. There was no hate left inside of me at this point when I looked into this innocent child's grey eyes, all I could think of was love and how I wanted to be strong and healthy for him. There are no words to explain how this man and baby changed me. They breathed love and light into me.

Body

While growing up, it was rare for us to sit at the dinner table and have a home-cooked meal. My mother was busy working to be able to support us as a single parent. Our dinner normally consisted of ramen noodles or a bag of chips. I was never taught proper nutrition at home nor the importance of having a family dinner. I was lucky that I was a healthy child for the most part, until the age of 14 where I developed an autoimmune disease. I started developing rashes on my legs, which were painful. The rash continued to spread until both my legs were completely covered with a raised rash. At times it burned and itched as if I had been stung by bees. I was never taken to a doctor, but the rash mysteriously disappeared after I ran away from home.

My next health problem was during the pregnancy of my first son. I was only 17 when I became pregnant and quickly developed preeclampsia during my 5th month. My blood pressure was elevated, I had protein in my urine, and my extremities were swollen. I was in and out of the hospital for most of my pregnancy and was placed on restricted diets. My pregnancy was rough, and my labor was very painful. I did deliver a healthy boy naturally. For the most part, I stayed physically healthy even though mentally I was falling apart.

During my second pregnancy, I was in a different mental state. I was happier, more stable and in a loving home. My pregnancy was great. I did not develop preeclampsia, but I did gain over 80 lbs. My husband who also ate as if he was pregnant too, gained 100 lbs. He also got very sick and had his gallbladder removed. After the baby was born, I immediately lost 125 lbs. I was the thinnest I had ever been. I feared being overweight to a point where I became obsessive with my training. I was training for hours twice a day. I also started eating Lean Cuisine TV dinners for lunch as they only contained 300 calories each, and I thought they were a healthy option.

A few months after giving birth, I started to develop heartburn and acid reflux. It felt as if I had an elephant sitting in the opening of my stomach. I went to visit my primary doctor who prescribed Carafate and told me to take Prevacid over the counter to help with the pain. None of this helped, I was still eating the wrong foods such as spicy chips, fried foods, tomato sauce, etc. I was not educated on nutrition, and the doctor didn't provide any nutritional advice.

The pain continued so I was referred to a Gastrointestinal specialist. They completed an endoscopy, and the results were impacted feces, and inflammation of the stomach lining. I was again prescribed more medication and told to take over the counter Nexium to alleviate the heartburn. I continued to enjoy my Cuban food, spicy chips, alcoholic drinks but was still being active. The pains continue, and I am now rushed to the hospital as the medication is no longer working. At this time, I was told that I had gallbladder stones and needed to have my gallbladder removed. I was now tired of doctors, medicines and their diagnosis. I refused the surgery, signed myself out of the hospital, and went home.

As soon as I got home, I dumped all medications, Lean Cuisines and snacks I had at home. I prayed for God to give me the wisdom to understand what was going on in my body and went to bed. The next morning, I woke up and decided to have a bowl of oatmeal instead of skipping breakfast and skipped my hour of cardio. I noticed that at lunchtime I felt a bit better and didn't have that burning feeling in my stomach. I went online to research what ingredient was in oatmeal and immediately noticed that it contained fiber.

For the following weeks, I implemented a high fiber diet and started drinking more water. I noticed that the heartburn was starting to go away, and I wasn't feeling so tired and bloated. I also wasn't constipated, that was the moment I realized that food could be medicine or poison. I started understanding that nutrition had a very important role in my health. I began incorporating healthier foods and eliminated processed foods from my diet. After a few months, my heartburn had completely vanished. I am now feeling healthier and stronger and ready to help my husband begin his weight loss journey.

Our Transformative Journey

I was not very supportive of my husband's weight gain. I was not nice at all! Since I had lost my first husband, I feared that I would also lose him and seeing him overweight and barely able to walk or breathe was terrifying. To cover up my fear, I would snap and call him names. I wanted him to snap out of it, and I wanted him to wake up skinny. In turn, I was doing the opposite. He was stuck in a vicious cycle, the less supportive I was, the more depressed he became, and the more he would overeat. He thought it was just impossible to lose 100 lbs. And that he might as well at least be happy eating his sweets.

I decided to take a different approach since being mean and nasty to him wasn't going to work. I decided that I would join a gym and start weight lifting and start incorporating more protein into my diet so that I could develop lean muscle. This didn't last long. A few days into my routine, he asked if he could join me at the gym, I obliged. I also started educating him on nutrition. We started making smarter choices together. We became gym partners and became known as the "Healthy Fit Couple."

We are now eating healthy, working out and feeling stronger but not quite as healthy as we should be. I am now working at a stressful job, going to school full time to obtain my bachelor's degree in International Business and am a mom to a newborn. My commute to work was an hour each way, and when I was home, I was busy studying for my courses. I eventually started to breakdown. One day while I was at work, I developed a migraine. It was intense and painful, and the migraine caused irregular heartbeats, which lead me to have my first panic attack. I drove myself to the hospital. I am now upset and wondering why? I am eating the right foods, I am active and working out, why am I at the hospital again? Doctors ran a few tests, and everything seemed normal, so they prescribed Imitrex for the migraine and send me on my way. I didn't bother filling the prescription. I went home and rested and the next day was back to work and school. This lasted for another year until I graduated from school and resigned from my job. I took time off from the workforce and started to help my husband grow his business.

On a busy day, while helping him at the office, I got another migraine and horrible back pain. This time instead of running to the hospital, I called my dad. He asked me to please go over his house and that he would have a holistic healer waiting for me. While I thought this was the funniest thing I had ever heard, I was also in pain and desperate for someone to help me find the root cause.

As soon as I arrived, I was asked to lay on a massage table. He first asked me a few questions and started his Reiki healing session. After he was done, he told me most of my problems are being caused by anger and stress. He told me that my anger was affecting my nervous system, stomach, back, and head. The stress was also affecting my health. He asked me to try to stick to a vegan diet, to drink lots of water and try to avoid negative people, places and things. I was startled by what he had told me. I never thought anger or stress could make anyone sick and I never knew I was angry. For the first time at least, I knew that my health issues could be cured and without medication.

I knew that it was time to do a complete overhaul, I was already taking baby steps and making healthy changes weekly, but I was ready to go all in. I wanted to feel energized, and healthy. I did not want to visit a doctor's office again unless it was for my annual examinations. Now I eliminated all processed foods, dairy, fried foods, and limited alcohol and red meats. I am now going to the gym six days a week, and incorporating more weight lifting. The greatest change was controlling my anger and letting go of the need to control others and situations. I knew to heal I had to forgive everyone who had hurt me including the man who had abused me when I was a child. It was rough, but I started attending mass in our local church and bible studies to help me with this process.

It took me a few months, but when the time was right, and I was ready I asked God to help me, and I was able to forgive everyone. It was as if a huge weight had been lifted from my shoulders. My jaw was no longer hurting from the clenching I was unconsciously doing, my back pains subsided. My stomach felt normal again, no more heartburn, nor heart palpitations.

Restored

There are many times in my life that I was ready to quit and many times I was tired of feeling pain. Many times, I wondered how others couldn't see through me and see that I was in despair. I would even resent those that would ask me for advice on their problems as if I was in any condition to help others when my own life was such a mess. I was a victim of sexual abuse, daughter of a single mother, a young widow, a depressed and angry woman who hated everyone including herself and I was a total mess. But God has a plan for me. He carried me through it all when I could barely hold myself together. Through the grace of God, I am now a wife, mother, daughter, friend, business owner, health coach, and motivator of many.

We went from financial hardships to become the owners of an investment property in Miami, Fl, which is mortgage free. We also own a beautiful home in Fort Lauderdale, Fl. We own several businesses, Geografixx Inc, a graphic design firm, and Vivire Wellness. Vivire Wellness is a holistic center that has helped many lose weight and start living a healthy happy life.

I went from being in the darkest of places to be in the most beautiful of cities. I have now traveled the world and visited France, England, Italy, Switzerland, and so many other places. I have visited places that I had always dreamt one day to visit.

I have not been back to a hospital in the last 12 years. I have not taken any medication either. Food is my medicine; the gym is my therapy, and my family and friends bring me pure joy. We lost a combined weight of over 100 lbs. and have continued to live a healthy lifestyle. My autoimmune disease is controlled. I do have my hormonal flare-ups, but by eating well-balanced meals and managing my stress, the flare-ups have been seldom.

We went from being overweight and sick to becoming a Health Coach who has helped thousands lose weight, get fit and feel happy and healthy. As a coach and influencer, I also motivate and inspire thousands around the world to start living a healthier lifestyle by creating new healthier habits and routines.

Spirituality I have learned that I do have a soul after all. I discovered that all though I appeared to be strong and emotionless, I was quite the opposite. I am a very loving and caring person. I love wholeheartedly. I believe in loving unconditionally and in forgiving others. My journey taught me that those that have hurt me were victims of others pain as well. It is a cycle that needed to stop, and I will not carry on this cycle. I choose to love others instead of causing them pain. I am a spiritual being.

While my journey has been a long and sad road, I do not look at my past with regret, it has taught me and led me to where I am today. The past does not define me. The past is what I have been through but not who I am. I know that my journey has just started, and I have a lot to accomplish. I know that I am here telling my story to help women who have been abused. I am here to help them tell their story, speak their truth. I lived in silence my whole life and always felt like I was living a double life as if that hurt little girl was not me. It is time to break the silence, break the chains, be free. My transformative journey has led me to speak my truth and be free of this shame I was carrying for decades. I once was silent, but now I roar!

Today I am fully restored, mind, body, and soul. As I have learned in my journey, you can't have complete healing nor live a healthy life if all aspects of your life are not in complete harmony. Love, nutrition, finances, emotions, health, fitness, career, family, and spirituality must all be balanced for us to live a completely happy and healthy life. It is important to value where you are in your journey and learn to enjoy the ride. Although it may seem like the ride is long and bumpy in reality, life is shorter than it appears!

About Evelyn Hernandez

Evelyn M Hernandez is the Co-founder of HealthyFitCouple, designed and created to help couples lose weight and get fit. She is also the founder of Vivire Wellness. Vivire Wellness was created to help busy professionals start living the healthy life they have always wanted. The "NO DIET" approach has helped many lose weight and get fit while enjoying delicious and healthier versions of their favorite dishes. This is a powerful program that has helped individuals emerge as a better version of themselves and has helped them reach their highest potential.

Evelyn M Hernandez is a Certified Holistic Health Coach and Wellness influencer. Evelyn earned a Bachelor of Arts, cum laude, in International Business from Florida International University. She is also a graduate of The Institute for Integrative Nutrition®, where she became a Certified Holistic Health Coach. Evelyn is a Personal Trainer and is certified with the American Council of Exercise. She continues to expand her knowledge and recently became certified in Reiki and hopes to become a Master in the future to be able to teach Reiki to others.

Evelyn struggled with health issues for several years, including gastrointestinal problem, depression, and anxiety. After years of being in the care of hospitals and doctors, she found that conventional medicine did not have the answer for her. She began her quest and started researching alternative and holistic treatments for both her and her husband. Together they discovered true healing with food and fitness. She and her husband together lost over 100 lbs.

Evelyn advocates health and wellbeing, and it is her transformation that bought her to holistic health coaching. She now motivates, influences, and coaches' individuals who want their own transformation and want to start living a healthy happy life. As a coach and influencer, she has also motivated and inspired thousands around the world to start living a healthier lifestyle by creating new healthier habits and routines. She and her husband run a support group for other couples having difficulties losing weight and are very well known on social media as the HealthyFitCouple. Her specialty is working with couples who are having a hard time losing weight, and busy women who do not have the time to meal prep or go to the gym. She creates a special program for these busy women, which allows them to stay active, and healthy with minimal time at the gym and kitchen.

Evelyn currently resides in Fort Lauderdale, Florida. She is married to her best friend and has two sons, Jordan and Giovanni. When she is not helping others live their healthiest happiest life, she enjoys cooking, traveling and working out at her local gym.

In addition to health coaching, she speaks to groups about health and wellness.

Contact Information

Evelyn Hernandez
Vivire Wellness
Website: www.virewellness.com
Email: info@virewellness.com

Chapter 14

Tears and Goosebumps

By: Christine Jenks

Feathers and Rhinestones

What appeared to be a glamorous life full of glitter and lights, was a life I allowed to bring me to my darkest depths. But fortunately, my story doesn't end there. There's this fantastic quality we all possess, and it's called resiliency. I am back to a life of sparkle and shine, but with a whole new meaning. I went from a go-with-the-flow party girl to an advocate of health; from tequila shots to smoothies, from late nights to early mornings, from "the golden arches" to home cooking. My transformation began when my feathers and rhinestones started to fall off one by one. I went from a Las Vegas Showgirl full of life to an ailing empty shell, to now a soul learning, discovering, and embracing what life has to offer. Join me as I take you on my journey of the exciting adventures of being a Las Vegas Showgirl, to losing the greatest important thing in my life, my health, and then to how I discovered my purpose.

Life on the Las Vegas Strip

It all started when I was completing my dance contract on the open seas, and I asked my fellow talented cast members what city they were headed to next for their dance careers. Several of them replied Las Vegas. I was feeling spunky and cheered back, "I'll see you there!" In 2001, I made a move to "The City of Lights." Upon arrival, I didn't think I would stay in the desert for too long. It was a climate I had never lived in, plus, I didn't feel as if my looks fit in. I was a short haired brunette with small breasts. I didn't know if I would get work here as a professional dancer, especially as a Showgirl. But rather quickly, I was taken in by the magical scene of Las Vegas and the doubts dissipated. The dazzling costumes, the lights, the incredible performers, the spectacular shows, the fantasies, and living life like a mini-celebrity; this was my new life.

Through a dear friend, I was introduced to a producer who hired me for my first gig on the famous Las Vegas strip as a Showgirl. There I stood at 5'9" smiling, wearing a glittery costume with fluffy pink feathers that came out of my headpiece when I had the pleasure to meet Mr. Miyagi from the Karate Kid, Pat Morita. My next audition was to be a ring girl. Remember my comment above about my breast size? Well, I didn't get the job. Instead, the producer hired me to be Cleopatra. I was adorned in jewels and gold, as I toured my magnificent palace with the glorious Julius Caesar by my side and with my two very large, handsome Centurions. A much-preferred role for me. I was in heaven and having the time of my life. It was so outside anything I could have imagined. In my high heels, long eyelashes, and a big smile on my face, I went on to my next audition; this time for a sizable theatrical show on the strip.

After a couple of auditions, I was hired into all the glitz and glamour this production had to offer. It took me two attempts because I didn't "look the part." I gave myself a makeover and auditioned the next go-around and was hired. The magnificence of the costumes in this production was brought to life with various colored jewels, feathers, and shapes. The set lowered and lifted with elevators. I can remember my opening night in the show. I was in the basement, pre-set on an elevator floor with a few other cast members, wearing a swooping decorative black hat, sparkling jewels surrounding my bosom, and a dazzling skirt to my ankles with a wide opening to allow my legs to extend in the showgirl walk while wearing three-inch heels.

The music began, and in anticipation after a few counts of eight, the elevator rose. My heart beating faster, praying I would remember all the choreography, my eyes suddenly cleared the stage floor. I saw the audience just an arm's length away, the stage evened out, and here I was in my very first Las Vegas Show. The audience lit up as the entire cast came into sight in the most stunning array of costumes and spectacular staging.

We performed twelve shows a week and climbed up and down two thousand stairs a night between the stairs onstage and backstage. After the second show, we would head out to the clubs; dancing, drinking and having a blast. I was living the life of a party girl; sleeping late, hanging by the pool during the day, napping, and then doing it all over again without a care in the world. Eventually this lifestyle caught up with me. I started to get dizzy on stage and not having the strength to complete the shows. I left one night, not knowing it was going to be my last show in this production. That evening when I left the show, I saw elephants walking down Tropicana Avenue. I was so baffled at first, and completely out of sorts until I realized the circus was in town. Thank goodness it was a real parade of elephants and not my illness getting the best of me.

It never occurred to me how extremely dehydrated I was, nor did I realize that I had developed a fear of heights. There I was, placed on the highest step of an extended staircase of the set, on the edge of a thirty-foot drop, in three-inch heels, wearing a showgirl backpack that required two stagehands to place it on me gently; one wrong step and it would be a long fall. Night after night, it wore me down, and I could no longer perform. I went to several doctors, and none of them could give me a diagnosis. I was extremely frustrated and wanted to get back to doing what I loved, dance. I flew back home to Western, Massachusetts to meet with the doctors my sister worked for, and they were able to provide an answer. After a tabletop test, the specialist discovered I had developed neurocardiogenic syncope, a condition where I could faint with a change in my blood pressure.

Diagnosed, and almost fully healed, I went back to "the City of Sin." I was once again wearing my high heels, long eyelashes, and swaying my hips as I glided across the stage in a very intimate, and incredibly sexy show at the pyramid. One would have thought I learned from my previous set back. The same routine of performing the shows, the late nights, and going to sleep when the sun came up. In between appearances, we ate the "fun meals" from "Mickey D's." Plus, we enjoyed the prize inside. Not every cast member ate fast food, but many of us did. At that time, I wasn't thinking of what I was putting into my body or the harmful effects of my actions. I was having fun and living a life so outside of what a small-town girl from Belchertown, Massachusetts could have envisioned. After two fun years and developing friendships that are lasting a lifetime, I chose to leave this cluster of beautiful, tall, slender women. An old ankle injury resurfaced, and it was time for a change. I entered the exciting world of cocktailing on the casino floor.

Serving tasty beverages to patrons gambling was sometimes tricky business, but I managed to do just fine for a while. I still had the pleasure to dance, this time just for three minutes at a time and once an hour. It took a moment to get used to dancing on small stages on top of noisy slot machines, but soon it became the norm. The money was fantastic, but I was now on the first level of promoting alcohol and gambling.

Still going out and doing up the town wearing high heels, I began to add more stress on my body. I worked in a smoky environment with long hours and carrying heavy full trays of beverages. I started to notice the swelling of my stomach and the severe pain in my gut after eating the food that was provided by the casino in the dining hall. I started my work shift looking slender in my revealing uniform, and then by the end of the night, I looked and felt like a sausage. A concerned and knowledgeable co-worker told me one night that her friend was sensitive to gluten and had similar symptoms. I gave it a brief thought but never pursued it. Unfortunately, instead of stopping to listen to my body, I ignored it and off to the next Las Vegas adventure as Manager of Casino Marketing.

Now in a suit and bustier, I leaped outside my comfort zone and into the world of business as Manager of Casino Marketing. I was hired for a large casino that was saying farewell to its long run and transitioning to new ownership and a familiar name. It was a stressful position but exciting all the same. I was well taken care of from those within the business. I guess they thought I had power and influence with my fancy title, and I went along for the ride. It was such an eye-opening experience to take a risk into the unknown, but what was too familiar was the incredible nightlife. The late nights and overindulging with food and drink brought back to the surface the same symptoms I had before, this time worse. It had gotten so bad that even a co-worker said that I smelled; how humiliating.

The Bottom of The Bucket

My symptoms would come and go, and I was eventually laid off from work. My role at the casino had served its purpose, and it was time to figure out what was next for me. It had been an incredibly intense fourteen months of hiring talent, managing the bar, assisting with marketing, jumping in last minute to emcee, and the list goes on. I felt incredibly lost after such a whirlwind expedition, so I went back to what I knew, serving cocktails on the casino floor. Within a month of my return to serving beverages to the guests, I received the biggest wake-up call of my life. I had been on a downward spiral with my health, and my body had finally had enough. I lost my health and the ability to function in everyday life. By April 2008, "The Gambling Capital of The World" had won. My lights went dim, the sparkle flitted away, and the exhaustion set in. This was seven and a half years after my enthusiastic arrival to the "City of Sin." All the late nights, living the rock star life, and not listening to my body, had finally caught up with me. I had gambled my health.

The glamorous life I had once known became an ailing empty shell. I had traveled into a constant state of migraine with severe bloating, body odor after eating, fatigue, dizziness, and depression. I was unable to work or collect unemployment. I could no longer function like a "normal" human being. My life echoed of emptiness as I was selling my clothes and belongings to make money to be able to eat and pay for doctor bills. I had been to numerous physicians in hopes of an answer, or the very least, relief. With no answer in sight, I started to question myself and my sanity, but I knew something wasn't right; I just couldn't pinpoint it. All I knew was how miserable I was feeling. The doctors with poor bedside manners would ask me "you're a showgirl, where are your breasts?" I had another tell me, "well if you don't like Vegas, why don't you just leave?"

The inappropriate questions were not appreciated at the time of my darkest of hours. I did not have the strength or energy to go into battle or defend myself; that was already happening inside of me. Instead, I would return home and put my head on my pillow and cry until there were no more tears. After so much weeping, numbness set in and I went into survival mode; I was idle in the heaviness of the fog with visibility to a minimum. I had been relying on the expertise of the physicians for answers, but instead, I received unhelpful questions. Months passed, and the financial loss increased with the inability to make mortgage payments or keep up with the inpouring amount of bills to be paid.

Finally, after numerous months of seeing various doctors and other alternative medicine practitioners, I was referred to an allergist. After receiving an extensive scratch test that left large welts, intense itchiness, and redness on my back, the answer prevailed. The allergist discovered the secret to my ailment; a gluten sensitivity (my co-worker had been right), along with a sensitivity to bananas, pork, corn, soy, kiwi, coconut, and some environmental allergies. I was digesting the very food that was keeping me sick every day without knowing it. I relayed this vital information to the acupuncturist I was seeing, and she guided me as I eliminated my "trigger foods." The treatment she provided gave me great relief and a safe place for my body to rest and begin its healing process.

I now had an answer to my incredible discomfort. However, I still had to manage the remnants of losing the single most important thing in my life, my health. Thank goodness for the bright lights in my life; my loving and dedicated family and friends. There were many long-distance phone calls back home with my parents who provided unconditional love and support. My amazing friends generously brought me to my appointments, kept me company, collected funds, and lifted my spirits. With so much being unknown during this time, they kept me grounded. By November 2008, I was forced to leave Las Vegas. I had exhausted all my resources and then some. I said farewell to my saviors, took a deep breath, and boarded a plane headed back to New England. As the plane flew east, I watched the lights of the Las Vegas Strip fade into darkness.

Rising Up

Back home in Belchertown, Massachusetts, living with my parents with not even a dime to name, was not how I envisioned turning forty would look like. I was embarrassed, defeated, and lost. I had worked hard for the financial achievement of owning my own home. My family was kind and patient. My nieces and nephews made crafts to lift my spirits and displayed their love. My mom had given up her bed for me so that I could rest peacefully. My sister, to share the burden, took me in to stay with her, her husband, and my nephew for a short time. It was very therapeutic to overwhelm my nephew with hugs and kisses. The fog began to clear, but this wasn't a permanent living situation. I still had a lot of healing to do.

While living with my sister, I had spoken with a longtime friend from Boston and shared my humiliating ordeal. He showered me with support and got me in touch with a mutual friend that I hadn't spoken to or seen in years. I remember I was standing in the kitchen of my sister's home in front of a sliding glass door, looking out into the darkness of the night, when I received her phone call. She was attentive while I shared my story, and with generosity and warmth, she invited me to stay with her in Rhode Island. Shortly after that phone call, she met my sister and me at the halfway mark between their homes, and the exchange was made. She took me in, even after I shared with her that I have nothing to offer. I officially moved to the Ocean State.

This move provided a nourishing and safe environment for me to shed many tears, and work through the challenges of having lost my health and belongings. My dear friend was my saving grace. She and I had been through some exciting, interesting times together in the past, and it was comforting to be in her presence again. She introduced me to various alternative medicine healers, but the one that resonated the most for me was the acupuncturist. Her work and energy brought me peace and was a major contributor to my healing journey. Mother Nature also became my new best friend, as I took her in while I walked along the East Bay bike path. There was such beauty in this area to absorb and being near the water was therapeutic. I would explore the shoreline, or just sit quietly and breath in the fresh ocean air.

With clean eating, a safe place to live, love and sacrifice from a friend, and the great outdoors, I regained my strength and confidence. I was becoming me again, yet different. From here on out, my life was to be painted drastically different than it had been in the past years. As the healing continued, the clarity arose that it was more than just the food that brought me to my ailing empty shell. The stress, dry climate, poor environment, lack of self-care, and living against my grain were great contributors to my decline in health. I had been promoting alcohol and gambling instead of health and wellness.

In the middle of 2009, I eagerly returned to work. With the recommendation of my dear friend who had taken me in, the owner graciously hired me at the consignment store up the street from where I was staying. However, this was only temporary because I was soon guided and utilized in a field I truly believed in; fitness. Once again, my champion friend came through, and after I was introduced to management, I was employed as a customer service representative at the local fitness facility. I commuted to work by bike or on foot in all weather. The only time I would reach out for a ride was when the weather was too challenging. I vividly remember a time getting on my bike at 4:30 am, and it was raining. I set off on my bike into the dark, chilly, and rainy early morning with one hand holding onto the handlebars and the other holding an umbrella.

It was rejuvenating to be outside and to be active. Being a former dancer who couldn't move her body for so long, I had felt like a bird with a broken wing. To have movement back in my everyday life, along with the ability to work again, were true blessings. A few months into my new job, I was promoted to assistant manager, and then eventually manager. I was meeting such beautiful, interesting people who were supportive and encouraging. I felt as if I was where I needed to be. I continued with my healing and became inspired to teach fitness.

I first became certified in spinning after falling in love with my very first spin class, thanks to the motivation and energy the fabulous instructor. Following spin, I became certified in Zumba, TRX, and Barre. I truly enjoyed teaching (and still do). I found a new meaning to my life; to teach and encourage others to live a healthy life. The community of people at the gym was fun loving and caring souls that made it easier for me to be me. It was nourishing to be amongst them.

Within the walls of the fitness facility, there was a studio in the back area which cultivated my longtime interest Pilates; physical exercise designed to improve strength, flexibility, posture, and an overall sense of well-being. Most importantly for me, I started to work from the inside out. My first introduction to Pilates came in the form of a mat class while I was living in "The Big Apple." I fell in love immediately; Pilates made sense to me. I knew at that moment that one day I would teach Pilates and make it a lifestyle, but I just didn't know when. The answer finally surfaced within the gym environment.

My long-lost love of Pilates finally had an opportunity to blossom. The openness and desire for change and growth lead me to do some research and discover a training center in a nearby city. I was thrilled and signed up to become certified in beginner and intermediate Pilates mat. After the mat certifications were complete, I took a quick breather, and then went full force and I became certified in all the Pilates apparatus by 2016.

The Health Journey Continues

To this day, I am still teaching Pilates in a thriving studio in Providence, Rhode Island. It is where I can share my knowledge and specialties to those who are willing and open to connecting mind and body and working from the inside out. It brings me great joy to witness my clients experience relief from chronic pain through being consistent and persistent with their work. They leave standing taller and prouder with a new sense of well-being. I could carry on forever regarding the benefits of Pilates, I won't, but I will recommend you try it at least a couple of times. This method keeps me grounded and connected to Self. I would be lost without it because it is my lifestyle.

To enhance my new chosen way of living and to provide a more holistic approach to my teaching, I enrolled with The Institute of Integrative Nutrition. The past year of being a student again has been undeniably overwhelming. There was so much information I was trying to process, in addition to experimenting with several dietary theories, facing my "uglies," and working through past traumas, that I have felt another minor decline in my health.

Fortunately, now I know the warning signs and can make the necessary changes before falling too deeply back into the depths of despair. I give myself no option, but to remain healthy. I take on the same goal as one of my clients, "to be able to radiate light out of every pore of my body." I have the ability and determination to live a life full of happiness, light, and laughter. You possess the same. It's a choice. I have heard comments from some of those around me with the sound of despair that it's "too late" for them. I'm here to remind you that it's never too late to make positive changes in your life. It may get dark for a moment, but you will rise and shine brightly.

Take it from someone who had mainly been living from the outside in, being a people pleaser and allowing external forces to dictate my next decision. It was fun for a while, going with the flow and seeing where the next big gust of wind would take me. I met some of my dearest friends through these explorations, but I now refuse to sacrifice so much of myself through self-neglect and will be kinder and gentler to this delicate gift I have been given. There is no more time for beating myself up. I've lived, I've learned, and will always be learning. I free myself at this very moment. As goosebumps start at the crown of my head and travel down my body, my eyes welling up with tears, I free myself of all guilt, shame, and embarrassment for who I was and the life I've lived. It's a beautiful thing.

It is vital for me to be uniquely me, as it is you to be uniquely you. It is vital for us not to conform to the cookie cutter shape. To let go of people pleasing and kindly kick it out the door and compare and despair don't serve either of us. Together, let's be the courageous and fabulous people we already are. As I enter the challenges of mid-life with Menopause, once again, I look loss straight in the eyes. This time, loss of my youth. I must trust my intuition as I search for answers to making this transition a glorious process. My desires and goals are to comfort and support other spectacular women going through this significant transition. Together we will have the strength, knowledge, and energy to bring about change in our own lives and of those around us.

A Story to Tell

We all have a story tell, and I hope that someday you will manifest the opportunity to share your story in some way that helps you continue on your healing journey while encouraging others to do the same. As a dear friend said to me, "We have so much to learn from each other." I am grateful to have this breathtaking moment to share my story with you and to be a part of this extraordinary group. We all have had a different path that has brought us here together, but we all share common threads; transformation and the desire to help others. I get goosebumps from deep within as I feel these inspirational souls are meant to be in my life at this time, as we support one another to bring this amazing gift to all of you. It's a clear reminder of how important the connections with others is essential and powerful.

I encourage you all to nourish the positive relationships in your life and gracefully let go of those that no longer bring you joy. My eyes fill with tears, and a single drop trickles down my left cheek. I am forever grateful and consider myself extremely fortunate as I reflect on the times in my life when I hit rock bottom. Many were there to support me, getting me through the toughest of times. I am reminded of resiliency, the power to overcome, and of family and friends. I was never alone even at times when I thought I was; I was provided with compassion, empathy, kindness, and unconditional love. My life transformed and continues to do so as I set on a journey to help others find their truth.

Transformation; there's no fixed path in which it occurs because it is unique to you. It can be something significant happening in your life that makes you take a 180-degree turn, or it can be small shifts that clear your path. The only guarantee we have is that we are always changing and "It is in change that we find purpose." - Heraclitus (Greek Philosopher)

About Christine Jenks

Christine Jenks is a certified Power Pilates Instructor, Integrative Nutrition Health Coach, and a lover of the word FABULOUS! She is passionate about helping others feel better from the inside out through physical activity, clean eating, and mindset. Movement and creativity have consistently played an essential role in Christine's everyday happiness. She believes life is meant to be enjoyed and to embrace the knowledge gained from the lows in life. Life is not perfect so letting go of "perfectionism" and facing your "uglies" are key to living a healthy and fulfilling life as she has discovered through her transformational journey.

As a small-town girl from Belchertown, Massachusetts, Christine said to her mother, "One day, I'm going to live in New York City and travel the world" and she strived until she did just that. This ambition ignited when she went to a girlfriend's dance class and was amazed at how they were moving their bodies in space to music. Her mom, having been a dancer herself, fully supported Christine with enrolling in dance classes; a pivotal point in her life which eventually lead her to earn a Bachelor of Fine Arts Degree in Dance from The Boston Conservatory of Music, Musical Theatre and Dance. With the intention of becoming a dance teacher, Christine was bitten by the "performance bug," and ventured into the world of performance. The excitement of performing in front of an audience; the lights, the theatrics, the vulnerability of putting it all out there through movement; swept her away.

With a professional dance career spanning over fifteen years, Christine's dreams came true and more. She performed in Boston, made it to "The Big Apple," traveled the world dancing with the Holland America Cruise Lines and her grande finale performing on the Las Vegas Strip. After being adorned in jewels and feathers, this former Las Vegas Showgirl leaped outside her comfort zone and into the world of business. She welcomed the title of Manager of Casino Marketing from a major casino on the famous Las Vegas Strip.

In 2008, Christine's health declined, and the repercussions of her inability to work went into effect. Thankfully Christine had a fantastic support system of friends and co-workers living in Las Vegas to help her through this challenging time. After numerous months of not knowing what was causing constant migraines, severe bloating, body odor after eating, fatigue, and depression, an allergist was finally able to provide Christine with an answer; she had developed food sensitivities. She removed the "trigger foods" from her diet while working simultaneously with an acupuncturist. Inevitably, Christine departed Las Vegas.

Once back in the New England area, her healing continued with a longtime friend providing a nourishing environment for Christine to shed some tears, work through the challenges of having lost her health and belongings, and to have the opportunity to be in nature and start to rebuild her life. In time Christine realized it was more than just the food that was preventing her from living a healthy life; stress, unhappiness, environment, and living against her grain were great contributors to her decline in health.

In the middle of 2009, Christine's health and spirit returned, and she was ready to get back to work in the field of fitness. She was hired as a customer service representative at a fitness facility and then soon promoted to manager. Inspired to encourage others to make health a number one priority, she became certified in spin, barre, TRX™, and Zumba ™. In this cultivating environment, her longtime interest in Pilates had an opportunity to blossom. She became Power Pilates certified in all the Pilates apparatus by 2016. With this method created by Joseph Pilates, she witnesses the progression of her clients relieving chronic pain, standing taller, developing more confidence and moving with more ease; creating an overall sense of well-being. To include a more holistic approach to her teaching, Christine enrolled with The Institute of Integrative Nutrition®. After a year of more self-growth and gaining knowledge, she graduated in March 2019.

With resiliency and sparkle, Christine continues this transformational journey as she enters mid-life with the ability to offer her clients insight, empathy, and a safe space to accomplish their goals. With her shift to more natural living, she understands that everyone is unique. Christine's focus includes hormonal health, stress management, bringing it back to basics and the power of relationships and community.

Contact Information

Christine Jenks
Althea Wellness Coaching
Website: www.christinejenks.life
Email: christine@christinejenks.life

Chapter 15

Follow the Lights

By: Tamara Samilenko

My Moroccan masks hung on the wall. The neatly folded sheets and towels stacked into the spacious linen closet. The clothes organized into the bedroom closets by purpose then by color. My favorite books, pictures, candles, and ceramics strategically surrounded me. I loved how I decorated my first New York City apartment. I was ready for the next exciting chapter of my life.

I was twenty-nine years old, single and ready to exchange the humdrum life of Long Island, for the electrifying and provocative life that New York City could offer. Interestingly, growing up, I knew I would never want to live in such a bustling, overcrowded, dirty environment. But here I was. I had been working in NYC for a while, and a residential opportunity presented itself, so it only seemed natural to make the transition. Rather, it seemed like the correct thing to do, for if I could make it there, I could make it anywhere, right? This move allowed for an easy commute to my respectable job dressed in my equally respectable (i.e., boring) wardrobe.

I was ready to be truly on my own. No one to monitor the company I kept or the number of drinks I consumed. This was a dream come true for someone who kept a very compartmentalized life: The Worker; the Daughter/Sister/Granddaughter; the faithful Friend; the dark Depressive; the unpredictable Drunk.

The Drunk left all others behind including her work ethic, family responsibilities, and even the sacred bonds of friendship. Don't bother introducing her to a nice guy, even if he was an Archeologist. The Drunk was increasingly incapable of holding down a remotely healthy relationship. She wanted to be "normal" and do things "correctly," but just couldn't. I pretended this didn't worry me, but the truth was that I watched my friends marry off one by one and that I had become the oddball out. I went stag to many of these events. I was the life of the party and was often remembered for my short and low-cut dresses and unsteady heels. I always cleaned up well, loved to talk to everyone, was charming, naive and fun - until things got out of hand – and they did. When they did, I was dangerous to myself and others. I credit my dear friends and kind strangers (Angels) who pulled me out of many precarious situations.

But now, it's April 2002 in a post-9/11 NYC. Rather suddenly, I had a tremendous sense of fatigue that lingered for days. Where was this intense lethargy coming from? I recall in middle school complaining about severe fatigue. The doctor diagnosed me with Chronic Fatigue Syndrome and suggested to my mother that I spend more time at the horse farm nearby with my friends.

I spent a good portion of my weekends there surrounded by horses, giggles, and friends -a great escape. But this was different as I was an adult with adult responsibilities and did not have time to be held down by this invisible force. I was also experiencing muscle and joint pain. Not only did it affect my social life, but I was becoming concerned as my busy season at work was fast-approaching. I was a meeting planner and thoroughly enjoyed crafting schedules, meeting with speakers and vendors and creating a positive experience for all. The summer season demanded all my focus and energy, but it just wasn't there. I was certain I had Mono. This merited a call to the respectable family physician.

"So, tell me, Tamara, how long have you been feeling this way?" he asked. I began to cry and insisted all was great in my life except this horrendous fatigue. I felt some relief after he ordered a battery of blood work. A week later the phone call came, "Tamara, you don't have Mono. Come in for more tests". Each time I came in for an appointment, and he asked how I was feeling, I always cried. What the hell was I crying about? I knew part of it was not understanding this fatigue. I felt like I had a wet, wool blanket thrown on top of me. My thoughts and movements were often running in slow motion. There were some days where I just could not keep up with conversations and therefore, kept to myself. I felt increasingly embarrassed by this condition and shameful that I could be brought down like this. I found some solace with my friends, the bartenders. Even though I experienced dreadful fatigue, I often found the energy to intoxicate myself.

The drink helped to alleviate my back and joint pain and often energized me until I crashed.

It was during that second or third appointment where the doctor asked that dreaded question, "…how much alcohol do you generally consume a week?". "Not too much," I responded. More tests.

The Dream

My nights were often occupied by a recurring dream I had throughout my life about looking for the sunshine. I'm at a lovely resort or the small beach from my childhood. I am playing in the water (sometimes amid very big waves), and the sun disappears behind angry clouds. I become cold instantly and obsess about the sun's return. I try to read the clouds to determine when it will be safe to go in the water again or when I can simply lay and soak up the sun's delicious rays. I have neither achieved my even tan nor do I feel content in the amount of sun I have absorbed before returning to my regular life. It's never enough sun. I always awoke from these dreams in a state of anxiety with the idea that I was not whole and not ready to partake in the world.

While my nights were negotiated over tall waves, the days were often filled with lethargy, confusion, and a feeling of being separated from my reality. But not all of the days. I truly looked forward to my work events where I collaborated with others. I gained energy from this, and it often sustained me for the day. I so enjoyed welcoming my guests and ensuring a positive experience for them and exceeding their needs. My colleague teased me sometimes about this and asked why I cared so much especially about the less-than-friendly guests. I explained that I believed that everything was made up of energy and that we all could help shift our energy and that of another. I so loved trying to shift the energy to help a person engage in a more loving experience of their current reality. I was always lifted by the exchange.

I first experienced this energy exchange phenomenon when working in a hotel in Midtown Manhattan. I was so naïve, gullible, and very young. My job necessitated me to deal with anything and everyone who came through the doors. I realized at some point that I could be anything to these people no matter what I believed about myself. I decided I would keep secret that I was quite anxious and cared far too much what others thought of me. I would only show them what I wanted them to see and hide the rest. Sure,

Our Transformative Journey

I was confident amongst friends and peers. But self-esteem was something I never learned and didn't have much of. To most people, I seemed like a perky, fun-loving, young woman, and that's what I would run with.

Along with an absence of self-esteem comes an absence of pride. Oh, there were times in my life that I was proud of myself like in the 3rd grade when I was the alternate for the Third Grade Spelling Bee. I was proud of myself in the 4th grade when I almost memorized my entire piano recital. I claimed "winner" in the 2nd grade as having the sharpest pencils, and I often got my schoolwork done first! Who was I racing? And I loved swinging the highest in 3rd grade on the playground. Tom Riley and I would swing ferociously during recess, and the victor was the one who was swinging the highest when the whistle blew indicating fun-time was over. I won every time! Or did I? Did Tommy let me win because I had to? Anyway, I excelled at swinging. I could swing for hours, and later during my high school years, I often did. Swinging saved my life, over and over again.

I certainly have many, many more memories of not being proud of myself. I felt awful snitching on my brother when we were little and getting him in trouble. I was embarrassed in the 3rd grade when I was caught cheating in reading comprehension class. I pushed myself to be in that highest reading level but knew I didn't deserve it because I struggled terribly with understanding what I read. Who was I competing with? I wasn't proud of myself for hiding from my grandparents on top of the garage or house, in the trees or on the swings at the local beach. I became an excellent climber. Swinging, climbing, and hiding, all became part of my usual secret routine.

As a child, I was curious, engaging, loving, and a bubble of laughter. My favorite color was yellow because it was the color of the sun and I often envisioned swallowing the sun – it gave me a yummy, warm, loving tickle in my belly every time. I loved that feeling. I taught myself a game called, "Now I'm Not Thinking." I was fascinated by thoughts and the idea of having no thoughts. I would close my eyes and try with all my might to not think. The result was always the same in that I would hear my voice repeat the words, "now I'm not thinking, now I'm not thinking." I found it all very interesting and amusing. I wondered what came first: emotions or feelings? How could I control myself so that I'd feel the tickle in my belly more and the scared feelings less? Could I learn to force myself to feel and think about what I wanted? What thoughts controlled my piano teacher when he would massage my shoulders during lessons and tell me how beautiful I was? I cannot say when it started or if it was cultural or societal conditioning or simply self-imposed fear that encouraged me to hide away. I started trying to hide my feelings, emotions, creativity, aspirations, and curiosities. I started hiding what I thought was inappropriate and began trying to fit into a mold I thought would be appropriate and acceptable and welcomed and loved.

I wasn't proud of myself when I started drinking at the age of 14 with my older girlfriends. Getting caught at 16 for shoplifting scared me. It was a relief to get caught for it broke the kleptomaniac cycle. Although this particular behavior ended here, addiction itself was only getting started.

Soon after, I picked up yet another self-deprecating habit of cutting myself with razor blades. I did this regularly and contained it mostly to my forearms. I had no clue where I picked up this painful and grotesque habit. I recall cutting when I felt particularly enraged. My feelings were so overwhelming, and I didn't understand them or know what to do with them. Ironically, I would re-carve a peace sign into my left arm until the blood oozed. This ritual often accompanied the music of The Doors. I was certain Jim Morrison would have understood my pain and questioning my reason to live. He would have approved my mind-expanding hallucinogenic drug experimentation and my drinking. He would have appreciated my breaking through the doors of perception with my blood-letting habit.

Surprisingly, all of this behavior was a well-kept secret. A couple of friends knew about suicidal tendencies, and a couple of teachers certainly recognized depression and anger. But I was also popular with my friends in that I could stay up all night drinking with the boys, and I was often a source of entertainment for all.

The D-word

Back to 2002. At the next appointment with the doctor, he mentioned the dreaded D-word: "depression." This was his diagnosis after all my labs were clear. Even though I cried through our appointments together, I proclaimed that I had nothing to be depressed about. I was too young. I had a nice place to live, a good job, a good family, good friends. How could this be? But, I was desperate. I was desperate for vitality, for strength, for energy, for creativity, for health. What I did not understand then was that I was most desperate for love, for self-love.

He enrolled me into the Star D trial sponsored by the National Institute for Mental Health. I started an antidepressant called Celexa (an SSRI). I remember he also suggesting I not consume any alcohol on the medication and again suggested I cease my pack-a-day Marlboro Light habit. I had no control over either habit but told him I'd oblige. It wouldn't be the first time I lied to a doctor. I had been lying to my OBGYN about my smoking so that he would continue my prescription for the birth control pill. So, at this point, I had been on the pill for ten years, starting on my SSRI journey, smoked at least a pack a day, and drank dangerously. I thought this new pill would be the magic I was looking for. I hoped it would give me a new life, a new brain, a new body, and that it would in general, fix me. What happened was the opposite. My blackouts became increasingly dangerous. It was frightening. Each day, I begged myself not to drink but to no avail. I couldn't stop even though the physical and emotional consequences were brutal.

The recurring dream was very prevalent during this dark time. I often went days without answering the phone. I feared that my downward spiraling behavior would be found out. What happened to that little girl that loved engaging with people? What happened to curiosity and innocence? It got to the point where I seldom looked in the mirror, for I saw something there that I no longer recognized nor wanted to acquaint myself with. I saw darkness. I begged to die for I could not handle the thought of waking up as myself one more day. I was a decent and well-intentioned, well-educated woman with seemingly everything going for her. But my inside story was very different from my outside story. My inside story was that of a dark emptiness. I drew a picture of it for my therapist at that time (a Teacher). My life became claustrophobic in this darkness. I couldn't breathe nor could I see a way out. I had constructed a life of secrets, lies, and shame. The separation from life darkened me further and eventually sucked out the fresh air. I couldn't think clearly, and my body was often slow and fatigued – like when you are trying to run in a dream. One night I prayed again. But this time instead of praying for death, I prayed for help.

The Grace

It was a Friday. I found myself literally on my knees praying for help. I recall receiving a strong feeling. That the Truth would lead to the Light. I so desperately wanted to be back in the Light. My desire for Freedom, Truth, and Light finally became stronger than the hold that the darkness had on me. It was then that I picked up the phone and made a call for help.

Our Transformative Journey

The addiction facility that I checked into conducted a routine medical examination. They said they had never seen someone on such a high dose of that drug and asked how long I was on it and if I thought it was helping me. I said I wasn't sure if it helped, but that I suppose it was that I was still alive. They did not make any changes to the dose. That was a glorious 28 days. Not once was I told that I asked too many questions. Not once was I told that I talked too much or laughed too much or cried too much. I relieved myself of secrets and lies and shame. I completely gave in to the experience and simply trusted in it. It was overwhelming to be with others who understood my self-inflicted torture.

Something else that I learned there was to self-soothe with sugar and coffee. I didn't have much of a taste for sweets before this but was told to indulge in it as my body needed to adjust from the loss of sugar in the alcohol I no longer consumed. I thought it was an interesting concept and ate the cake. And did so the next day, and the next day and so on.

Leaving the facility was difficult, but I immediately dove in 12 Step life and made lots of new friends and had lots of great adventures. I got a Sponsor (an Angel) and totally committed to this new life. There were numerous times while engaging with other recovering addicts, feeling vulnerable, unjudged, and accepted that I felt that familiar tickle in my tummy. It was blissful to begin to feel that again! This program saved my life. My life started to get bigger again. Unfortunately, lethargy and confusion continued. I started seeing a highly rated, board-certified pharmacologist. It was with her that I began the 13-year odyssey of SSRI trial life. We tried many different medications including Lamictal, Paxil, Wellbutrin, Cymbalta, and combinations of these and others.

The next few years were often unpredictable. I often had to cancel plans with friends or family because I was too tired and couldn't think straight. My brain fog would mysteriously appear and fill my brain. I was so grateful to be sober, but for what? To sleep through the rest of my life? I became so despondent with my work and longed for more. I did not know what I wanted, but that life was not it. What was the point of being sober if I was so dissatisfied with my life and slept through much of it? Relationships came and went, and I was able to dive into new hobbies and interests but was only able to keep up for short bursts. Headaches were a regular part of my life. I was bloated, addicted to sugar and coffee and my sleep was horrendous. I stopped exercising for the most part and stayed in more and more. Bouts of depression and suicidal thoughts still frequented me way too regularly. How could this be if I was taking this magic pill and living a sober life??

I worked with my doctor, and we changed medications often. Some of those times were excruciating, and I didn't know if I would live through them. Why couldn't my doctor get the damn correct concoction that worked!? I went to the doctor, after doctor in my quest to discover what was wrong with me. I spent thousands of dollars. I went to internists, specialists, and integrative doctors. I also sought the help of alternative practitioners such as a naturopath, acupuncturists, a medical intuitive (an Angel), mental therapists, physical therapists, and more. The infrared sauna became my happy place. The deep heat mimicked the love of the sun for me. I always felt hugged in love while in the infrared sauna.

The Quest

I finally concluded that the magic formula was never going to be found in the "magic pills." But that I had to find the answer in myself. Just like Dorothy and the red, ruby slippers. I knew that I had the answers in me and I had to learn how to tap into where those answers lay waiting. I began with a meditation cd and a spiritual quest to Miami Beach. I loved going to Miami alone to catch up with my thoughts. On that particular trip, I did things very differently -I prayed a lot. I sat by the ocean with the warm healing of the sun, and I prayed for clarity and then I'd listen for the answers. I prayed for the strength to help change my life and the clarity to see the direction in which to go. I repeated positive affirmations with the incoming surf and allowed the negative thoughts to be pulled out to sea. I was up with the sunrise daily. That morning light was tremendously invigorating and has remained a sacred time for me.

I was like an energetic sponge that week. There was a clarity I had never experienced before. There was a tremendous shift that took place that week, and I was never quite the same. When I got home, I was determined to continue on this path of expansion. I learned more deeply about meditation. It all made such good sense to me! This brought me back to my little nine-year-old girl and her game, "Now I'm Not Thinking." It felt so wonderful to finally start connecting some dots to my childhood- to that pure mindset that knew better. I declared that week that I no longer hated myself and that I would show up for myself with love in a way I never knew or did before. I was resolute to live out the lessons that my soul contracted to learn. My soul chose this life, and I was determined to honor that. I declared that I was ready to receive and prayed for Light.

After that week, life started to change. I faced many fears; I changed jobs; I learned to stand up for myself and fulfilled a life-long journey of moving to southern California. Tremendous learning came from this move. While working at the Chopra Center, I started learning more about the scientific proof that meditation changes your brain. This was fascinating! More dots connected to my childhood. The life lessons that came (and continue to come) when I made myself ready to receive, were momentous. Perhaps not so much from the eyes of a stranger, but from my point of view, the changes were huge. My 12 Step Sponsor always told me that "if I compare myself to others, I will always come up short but that I had to compare myself to where I have come from" to see the growth. I still totally love that.

I knew that I wanted to try being me without the anti-depressants. My fatigue and brain fog were increasing as my short-term memory and libido were steadily decreasing. I saw such hope for my future but needed to tap into that authentic part of myself. By this point, I was practicing yoga and incorporated a spiritual practice, learned a lot about nutrition, became very interested in Ayurveda and loved trying out the newest bio hacks. I repeatedly tried to relieve my body of gluten, dairy, and sugar, but time and time again, I failed. I had rid myself of alcohol, drugs, cigarettes, and emotionally abusive guys, but why couldn't I kick these addictions? I knew that I had to change what I was putting in me so that the real me could come out. But how? I prayed on this for some time. Meanwhile, my doctor could not support my medication taper. How could it be so incredibly easy to put me on the meds, but find no one that would help me get off them?? More praying.

The Light

I came across the work of Dr. Kelly Brogan, Holistic Psychiatrist. Game Changer. It was becoming clearer that these SSRIs were not only no longer serving me, but rather hurting me. I learned that there was never any long-term testing done on them and certainly they weren't tested with other medications. I learned that the U.S is one of only two countries in the entire world where direct-to-consumer advertising is permitted within the pharmaceutical industry. This infuriated me! I learned that to date, there has never been any proof that low serotonin contributes to depression. I learned that over 70% of our immunity and brain health starts in our gut. I wanted to learn how to assist my body in its intuitive healing capabilities rather than manipulating its symptoms.

I enrolled and graduated from the Institute of Integrative Nutrition. Since then, I have altered my nutrition to best support my depression, end cravings and to restore my microbiome. I am learning how best to support my physical, emotional and spiritual health. I continue to learn about self-care and self-love. I am continuing to honor my soul's contracts. I am no longer living a life of secrets and shame. This has all been challenging. Contributing to this writing collaborative is in direct contrast to how I lived. But I feel that this vulnerability is greatly progressing my healing and I pray that it will touch at least one person out there – one person desperate to get out of their darkness and back to the Light. I also became a Certified Light Therapist. I learned how to funnel my love for Light and its limitless healing properties to help the body help itself.

I have the honor of assisting clients with their physical and emotional concerns. I believe there are no coincidences. When I found the Lights and began incorporating them into my daily wellness practice, I had no idea what a tidal wave was about to hit my personal life. The Light has saved me again. I see how they have helped me to more easily shift my thoughts to serve me better and to help me stay focused. I love meditating with the lights on me and from there developed what I call *Light Journey*. After consulting with a client, I take them through a guided visualization and let the lights "show me" where the energy needs to go. I can say that each time I have the absolute honor of taking a client on a *Light Journey*, my tummy tickles. I am in love with the body utilizing the light to release blockages and deliver balance. From this balance, we heal.

I understand now that when my tummy tickles, I am working with my true nature. It is this Source Energy in the form of my Soul that chose to come into this life and have certain experiences. For much of my life, I hid my authentic self, and this contributed me moving into darkness. No magic pill or doctor could ever pull me out of that darkness. I had to make this movement into Freedom, Truth, and Light myself. This is the place of self-love, and that is our birthright.

It's been a while since I had the dream of the sunless sky. I hope I never do again. I am eternally grateful for the Light and for always being there even when I couldn't see it. I am eternally grateful for the Light to shine when I begged for clarity. I am eternally grateful for the journey of my soul to unfold in my truth each day, even when those days seem insurmountable. I am eternally grateful for my Teachers and Angels. I am grateful to the tree-swing in the yard of my future home.

About Tamara Samilenko

Tamara Samilenko, INHC, CLT, is founder and owner of SolGuide, providing Integrative Health Coaching as well as Light Therapy. She is passionate about helping others to help themselves. Tamara collaborates with her clients to evaluate their goals and uniqueness and creates a mind-body-spirit approach to wellness. She coaches with compassion, empathy, and accountability. She guides clients in helping to journey them to their inner truth to find their vital, joyful selves.

As a Certified Light Therapist, Tamara enjoys working with the Energetic Body and helping to bring it back to balance. LED Light Therapy (aka, Photobiomodulation) is a form of Vibrational Medicine and is a proven method to reduce pain and increase circulation. It can assist with all pain including wound healing, concussions, skin issues, cosmetic improvements, inflammatory issues, dental health, and digestive relief. It can also aid in reducing anxiety and depression. In addition to utilizing Light Therapy in its conventional methods, Tamara has developed her technique called *Light Journey*. She works with the client to identify possible emotional blocks and together with her intuition, and life training journeys the client on a guided visualization to assist the body to release such blockages and allow it to come back to balance. Tamara combines Integrative Health Coaching with Light Therapy and also uses each modality separately with clients.

Her specific passion is working with recovering addicts to help them move into a life of vitality, health, and self-love. As a sober woman herself, she battled many years of first kicking her addictions and then piecing together a vital, meaningful life. She was medicated on antidepressants for many years after sobriety and was held hostage to them as they were deteriorating her mind and body. She decided to begin to empower herself with knowledge and the trial and error with how to heal herself. Part of that journey has been graduating from the Institute of Integrative Nutrition. It has been a winding road of self-discovery, and she feels blessed to come into contact with the many Teachers and Angels that have helped her navigate along the way. The journey is still unfolding, and she remains open to the teachings. Her goal is to help others make the journey after sobriety be less painful than it was for her.

Tamara's passion for human relations and helping people stems to her childhood. She graduated with her B.S in Anthropology from S.U.N.Y New Paltz and received her MS in Travel and Tourism Management from New York University. She spent more than 20 years devoted to the hospitality industry including as an Event Planner for the Advertising department at The New York Times and a Guest Services agent at the Chopra Center.

Tamara Samilenko is a first-generation Ukrainian American and grew up in Long Island, New York in an extended family. Her grandfather taught her Ukrainian language and history while her grandmother enjoyed cooking the cultural delicacies and making Easter Eggs with her and her brother. Her parents and grandparents remained part of the Ukrainian community and instilled the importance of ancestry and cultural traditions. Both Tamara and her brother spoke only Ukrainian when they started pre-school.

Tamara thoroughly enjoys being in the sunshine, traveling, meeting and engaging with people, laughing with good friends, experimenting with the newest wellness hack, practicing yoga, watching Bigfoot documentaries, listening to the music of #DonnaDelory, and being around animals and nature. She currently lives in New York City.

Contact Information

Tamara Samilenko
SolGuide LLC
Website: www.SolGuide.com
Email: Tamara@Solguide.com

Chapter 16

The Metamorphosis of a Healthy Smile

By: Chenicka Huguley

I was born and raised in a small town in Alabama called Lanett, you know one of those towns that if you blink you miss it. Being raised in a semi-traditional Baptist home that was right next door to the church, I had no excuse for missing any of the Sunday or Wednesday services. My brother and I often fought over the most mundane things as most siblings do, and I was considered a tomboy by all standards of the word. From the outside looking in you would think that I lived a healthy happy life. I was always smiling, so much so that it became my moniker, the girl with the pretty smile. But I learned to plaster that smile on my face from an early age to keep people from really seeing what was on the inside and this is the story of the metamorphosis of my smile.

During my childhood, I went through a lot of things and seen a lot of stuff that had become so commonplace for children these days, just open a paper or turn on the news, but back when I was growing up, it did not seem so ordinary. You see I was raised by my grandparents, and this was the topic of many jokes and cruel comments when I was growing up. Things such as "your parents didn't want you" or "your mom in a crackhead."

Well as ugly as those comments were, they were right, and when someone makes a real statement about your situation, and you cannot give an argument of defense you tend to create a safe place for yourself in your mind to escape the pain, and you withdraw yourself from the real world. That was my solace as a child. I had to find a safe place for me to run to when the pain of being picked on was so intense, that I could hardly bear it. You know how the old saying goes of "stick and stone may break my bone, but words will never hurt me," but when you are actually in that situation can you honestly say they don't hurt. My skin was not thick, and

Our Transformative Journey

I could not just ignore the comments or think of witty things to reply to them to offset my pain.

Now home life was a little different than most people, as I mentioned I was raised by my grandparents and this was because my brother and I were born into the home. My mother had my brother while still in high school, and she had me the year after she graduated. My brother and I have different fathers and while his father would come to see him, my father would not. The first memory I have of seeing my father's face was when we had to go and do a blood test to determine if I was his daughter. We had to pose for this family picture for the records, and this was the first time I saw him.

After that day it would be 15 years before I would see him again. I can remember thinking that I did something wrong for him to not want me. You know how kids always think that it is their fault when parents are not together. Here I have my brother, and his father comes to visit him regularly, and I watch from the screen door as they spend time with each other and play and my father will not even give me the time of day, even after confirming that I am his daughter.

People used always to tell me, "you look just like your mother," and again I would smile, say thank you and keep moving. My mother was a very sore spot for me because you grow up thinking that she is supposed to be there for you when nobody else is right? Well, my mother had an addiction, and it took up the majority of life. The only good thing I can say about the situation is that I never saw her actively using drugs, but I can remember seeing drugs around the apartment early on when we would spend time with her outside of my grandparents' home.

We never stayed for more than a few days, but they were very emotional experiences. Imagine coming come from the neighborhood candy lady ready to play video games and have fun with your brother. You set your bag down on the couch, and when you come back, not looking, you pick up the bag open it, and you see needles, little small rocks, spoons, and other paraphernalia. When you go to your mom and ask her what it is, and she just snatches it from your hand and says mind your business. It leaves emotional scars especially when you love your mother and think the world of her, but shortly after this, she began to spend less time with us and more time in the streets.

It was during this time that the real abandonment issue started to arise. I began to feel neglected by the people who are supposed to nurture you the most. I had my grandmother, but it was not the same as having your mother there. I began to have hateful feeling towards her because I felt that she was not fighting enough for her children and that she wanted the streets more.

The Fake Smile

This began a long journey of creating my happy façade and trying to find something I could be good at and get recognized for, or at least wanted for me. I loved my grandmother, and she was lovingly raising her oldest child's children and doing the best she could, but I still felt neglected and abandoned by my mother and father. When I would come home after being picked on during school, my grandmother would talk to me and tell me what a wonderful person I was, and this was usually associated with sweet. So, from an early age, I began to associate the bad feeling with eating food, and it became a crutch for me for the majority of my life. Whenever I feel bad or if I was having a good time, I would eat sweets to help satisfy the emotions I was feeling. I often felt like a burden to her, so I immersed myself in reading and learning to at least get good grades to make her proud.

Throughout school, I studied, made good grades and tried to make friends. However, it did not turn out the way that I wanted it to turn out. My feelings of abandonment prevented me from making lasting friends. You see if I did not put myself into a friendship then when they left me, I would not be hurt. That was my plan, to cut myself off emotionally so that when the person eventually abandoned me because they would move on in my mind, that I would not feel the feelings of abandonment or rejection. I hid behind my smile, associated at school but never made any lasting friendships due to my thinking that I did not want to be hurt by putting my real self out there because no one would accept the real me. But with all this hiding, I did not realize that it was causing the situation to get worse. I was digging the hole of my emotional breakdown deeper, and instead of safeguarding myself I created a more vulnerable environment that festered and spiraled out of control.

I did not realize I was dealing with critical depression until I was a junior in high school. This is around the time that people start talking about the prom, they were really into the opposite sex and having intimate relationships and experiencing all the fun of having after school parties and the social scene. People started to pay more attention to their bodies, and being skinny was really in, and I did not fit into any of those categories. I was a year younger than anyone else in my class, I was chubby due to always relying on food to help me with my emotions, and I was not desirable to the opposite sex. To me I was fine, I did not want those relationships because I set myself up to not want them for fear of being rejected, so I thought I was doing fine. Even when speaking with counselors during their wellness check after the death of my grandfather during my sophomore year they did not notice my depression or suppressed feelings, this was due to me perfecting my fake smile and happy disposition.

But during my junior year in high school, my grandmother started slowing down, getting sick and having to spend time in the hospital and could no longer work the way she uses to, and I began to get scared. You see my grandfather past away during my sophomore year, and while I was hurt and devastated I had already set up my feeling to accept that he was going to pass away due to having been with him during his illness, but my grandmother was another story. She was the only person that I let into my world because she was the only one that showed any type of love for my brother and I and no matter how hard I tried to put her in the category as everyone else, I just could not.

She was sick and going to work less and less, and I did not want to put any more burden on her, so I got a job in my junior year after school and began to take some of the responsibility of household expenses. I thought I was helping to take some of the pressure off her and in my mind that would make everything ok. She would get better and then things would go back to normal. I was adding pressure on myself, but I would continue to smile and act like I was handling things the way that they needed to be managed and everything was ok, but on the inside, I finally understood that something was wrong, but I had no idea of how to get help.

I wanted to make sure that everyone thought that I was ok because I had this persona to keep up, I had created this smiling façade, and even though I was miserable inside, I had to continue to the show I was ok on the outside. I began to use food as a way to deal with my feeling again, and I also started to socialize less. It was my thought that if nobody saw me, they would not figure out anything was wrong. It started with going directly home after school or work and only coming out to prepare food or help my grandmother with her needs. I was still functioning, and I was being seen so no one thought anything about it and there was the fact that I was always smiling.

By this time, I had perfected the smile, and it was foolproof. I continued to get worse, and my grandmother did not get better. My grandmother had to retire from work early due to her medical issues, and I felt like a failure. I was trying so hard to help her by taking some of the burdens off of her, but she did not get any better. Sure, I knew I did not cause her illnesses, but I felt I had failed in helping her to get better. At this point, the only thing I had to keep me emotionally sane was food, working, and my grandmother.

My plan to get better was simple in my mind, perfect my happy personality, which was harder than it seemed, well it was harder during the daylight hours. However, an opportunity came that would change everything. After graduation, I was offered to take another shift at work that would put me working all night and sleeping all day. It was perfect. I worked at night and did not have to interact with many customers due to it being the slow time for shoppers, and I had the perfect excuse to be in my room all day, I had to sleep so I could work the next night. I felt that I had it all figured out. I was making extra money and could take more household responsibilities, and I had the perfect excuse, not to have to associate during the day. I had been working the night shift for a few months when it comes to the person who would change my whole world and start the process of my metamorphosis.

The One

He was one of the bad boys in the school that would stand on the walls during the change in classes and most often than not would be in the principal office for something. I can remember having a crush on him in my junior high school years but never really pursued it because I felt that no one would want me, and I did not wish to experience that rejection again. But now he was back in my life. We started as friends because I was not interested in letting anyone into my world. I had built my fortress, and I was not allowing anyone inside to breakdown my walls. But he made himself a fixture in my life, and he began to pull me out of my world more often.

In the beginning, I was like a fish out of water. Here I was 19 years old and had never been to a party outside of family functions and had never had anyone to show me any real attention besides my grandmother. It was different, and I didn't know how to handle any type of male friendship, well any kind of association. But, it made me feel things I had never felt before. He became my first real relationship, and the experiences that I had with him taught me a lot about myself and the world outside of the mind.

As you can probably imagine, I fell head over hills in love with him, and he morphed into the main thing in my life. Being my first real intimate relationship where we both had feelings for each other, I can say now that I let him get away with a lot of things that I would not let anyone get away with now. At one point I would even say that he had way more influence over me than I had on myself and a lot of the decisions hinged on how he would react to the outcome. This was done because I wanted to hold on to the relationship that I had let form.

All of my life up to this point was centered around me not allowing anyone to get close to me, not letting anyone into my world because I have experience with abandonment. But, he was different, and he was persistent, charming, and attentive, all the things that I had not yet experienced from the opposite sex. My family members did not too much care for him, and they all hated him except for my grandmother. This was due to him letting me know I could say no to them when I did not want to do what they asked me to do. You see I use to be a pushover for my family and I use to do just about anything they asked, even if I didn't want to because once I gave in they would leave me alone and I could return to my solitude. We were together for five years, and during this time we did move in together, and it was just us against the world. I thought I was happy and that nothing could come between us because I finally had someone who had seen me in my most vulnerable and loved me despite my flaws. But as all stories go, they always have their trials and heartache, and mine was just around the corner.

Once you live with someone, you begin to see a lot of things that you would not usually witness if you were just dating and they returned to their home after the date. You begin to notice patterns and get to know the person's mood and what triggers them, and once you learn these, you see when those patterns change. It took about a year of living together to get his habits down and then about a few months to notice when they deviated.

It started small with being later coming from work, the excuse of working overtime and wanting to hang out with his friends more. I was new the whole relationship thing, especially the living together part. So, I let a lot of things slide and stayed home waiting. Then it got worse, he would start to say he was spending the night with his friends or staying home with his parents, and again I just let it go. I wanted to keep him because at this point I had put my all into this relationship and he was my world. Everything I did was centered around him, and I just wanted to keep the peace, be the dutiful woman and be waiting at home with open arms. It was all that I had learned to this point about how to maintain a relationship.

Well as you can imagine, there was infidelity, and I was devasted. Once again, I felt rejected, and all the old feelings come back to the forefront. I was lost and furious with myself. All this time in the back of my mind I was telling myself that this was a mistake, but my heart won out, and I allowed the relationship. I had given him full control over my life, and I did not know how to take the control back. I did not even know where to start. Even with all of this devastation when he came back, I wanted to work it out, not be a failure, not hear the words "I told you so" from within my mind. He said he wanted to work things out and I jumped at the chance. Here I was a 23-Year-old, and in my opinion, an undesirable overweight woman and I had to hold on to what I had, I could not let it go.

So, we tried to self-counsel ourselves through the Bible and as crazy as this sounds this was what started my healing, not just for the relationship but for my life as a whole. We began to read the Bible together every night, and I learned something new about him. He knew the Bible. This was never anything that had been discussed before with him, so I did not know what religion he was or even if he went to church. I was raised Baptist and had long since stopped going to any services. But I had a love for the Bible, so this made me happy, and we began to heal our relationship.

The Metamorphosis

The moment that changed my life was one night we were reading the Bible, and we came to a passage that I was passionate about, and I was excited to share my knowledge with him. So, after my enthusiastic explanation, he said I was interpreting the passage wrong, and we went back and forth for a minute about how who was right or wrong. In the end, I said well show me in the Bible where I am wrong, and he said: "I can't but my mother can." That night I found out that his parents were Jehovah's Witnesses.

I was floored, but I called his mom, and we discussed the passage, and we talked that night for about two hours, going over many Bible passages and I learned so much that night. We planned to meet the next day, and after many meetings and a lot of thoughtful discussions with myself, I finally agreed to a formal Bible study. I was learning so much and breaking down so many ingrained misconceptions that have been with me since I was a young child. I learned how relationships are supposed to be a team effort and not just one taking total control, that we complement each other to make it work.

Girded with this knowledge and other issues within our relationship, I had to break away from him completely. Granted we were already drifting apart, but after having an accurate understanding of the way that a healthy, chaste, and wholesome relationship is supposed to be, I was able to make one of the toughest decisions of my life. I gave him up, the one thing that I threw away all control for I gave it up. Was I scared, yes, was I concerned about my future, of course, but the knowledge I was learning and the association I was having with the members of the congregation went a long way to assure me that I was no longer alone? Yes, I still had my issues with my image, trust, and rejection but I was learning that it was ok to have those as long as they are in the proper perspective.

After a year of studying, I was baptized as a Jehovah's Witnesses. Most of my family questioned my decision to not only study but to change my religion. However, I made my decision after studying the Bible with the Witnesses, learning about their organization and my grandmother telling me that she did not care what I was she would love me anyway. I can say with certainty that this was the best decision I have ever made. I have no regrets. My grandmother died about three months before I was baptized, and I can honestly say knowing the promise of seeing her again helped me to deal with the devastation of losing the first person who loved and took care of me.

I was learning so much about myself and how to cope with life, but I still had the perfect fake smile. It was something that I had perfected, and I stilled used it out of habit. Even though I knew I had found, people who I could share my concerns with I still judged myself, and harshly. So even though I was socializing more, when I would go home, I would still have to face my inner struggles. I was 5'2" and over 200lbs and almost tipping the scale to 300lbs. But I hid behind all the smiles and the fake happy persona. I was truly happy with my congregation, and I loved learning about Jehovah, but I was still so critical of myself, and I did not know how to cope. But one traumatic event would bring everything to light and leave me bare.

True Smile

One evening I was invited to a fair with some of my friends, and I was having fun. We were riding the fair rides and having a good time eating all of the great foods. Until the one ride, the one that would finally break my façade in front of my friends. We all decided to ride this ride, and we had to bring the bar down over our head and clasp it between our legs. Everybody else could get clasped but me, I could not fit in the seat. Even with the operator trying to force it down it would not clasp, so I had to get off the ride and wait for the others. I could not stop the tears from coursing down my face, and I wanted to hide in a hole and never show my face again. The ride home was pure torture because no one wanted to talk for the entire trip. Once I arrived back, I barricaded myself into my apartment and did not come out for weeks. I did not answer calls or return any text messages. My rouse was uncovered, I was not the happy go lucky girl anymore, I was someone I thought they would look down upon for being the fat, unhappy girl. I was at the lowest point of my life. I could not call my grandmother for advice, and at that very moment I felt truly alone and abandoned.

I prayed and asked for clarity and help because I was so depressed, and I did not know how I was going to make it. I knew I needed to lose the weight and I knew that I needed to get a better picture of myself. I knew I needed to talk to some but talking about my issues has always been a struggle. But with my Bible trained mind,

I knew I needed to speak about my issues honestly with someone. My next step was to schedule a meeting with a therapist and get to the bottom of my problems. Through my sessions, I was commended for finding a foundation that I could have faith in and finding spiritual balance. My issue was my emotional balance, and I had to forgive three people in my life so that I could heal emotionally. I had to forgive my mother, father and myself. I had to come to terms with the fact that I was not responsible for how they treated me as a child and that it was not my fault that they were not in my life as I grew up.

Then I had to forgive myself and begin to take care of myself, also understanding that this would take time and that it would not happen overnight. I think that the hardest lesson to learn was patience. Then came the journey of cleaning up my diet, moving more and loving myself more. In the end, we must learn from our experiences and use them to continue to help ourselves and others, remembering them, so we don't fall back into old habits. But the most important thing that I achieved was a healthy and real smile. One that I still use often. I have been using my experiences to help others cope with similar issues in their lives such as self-love, forgiveness and their health and wellness and I will strive to continue to help as many people as I can.

About Chenicka Huguley

Chenicka Huguley is a 2019 graduate of the Institute of Integrative Nutrition® and is a practicing Holistic Health Coach. She is the owner of Better Health and Life Achieved and CEO of The Firm Huguley, LLC. Her main concentration is helping people with emotional eating issue learn to deal with their emotions and begin the journey of repairing their relationship with food. She also specializes in detox and clean eating for a healthy lifestyle. She is an advocate of self-love and the journey to emotional and physical wellbeing and uses her experiences and recovery to help her clients.

After 15 + years of emotional eating and the subsequent yo-yo dieting that was not working, she realized that she had to stop just trying things and find something that worked. For her to find out what works, she had to discover what her body needed to be on the journey of health and wellness. Throughout this process, she found a system that worked for her and as a result had done something extraordinary in her health and wellness. Her passion now is to help as many people as possible to embark on their journey to achieve the best health and life they can. Her goal is to help the ordinary achieve something extraordinary in their health and wellness.

Before starting her business, Chenicka spent 21 years in the customer service field with the last nine years as a Client Relationship Manager and Project Manager with a large telecommunication company specializing in providing all forms of conferencing solution to fortune 500 companies.

Chenicka is an Alabama native currently living in Houston Texas. In addition to working as a holistic health coach, Chenicka is also an avid reader with a great love for mystery and suspense novels, loves to walk in the park and on trails, as well writing poetry. She also thinks she has a beautiful voice and loves to sing in the car. She is a photography novice and loves to photograph nature on her nature walks. Her faith is made strong by being an active Jehovah's Witness and studying, practicing and sharing her faith with others. She loves to cook and travel abroad, learning about the many different cultures all around the world and what their signature dishes are so she can recreate them in her kitchen.

Contact Information

Chenicka Huguley
Better Health and Life Achieved
Website: www.bhlachieved.com
Email: chenicka@bhlachieved.com

Chapter 17

The Longest Goodbye

By: Narkide Andre'

Food for Thought

I have always been that person who was very curious about health and wellness. A long time ago I realized that quality of life and the ability to fight disease were directly related to nutrition. I had heard adults talking about friends and family who were sick with diseases such as high blood pressure, diabetes, hypertension and elevated levels of cholesterol. I hated to see them suffering. In my teenage years, I was lucky to be in Brooklyn at a time when people were exploring dietary changes such as Vegetarianism and Veganism.

In the '80s small local businesses were popping up all over Brooklyn, businesses that began catering to people interested in these new ideas about food and nutrition, and overall wellness. There were juice bars, and restaurants that were adding vegetarian alternatives to traditional foods, dishes like vegan mac n cheese, and plant-based meat alternatives. Health food stores opened their doors and began addressing people's ailments with natural remedies, and natural supplements.

I started experimenting with new foods. Other than the local Chinese Restaurant and the local West Indian restaurants, my experience with eating foods from other cultures was limited. Coincidently, at this time several gyms and fitness centers also began opening in my neighborhood. Gyms like Lucille Roberts, Jack La Lane, and Bally's Total Fitness. Fitness had even infiltrated the fashion industry. After the release of the movie, Flash Dance clothing started to resemble workout clothes headbands, warm-up suits, leggings, and leg warmers. Everyone wanted to look like they had an active lifestyle even if they didn't. It was at this time that a local entrepreneur opened a gym that offered aerobics classes and Nautilus equipment.

It was walking distance from my home, and everyone knows convenience is always a key factor in maintaining regular visits to your gym. Once there, I met like-minded people who wanted to eat healthily and understood the benefits of regular exercise. Since then, I have always had a gym membership. Even when I didn't have time to exercise at a gym, I purchased videos, free weights, and a treadmill so that I could exercise at home. Regular exercise became part of my everyday life, so much so that I felt as if something was missing from my routine whenever I could not work out. Although I didn't become a pescatarian until many years after, I was always mindful of what I ate and its effect on my health. I started experimenting with vegetarian foods. My first non-meat burger was the Boca Burger, and I was surprised that I liked it. I wasn't ready to be a vegetarian, so I started eating less meat and more fish and chicken, figuring I'd at least try and be healthier in my journey to becoming vegetarian.

What's for Lunch?

I went to a huge high school in Brooklyn New York; Brooklyn Technical High School with about 5,000 students. Lunch was an event. Lunchtime schedules began as early as 11 am, the lunchroom was divided into three sections, and the food was in one. Back in those days, I was still a meat eater, so this allowed me to have a variety of choices from the menu. The school had begun using a new company that provided a fast food menu, and we were very excited about the change. Lunchtime now resembled eating at a fast food restaurant or the food court at the mall. On any given day the menu consisted of pizza, burgers (including cheeseburgers), fried chicken and a variety of fast foods. At first, it was great because it was like going to the food court at the mall every day. We eventually got tired of it which was evidenced by all the food that was piling up in the garbage cans. It was around this time that I started to expand my food menu by trying out different food from other cultures.

During Senior year I was looking into adding extracurricular activities to my college applications when I noticed a bulletin board with a flyer about the formation of a Nutrition Committee. The Committee consisted of the school nutritionist, three other students and me. We met once a month to discuss ideas about additions to the menu as well as to sample different options and give feedback. Together we made some great selections most of which was well received. This experience served as a springboard to my interest in food and nutrition. It also opened up my palate so that I was more willing to try different foods. Unfortunately, trying out new foods and changing my diet caused friction at home with my Mom. My Mom mostly cooked traditional foods from Haiti and much of that included foods that I had begun to eliminate from my diet

Metamorphosis

By the time my oldest son was born, I had already begun to make changes to my diet. I had always suffered from gastrointestinal issues like constipation, and after reading a few articles about the evils of red meat, I decided to remove it from my diet, in the hopes that it would help with these issues.

Along with red meat and pork, I also gave up dairy and introduced whole grains in bread, pasta, and rice to my new diet. Essentially, I had started reading about nutrition and making changes to my diet and now for my children, eating out became challenging. There weren't always healthy options at the places I frequented and going to social events became difficult. Most of my friends and family did not understand my reason for making these dietary changes. I heard a lot of, "We have been eating these foods for generations, and we are all fine." Truthfully, we were not. Trying to explain that most of the food we ate was not healthy nor were we "fine" met with a great deal of opposition.

Almost simultaneously, my sisters began to make changes to their diets too. My Mom was not happy with these changes. I was old enough to cook my food, and so I began cooking meals that incorporated my new dietary needs but, I still ate certain foods like white rice at home to make my Mom happy. I tried to modify recipes to use whole grains and lean poultry and more fish. I also began to prepare my food differently by frying less and less and using cooking methods such as baking, broiling and steaming to reduce my caloric intake and watch my weight. I was now a young adult and wanted to remain "Sexy"! Staying consistent with my diet was difficult because whenever I ate out, the healthy options on the menu were limited to salads or a plate of side dishes. Although I love salads, I wanted to have a variety of foods and enjoy my food. I am a very social person and enjoy spending time with friends and family.

Our Transformative Journey

When I turned 22yrs old, I decided to move away from home and found an affordable studio apartment in Harlem, NYC on 145th Street. I was so excited to be moving out and starting a new life. My new place was not much bigger then my room at home, I bought a futon so that I could set the main space as a living room when I had friends over and open it up into a bed when I was ready to go to bed at night. I was all grown up. I was especially excited about decorating my new place and having friends over. I saw this as an opportunity to try out new recipes and to continue to experiment with new foods in my very tiny kitchen. I often had friends over for casual dinner parties, and they always raved about the food, asking me for the recipes. I only lived in that apartment for two years. My landlord decided to sell the brownstone and did not renew my lease. I was not able to find another apartment before my lease expired so I moved back to Brooklyn to stay with my sister Leila while I apartment hunted.

While at my sister's house I found out that I was pregnant with my first child. My then boyfriend and I had just broken up, and he had moved to Texas to be with his new love. I was ready to embrace single motherhood and needed to find my place ASAP! I registered with the local real estate office and soon found a large studio apartment only blocks away from my sister's apartment. I moved into a beautiful prewar building in a really, cool part of Brooklyn; Clinton Hill. There were great shops, galleries, entertainment, and restaurants; a lot of cultural things to do right outside my door. On February 14, 1992, I went into labor and delivered my son Masai Ahmir, and I was immediately in love. Although he was delivered by cesarean section, his birth was the most wonderful experience of my life. His Dad and I briefly reunited to work things out, but unfortunately, that reunion was short-lived. We co-parented, and he has been a great father to our son and a blessing to our family. We are good friends.

We are Family

Determined to eat healthily and to pass these values on to my son, we ate mostly fish and poultry, a lot of vegetables and even way back then we avoided dairy. Shortly after the breakup, I met my now ex-husband. We met while I was taking a Computer Networking class in New Jersey. We became fast friends traveling to Brooklyn after class together and realized we had a lot in common. Similar religious, cultural, nutrition, and lifestyle beliefs. After just three months of dating he asked me to marry him, and one year to the day later we were married. We both mostly ate vegetarian meals. Soon after we were married, I became pregnant with our Daughter,

Our Transformative Journey

Nailah who even as a child she exhibited a self-awareness that many adults still struggle with. A bit of a "Tom Boy," she loved sports, watched games on tv, and played basketball, soccer, rode her bike and even skateboarded.

One day she came home from school, (at the time we were still eating chicken) explaining she had watched a film at school about the mistreatment of animals. It was that day, she refused to eat the chicken and declared herself to be a vegetarian! She became a self-proclaimed vegetarian at the age of 7 until about the age of 18 when she began eating fish again and switched to being a pescatarian. My youngest son is a rebel. Although he does not eat red meat, he does eat chicken. Both of my boys do, and when I cook chicken, it's organic and free range. For the sake of my sanity, I pick my battles because after all, I do believe in bio-individuality! I try to cook a variety of dishes so that everyone is satisfied, but there are always plenty of vegetables!

My Ex-husband Stanley is a bit of a "Health Nut," he had his cabinet in our kitchen in which he kept all his supplements and herbs and solutions. I believe that he is single-handedly responsible for his good health because he seeks out things that he believes will both keep him healthy and ward off preventable diseases. He is the perfect example of what happens when you take charge of your health. Back then, we also had a lot of workout equipment at home despite us both belonging to a gym. We wanted the option to work out at home if we could not make it to the gym regularly. He believed in taking supplements and was very knowledgeable about nutrition. He was a great influence. I learned a lot from him about eating healthier as we shopped together for groceries and he would tell me the different benefits of herbs, spices, fruits, and vegetables.

We often detoxed by juicing too. We would go to the grocery store and buy fruits, vegetable nuts and other food to use during our regular detoxes. It was at that time that I started to become more interested in the direct connection between food and overall health. Stanley was born premature and as a result, had many health issues related to his birth. Born at just seven months in the year 1965, when certain advancements in medicine were not yet perfected, as a child he suffered from terrible asthma attacks that caused him to be hospitalized often. He also had a hearing impairment which later required the use of a hearing aid. He is still a great influence and often tells me about new herbal cures for my ailments.

Learning the benefits of frequenting the local Farmer's Markets and of eating organic foods and cage-free eggs, all began to become a part of my daily life. I often described his health by using the analogy of baking a cake. One of his doctors asked me what I meant by that. I explained that when you bake a cake and decide to take it out before it is ready, the outside may seem done but when you cut it open, you'll find that the inside was not quite ready and you aren't able to put it back in the oven to continue baking.

We were avid juicers and later purchased a Vitamix which I enjoyed regularly. I liked the minimal cleanup and benefitted from the high fiber smoothies, (if you know what I mean). We ate almost all of our meals from home, and although we were steady with our healthy eating habits, we did allow ourselves to indulge occasionally in sugary desserts, "junk food," and the popular fast food restaurants (most people don't know that Burger King has a veggie burger). Although I wanted the children to understand and appreciate eating a healthy diet, I also wanted to try and maintain a balance.

Who are you and what have you done with my Dad?

It was at this time that we started to notice changes in my Dad's behavior. My Dad had been an accountant, but when he was forced to retire early, he decided to get his CDL license so that he could continue earning a paycheck and build towards his retirement. He began his second career as a School Bus Driver. My Dad loved being a School Bus Driver; he loved to hear the laughter of the children as he drove them to and from school.

My Dad worked hard getting up every day at 3:00 am to get ready to go to work. He planned everything out, he was very disciplined and focused but after all, he was an Accountant, and those qualities had worked well with his first chosen career. He had made plans for his retirement by paying off all his debts including every credit card, car payment as well as the house. He always said that he didn't want any financial commitments to keep him from enjoying his retirement. Around 2012 I noticed a change in my Dad; he was becoming forgetful and exhibited some paranoid-like behaviors. He would forget to pay a bill but would insist that he had made the payment and that the error was on the part of the company to which he had paid the bill. My Mom made me aware of discrepancies in his billpaying practices. This was very noticeable because he was always so meticulous about his recordkeeping.

My Mom and I had a tradition, she would host Thanksgiving, and I would host dinner on Christmas Day. We have a relatively small family in attendance at Christmas dinner, which consisted of my Mom and Dad, my sisters Leila and Marjorie and my family of five who were the bulk of the attendees. Occasionally, there would be one or two other guests. My Sisters would tease me about making a big dinner, they called me Martha Stewart, but I liked that. I would use one of my many sets of china and set the table with full place settings and a fresh floral arrangement. My sisters would call when they were nearing my exit to my house, and that would be my queue to put the hors d'oeuvres in the oven so that by the time they reached our house the hors d'oeuvres would be fresh out of the oven.

I looked forward to Christmas dinner because it gave me a chance to show off my cooking skills and spoil my family. I would start planning the menu about early December so that I could make sure the menu was irresistible! During the time I noticed that my Dad was not keeping up with the bills, was around the same time the first incident occurred where he started to lose his way and get lost while driving. The Christmas of 2011 my sisters called from the highway to tell me that they were lost, and my Dad could not find his way to my house. I stayed on the phone with them giving them instructions until they were able to arrive at my house. Although we were concerned, we had no clue how many other times this would happen in the years to come

A Beautiful Mind

After speaking to a friend, who is a medical Doctor, about some of my concerns, she advised me to have my Dad evaluated for Alzheimer's and Dementia. We made an appointment to see a specialist in New York City. The doctor performed a physical exam on my Dad and referred him for a CT scan of his head. He gave my Dad a series of tests which included him having to repeat the words he had said in sequence and my Dad didn't do so well. At the end of the visit, he was diagnosed with beginning stage Dementia. Although I was not surprised, I was stunned. We walked out of that office, and all I could think was that my Dad had just been given a death sentence. There was silence on that long ride to my parent's home that was deafening. We were unable to speak the unspeakable.

After I dropped them off, I drove home thinking my Dad had just been diagnosed with a disease that would eventually take his life. I knew that there were no documented survivors and that he had been given a prescription that would at best, slow down the progress of the disease.

My Mom called me one day to ask me to try and reason with my Dad. He refused to let her take over the bill payments, and many household bills were late. My Mom was concerned that he was falling victim to scams and that the money that they needed to live and pay bills was being wasted.

The next time I went to visit, I found him sitting in the dining room with a bunch of envelopes that already had stamps on them. I asked him what he was doing to which he answered he was paying bills and making charitable contributions because they would be good deductions on his taxes. While he was filling out the info on the inserts, I picked up his checkbook ledger to take a look, and I was shocked and in disbelief at what I was reading. There were pages and pages of contributions to dozens of charities as well as checks to different sweepstakes.

I asked him why he was spending so much money on the charities and sweepstakes that required him to give them money to cash in his winnings. He answered that it was not a great deal of money only a few dollars here and there. I tried to explain to him that it was not just a few dollars here and there, but he did not believe me. I asked him if he would add the amounts if I read the numbers to him and he said, "Yes." You see, my Dad was a mathematical genius and could add a long string of numbers in his head, a skill he had not passed down to me. As I read the amounts out loud, he began to add them in his head and say the totals out loud. When the totals reached beyond $500.00, I stopped. I looked at him and said, "That's not just a few dollars here, and there is it?" and with a sad look on his face he replied, "No." After that day, I started taking the checkbooks home without his knowledge and shredding them. Eventually this all stopped, but unfortunately, we had already lost thousands of dollars.

In Search Of

My Dad was always a jolly person. He loved to laugh, but he did, however, have a wicked temper, and when he was angry, it was best to stay out of his way. As the days and months and eventually years rolled passed, there were countless numbers of examples and incidents that occurred as a direct result of my Dad's struggle to live with a disease that was robbing him of himself. There were countless times that he parked the car and could not remember where he had parked it; we had to go out and drive around until we were able to find it. There were other times that he would get lost and drive until he had run out of gas and we would call him and find out where he was so we could bring gas and drive him home safely. These things happened often, and every time, we held our breaths and prayed for the best outcome.

One day, he went for a walk and got lost, and we had no idea where he had gone. He was lost for hours when finally, a stranger found him on the ground; he had fallen. The stranger called for an ambulance, and when the paramedics came, they used his phone to contact us to let us know that they were taking him to the hospital. When I arrived at the hospital and was finally allowed to see him, I was shocked to see the state he was in. He always wore dress pants, a shirt, and shoes whenever he left the house. He was sitting up in the hospital bed, his face was a bloody mess, and the blood had soiled his shirt. His mouth was bleeding, and it was obvious that he had lost a few teeth. His pants were dirty from having fallen too. When he saw me, he asked me what I was doing there, and I told him that I came to see how he was doing. He was surprised to see me, and when I asked him if he knew where he was, and he replied, "I'm here for the wedding." My heart sunk. When we became afraid for his life, the safety of others, both on the road as well as pedestrians, my sister and I devised a plan to steal the car while he was in the hospital. Much like a Mission Impossible episode my sister, who did not drive, found a friend who took the car out of the driveway only after breaking the lock on the gate and drove it to a parking garage. The next day I took a bus to NYC and then a train to the garage and drove the car to my house where it stayed in my driveway until we were able to sell it. We used the money to pay fines against the house since we were about to lose the house due to violations that mounted into the tens of thousands of dollars of which my Dad was not capable of taking care.

There were many more times when my Dad would get lost, and my sisters and I would drive around for hours looking for him. He would say that he needed to get to work and my Mom could not stop him, so by the time we would go out looking for him, he would be long gone. The last time my Dad got lost was November 8, 2017, when he left the house at 8 pm in the evening and disappeared into the night. I left home to go to NYC to help to look for him.

The police came to help us search for him as the Police Captain came with three squad cars, search dogs, and a helicopter. This time was different, it was nighttime, 40 degrees and he had left the house without a coat wearing only his pajamas. An officer asked us if he could pray with us and they stood outside under the night sky and prayed for our father's safe return. My sister and I drove around all night, going to places where we had found him before, but we could not find him.

As the sun rose, we were struck with fear. Fear that we would not find him alive this time. Every time we saw a police car, we would ask the officers if they had heard anything about him and although they knew about the BOLO (be on the lookout) about an elderly Black man who was missing, they had not seen him. Finally, we got the call that he had been found on the other side of Brooklyn. Someone saw him after the sun had come up and called the police. They sent a squad car for him, and we waited at the house to see him. He was shivering, and his feet were filthy, I was so happy to see him and know he was ok. The same day we found him was his 77th birthday and my Mom had baked him a cake. I had the locks changed so that he could not leave the house and although that type of lock was dangerous and unsafe because it meant it had to be locked from the inside, I felt I had no choice. I was able to hire an amazing woman who took care of my Dad who also helped my Mom around the house. She became family.

The End Makes Way for New Beginnings

I did not know that would be my Dad's last birthday as he passed away on August 25, 2018, at 3:18 am. I began studying at the Institute for Integrative Nutrition in February 2018 in efforts to find ways to help heal my Dad. I believe that the illness that took his mind and eventually his life began with gastrointestinal issues that he had his whole life. Something from which my sisters and I also suffer. My Dad, Pierre Borgella, lived a rich, full, and beautiful life and always wanted the best for me; for all of us. I know that an unhealthy gut will poison your entire body and that the microbiome is the key to good health. I am committed to helping others take care of their health to live their best lives. After taking a leave of absence to pursue my dream of becoming a Health Coach, I quit my job after my Dad's passing and have been living My Best Life in honor of his. Forever in my heart, "I love you Pop!"

About Narkide Andre'

Narkide was born in the West Indies on the island of Haiti, to Pierre and Ninon Borgella. When she was three years old, her Mom left Haiti and moved to the United States to prepare for the rest of the family to join her after that, in Brooklyn NY. Her father, affectionately called "Pop" to her and her siblings, would join her mother a year later. Narkide eventually immigrated to the US when she was five years old with her younger sister Leila. In the days before they left Haiti, they were saddened because although they were eager to see their parents, they would be leaving behind everyone and everything they knew and loved.

Her parents rented a beautiful brownstone apartment in the Park Slope neighborhood of Brooklyn, NY, where they shared a bathroom and kitchen with another couple. When she arrived in the United States, Narkide did not speak any English. Her parents spent the summer before she started school, speaking to both children in English and insisting that they watch television so they could familiarize themselves with the new language. That Fall, Narkide was placed in a bilingual class at the local elementary school, to which her parents were not happy with the school's decision to place Narkide in such classes. They wanted their children to assimilate so they would not stand out, and all the opportunities that were afforded to American children would be available to them as well.

The following school year her parents removed her from the public school, and Narkide began 1st grade at the local private Catholic School, where they placed her in mainstream classes and was left to figure things out on her own. Although her English language skills were better than they had been, she was not mentally nor proficient enough to handle what was expected. In an incident wherein Narkide did not answer her teacher's questions, she was humiliated, thrown out the classroom and made to stand outside the door. Her teacher thought she was being defiant and refusing to answer her questions; however, the reason for her noncompliance was because she was too embarrassed to admit she did not understand what was being asked. After that, she was determined to become fluent, so she read every book she could get her hands on and voraciously watched television so that she could perfect the pronunciation of words. Narkide soon rose to the head of the class and became one of the smartest students of her class. It is Narkide's strive for excellence, determination to persevere and passion for the work she does and the people she serves that makes her a not only an extraordinary human but effective in her delivery.

Narkide currently lives in Central New Jersey with her three children; son, Masai 26, daughter Nailah, 21, and son Jawhar 16. She has three sisters Nadege, Leila and Marjorie, and an amazing Niece, Niara. She is the Proprietor of her Interior Decorating business *Outstanding Interiors*, which is her first passion. She creates both commercial and residential design as well as home staging. She is obsessed with both art and architecture and is a self-proclaimed "Museum Geek." She currently works as a Health Coach with a company specializing in weight loss programs, where she coaches patients and assists them in maneuvering through their weight loss journey while working on their health goals.

Contact Information

Narkide Borgella Nutrition
Website: www.narkideborgellanutrition.com
Email: narkideborgella@gmail.com

Chapter 18

Progress Over Perfection

By: Sneha Sharma

The Travelers

Two people are beholding a happily ever after, with two suitcases full of dreams, migrating between two countries transversely different and maybe, with too little an understanding of the journey that lies ahead. From New Delhi to New Jersey we traversed riding on the wave of hopes and dreams. From effortlessly crossing a tumultuous ocean to standing helpless before a gentle river, when I started this journey, I could never have imagined what was impending.

It was the fall of 2012 when my husband Ashu and I decided to leave behind our comfortable lives in India, our homeland, our loving families and the culture that molded us, all for the American dream. I said goodbye to my rewarding career as an investment banker in one of India's leading banks. I boarded a 15-hour flight, leaving behind gratifying days filled with important business meetings. I also said goodbye to daily family gatherings, and I bid trifle sad, yet excited for the future farewell to friends of a lifetime.

I landed in America thrilled, yet my heart had few misgivings. I was not sure if I would ever work again, how long it will be before I see my family in India or if I would ever find a true friend in the new country. But there I was, in the USA, starting anew, studying the New Jersey driver's manual, navigating giant supermarkets, and trying to figure out the fascination that Americans had for Halloween.

The Baby Question

Two years into our American dream and I was enjoying my new life in this beautiful country. I was 29 years old and content with our twosome, not sure we should be rocking our comfortable boat with a baby in the scene. Frankly, we did not have a burning desire to add to our family until now. However, the ticking biological clock made me nervous. We started trying, but also not trying to get pregnant. We were ready to accept whatever the future had in store. Motherhood, after all, had not been high on my to-do list, but as I approached 30, I also knew that with passing time fertility could become an issue.

To start a family, we had the same questions as any other couple would, did we have the time and the money for parenthood? My husband had a work visa, but I was not eligible for one, which also meant that I had the free time to spend months happily pregnant. We were still rummaging with the idea when things materialized faster than we anticipated. It seemed the universe had decided for us when the word 'pregnant' showed up on the Clear Blue pregnancy test that August 6th morning in our temporary hotel home and my first reaction was goosebumps and fear.

Suddenly, we felt that we were not ready to become parents yet, and the prospect of becoming one was terrifying. I had no idea what the next year would bring, and maybe, as it turned out, it was a good thing that I did not know then. All I could see in the word 'pregnant' was uncertainty - us in a new country, with no permanent job, no permanent home, and no family, besides the one growing inside me. Slowly as the truth sank in and the thrilled congratulations poured in, I became more relaxed and warmed up to the whole idea of pregnancy. I looked forward to being more pampered by my already adoring husband. My mother would come and stay for six-months to help with the newborn and the fact that my house will be filled with cooing and gurgling of an angelic baby.

The Last Minute Rollercoaster

The baby bump grew as time passed. So far, my pregnancy had been a breeze, and I enjoyed the attention showered on me and our daily conversations with my baby bump. However, when I was three weeks from my due date in April my yearning to see my mother surpassed my desire to see my baby. My mother made the same 15-hours flight that had brought Ashu and me to this country two years ago, and I had not seen her since. Our joyous reunion set a relaxed and loving mood for the last weeks of my pregnancy and my upcoming baby shower.

With my ma around I felt great. We chatted and laughed and caught up with the family gossip, together we took care of the last-minute chores for the upcoming baby shower. And then, like a bolt out of the blue everything changed. The night before my baby shower, I had such an intense itch all over my body that I had no choice but to go to the ER. I fully expected to get a prescription cream and come back home within a few hours, at the tops. Imagine my shock, when I learned that the doctors were going to admit me for observation. A blood test revealed some problem with my liver function.

The doctors feared Hepatitis A and refused to discharge me until they were sure of the diagnosis. Around midnight, a doctor came into the room to tell us that my results didn't look good and more tests were needed before they'd know anything definitive. I felt like a prisoner and would have signed any release form to get out of there.

In a few hours, it was my baby shower, with more than fifty guests invited. I was adamant about leaving the hospital and Ashu was fully aware of my fierce determination and stubbornness. He held one of my hands and put his other hand on my baby bump and looked into my eyes. Very gently yet firmly he said "honey, I know how you are feeling, but you know what? You are a mom, and a mom will always choose what's right for her children". As usual, his words calmed me down, and I realized that no matter how excited I was to attend my baby shower, I would never do anything that jeopardizes the wellbeing of the baby herself. I was asked to prepare for the delivery of my baby within days. Thankfully the results came in negative for Hepatitis A, and mercifully the itching also stopped.

The Rollercoaster Continues

On March 15, 2015, five days after being admitted to the hospital for unexplained itching, the doctors induced my labor. Hours later, we were holding our first born in our arms. We decided to name her 'Aisha,' meaning full of life. I'd always heard people say, "When you become a mother, life changes forever." And change did come to my life albeit not in a predictable manner. Unlike the movies or mommy blogs, where the fawning new moms are absolutely in love with their newborns, to my dismay, I felt absolutely nothing when the nurse put my five-pound three-ounce daughter on my chest. I was both confused and ashamed at the same time, for my lack of feelings, let alone the surge of love I was supposed to feel.

As I looked at my precious child, I kept thinking why don't I feel that gush of love, those emotions you see in every commercial for diapers? What's wrong with me? She was in perfect health and looked so cute in a beanie over her little head. I couldn't take my eyes off that peanut, but inside I felt nothing. For our hospital photographer, I faked what I thought would pass as a loving new mom look – goodness knows I'd seen enough of them on TV. I didn't stop the new mom impersonation there. I wrote gushingly about how wonderful motherhood was, the same stuff I'd read in every new mom Facebook post. We drove this tiny baby from the hospital in a large car seat to our rented apartment. During the drive home, I kept wondering what was wrong with me; why did I feel so hollow.

Fortunately, at home, I had my family around me to help, or so I had hoped. My mother-in-law had joined my mother in America for the birth, but it seemed that neither of these mothers who had reared five children between them remembered much about how to take care of a newborn. While they tried to contribute with taking over the housework, neither were too comfortable doing what this novice mom needed most - help taking care of the baby. I can only compare the first few days of being home with the baby to being hit by a truck and to my utter dismay, I find the latter a preferable and more comfortable option. I struggled to keep my head above water, a prophetic analogy as it turned out a mere month later. For now, in the exhausting, sleep deprived first four weeks, I came to understand why no sleep is considered a third-degree torture method. On top of that, I also became a charter member of the La Leche League Losers.

Despite trying everything, I could not breastfeed my baby. I tried latches, supplemental nurses, lactation consultants, herbs, diets, hospital grade pumps but nothing helped me lactate. Why couldn't I do something as natural as breastfeeding? No matter how much I tried and obsessed over it and tried again, I couldn't fix it, and no one could help me either. But, I'm not a quitter, and I pushed on, trying to do the impossible for my daughter somehow.

While I was still trying to find my feet as a new mom, there started a constant background soundtrack of colic. Ironically, I had never even heard of the term colic before my daughter suffered from it. That precious baby in the beanie who started life at just over five pounds screamed like a giant monster, as waves of pain washed over her little insides. Babies with colic cry and cry for more than three hours a day, for more than three days a week, for weeks and months.

My daughter cried 15-hours daily at such intensity that my husband feared the neighbors would call child protective services for some horrible cruelty we must be inflicting on her. Too rarely, she slept and ate, and only then would the noise and the household settle down for a moment. At all other times, hysterical crying filled the air. After two weeks of this horrible noise, her pediatrician informed us that the colic and the intense crying could continue until she was three months old. I felt terrified at the thought. I could barely get through an hour with this nonstop wailing child, how I would ever survive months more of it. Ashu and I comforted each other saying with time 'this too shall pass.'

However, no matter how well we simple humans try to cope, the universe comes up with its plans. Although, I knew my mother-in-law had to leave within a few weeks, what I did not anticipate was that my mom would also have to go back to India so soon. We learned of my father's heart attack, and I had to say goodbye to my mom, with the persistent soundtrack of colic in the background. I tearfully kissed my mother farewell for her journey back to my father in India and watched my husband leave for work, a world where no one cried persistently.

What descended on me in that little apartment with a screaming infant was a life of isolation I had never felt before. My baby in her world of colic pain gratefully tried to accept whatever love and drops of breast milk her mother could painfully squeeze out of her exhausted self. I felt like a failure, beating myself for struggling to keep myself or my baby calm. I found myself in a state of unfathomable sadness and crying almost every day. I hated stepping out of the house as I couldn't find the motivation to dress up. If I limped through motherhood earlier, now I was legless and crawling. Things were getting worse. In Hindi, there is an expression that means "this night has no dawn'. My whole life was like that night.

Sadness

A few days later, the 6-week postpartum checkup was my first visit out of the house without my newborn. It felt good to have a moment to myself. I went to the appointment expecting the doctor to announce that I was physically healing and send me home. However, something far darker awaited both of us before I left the doctor's office. After giving me a clean physical bill of health, the doctor asked me a simple question, "Sneha, how are you feeling these days? Do you ever feel overwhelmed?" For some reason, this question hit my core. It made me burst into tears and cry out loudly as if someone had died. I felt that the doctor, probably as another mom knew of my pain and was genuinely concerned about me. No one had asked me until now how I was coping. I guess everyone assumed I was managing. My tears flowed freely in that office. I've never cried like that in my entire life.

Despite my blinding tears and her insightful question, I also felt a troubling disconnect. She regarded me with such a detached look and lack of empathy that it made me wonder if she suspected that I was going crazy. I tried to control my sobbing as she handed me a questionnaire, asking if I'd cried most of the days, if I can laugh or see the funny side of things, and whether the thought of harming myself or the baby ever occurred. I answered every question honestly, marking 'yes' to more than 90 % of the questions. The doctor checked the answers and confirmed what I had just begun to realize, that I was severely depressed, and my depression had a name - Postpartum Depression.

The doctor said that I needed to see a mental health specialist. I left the office feeling worse than before. Not only was I exhausted, unable to breastfeed or stop round the clock colic crying of my baby, but I was also so depressed that I needed to see a shrink. My husband and I, still new to this country and its ways, felt petrified that officials could take our daughter away because of my depression. I had reached a new low. How did I, once such an upbeat, accomplished career woman become this sobbing mass of insecurities, fears, and sadness? I couldn't imagine someone being depressed after having a baby before it happened to me. Remember, my frame of reference was the picture society, social media, and most women painted, of the radiance of motherly love and a gurgling baby.

I started reading on PPDS, trying to find out, what the hell was happening to me. To my shock, I found out that postpartum depression affects one in every eight mothers. It is a real, clinical form of depression and requires treatment and attention, just like any other mental illness. Knowing how common it is, lifted some weight from my shoulders, but I wasn't anywhere back to normal. Extreme PPSD, studies reveal, can cause a mother to harm her baby or herself. To my eternal gratitude, even on my craziest days, I never felt like hurting my baby, but what I didn't know then, as terrible as I thought, that I was about to embark on an even more terrifying moment of my postpartum depression journey.

One evening, my mild-mannered husband and I got into a fight about his lack of understanding of how I felt. I raged that he had it easy; he got to leave the house all day and not hear the screams of an inconsolable infant. I grabbed the car keys and started to drive with no specific destination in mind. I just wanted to find a peaceful place to get away from it all. Usually, that place would have water nearby. As I drove in the darkening evening, I had hoped to find a spot to park the car, cool my emotions and have an honest dialogue with myself. I drove two towns away from ours and stopped the car near the beautiful banks of the Delaware River.

In this watery setting, the self-talk started where a chain of racing thoughts crossed my mind. I talked to my self about what is going on in my life and how I have ended up at this point where I have no control over when I could sleep, eat, bathe or even go to the bathroom. I told myself that no one understood my pain no matter how much they loved me and that even if they did, no one could save me from either this life or these feelings. I convinced myself that this feeling of hopelessness and despair was here to stay for a long, long time. Then my dialogue with self-changed to one of action. "Be your hero, Sneha," I told myself staring at the river as tears streamed down my face. "Save yourself from drowning in a life you find so joyless and un-livable. End that feeling of drowning you carry every day with a real drowning tonight, Sneha". "Walk into the river, and all that pain can end forever in a matter of minutes." I got out of the car and started to walk to the river's edge.

I stood there with dusk around me, the river in front of me and the dialogue continued. The only people affected by this suicide would be my innocent newborn daughter, who would never remember me at this young age, and my husband, who in my depressed state, I had decided didn't care about me. While facing the river and the most significant decision of my life, my silence broke with a new burst of sobbing, a cry so primal and deep that I had to cover my mouth with my hands to avoid attention. If I walked straight ahead instead of turning back, I would end my struggle but start another for the people I loved most in life.

At the most critical time in my life, I knew I could not put myself before them. I returned to the car, shaken to my soul. How did this journey that started with such high hopes while crossing the Atlantic Ocean get me to the banks of Delaware in such a fragile state of mind? How did the optimistic, the life of the party, the non-stop laughter comedian, the competitive kick-ass professional, the wise advisor to many friends, and the powerhouse of energy, ended up on these muddy banks contemplating such a catastrophic step?

Phoenix Rising

One thing for sure, willpower alone will not get anyone out of PPSD. What helps is acknowledging and talking about it, and I decided I'd be the one to speak truthfully about it in my circle, and beyond if I ever had the chance. This transformation had to start from within. When I challenged the Hollywood (or Bollywood) version of early motherhood with my friends, I learned I was being ridiculed and judged by some in the group. Was this why women did not let on just how bad things are? But that didn't deter me; I knew there were many like me!

During pregnancy, before I knew about PPSD, I had smugly laid out plans about when I would return to work and resume my normal life. I felt I could not identify with a woman who stayed home to care of her family. I had to find an innovative way to add value to my life in my new country. While I thought the value would come from working, making money and connections, I got healthy enough to reconsider. Maybe the scare at the river did it, but I finally told myself to let go of the need to work just to fit in with my peer group. When I finally decided I didn't care what people said or thought about my life, I had a rebirth.

Gradually and painfully slowly, I understood that my depression stemmed from a witch's brew of non-existent support and lack of social connection. I forced myself to think hard as to why things turned so ugly. When I dug deep, I realized there was a big gap in my expectations versus reality. I couldn't help but imagine how my life post the baby could have been entirely different had I been in India.

Back home, there's a remarkable contrast. You have a village to take care of you including your immediate and extended family. Some Au-pairs can come and live-in with you to take care of the baby, for as long as you want. Most sub-urban households have permanent domestic help that takes care of everything from meals to housekeeping. You have your circle of friends, with whom you can relate to and share your feelings. That culture was a part of my upbringing as I grew up witnessing ample support around my family and me. Being in America, raising a baby on my own without my Indian support system was a recipe for disaster. Also, the image I had in my head of a newborn baby was of one who would fill the house with its coo's and gurgles as opposed to the infant in extreme colic pain whose screaming would fill the house.

Eventually, I accepted my circumstances and decided to work with what I had and reinvent myself. I resolved to look forward and find my way out of the depression. Time began to pass, not in hours of crying, but bigger chunks of calmness both for me and my little one. As a growing baby, no phase-in Aisha's life was permanent. Every phase was like a season. She grew in control and ability, and so did I. We became more independent and bonded with each other at the same time. I started to treat motherhood as a job, in the most positive sense. I resolved to make life interesting, worthwhile and loving for my child and me. Just as the old Sneha excelled at maintaining client relations, strategizing, and meeting targets, the new Sneha, with the depression lifting, adapted those skills to shine as a mom for her one and only daughter, Aisha. I started remembering my past life more clearly and reminded myself that I did not love my downtown job every day and similarly did not have to beat myself for not enjoying motherhood every single day, either.

As I started to get out of the black hole of depression, I looked for ways that might help my transformation and also what I would tell others who suffer from PPDS, especially in the early months of motherhood. I finally stopped obsessing over breastfeeding. I did my best, and if that didn't work I did what's second best, and it's called 'formula.' You must find help early on, whether it is your family or outside. Ask for assistance, hire if you need to and make arrangements before you get the baby home.

There are some things I could have done if someone would have pointed me in the right direction. My experience tells me that a new mother should stop feeling guilty about prioritizing her basic needs, as a drowning person cannot help anyone least of all herself.

There are some lessons out of my experience that you can take as a reader or give to an expecting mother. You can always negotiate with your partner and work out a schedule to take turns to sleep with the baby so that each parent can get a good night of sleep. Look for social connections and seek out women with same age children as yours as there's nothing more comforting than to have a friend who can empathize with you. It is essential to find some 'Me' time, whether it is a ten-minute stroll around the block or an uninterrupted phone chat with your bestie. Your entire family will benefit far more from your sanity than your stressed-out persona 24/7. Let go of the need for perfection, your overflowing sink of dishes can and will have to wait. Remember, with an infant in the house you are in survival mode, loosen that grip on control. And yes, when your colicky baby cries, and everything you try fails, sing a lullaby with headphones on while praying your husband gets home soon.

Before the dark clouds of postpartum depression engulf you, reach out for help, paid or otherwise. Anyone who has suffered from PPSD will never forget how terrible it was, but the survivors should also remember their duty to share the experience with the next desperate woman who cannot fathom what is happening to her. Finally, from a time when you could not contemplate how you could survive the next minute, there would be milestones you would reach that looked impossible only a few months back. She would sleep uninterrupted all night in her room. Contently play with her toys while you work. Tiny teeth of a toddler will soon replace her toothless grin. She will become a preschooler loving her new friends and a kindergartner waving at you from the school bus.

Today Aisha is four years old, and I am in awe of her, every waking minute! My husband and I can't get over her sweet voice, kind ways and angelic face. We can't imagine our lives without her. Every day we ask her, and ourselves, how did we get this lucky and she answers in that lilting little voice "God sent me for you!"

When Aisha started preschool, I had time to consider a second inning in my career, and I looked for something more in keeping with my changing interests and passions. I enrolled with the Institute of Integrative Nutrition in New York City and got my certification as an Integrative Nutrition health coach. While still in school, I started a health-coaching practice, called Between Cheat Days. Here, I help my client's un-complicate nutrition, I encourage them to feel great about themselves and live a joyous life that's true to their purpose or as I call it their 'WHY?'

As for me, I needed to reclaim my identity, and I realized my new individuality by becoming a health coach. As a graduate from one of the top nutrition schools in the world, I want to guide others on a path to their best and healthiest self. I also want to share what I lived through and my transformation from one of the most depressed moms to one of the happiest, from struggling to keep up with my toddler to feeling my best-energized self, from being stuck in my maternity wardrobe forever to being back in my pre-baby skinny jeans. I have found the answer to my calling in helping others. It took a leap of faith, in a series of leaps of faith in my life, but I knew I would not falter anymore.

So, go for it, and don't let setbacks on the path stop you from your goals and your purpose. Pack light and remember where you came from and carry big dreams wherever you go. Namaste!

About Sneha Sharma

Sneha Sharma is a health and wellness expert and the creator of Between Cheat Days - A holistic health coaching practice with its mission to inspire people to live their best life by finding the right balance of optimal health, quality Sleep, quantified Nutrition, adequate physical Exercise, and emotional wellbeing.

As an integrative nutritional health coach, her role is to bridge the gap between knowledge and execution. She believes that most people know what they need to do but lack the necessary support, mentorship and accountability that leads to any real transformation.

Her passion for holistic health and wellness stems from her success in overcoming her health struggles with PCOS, Hypothyroidism, Vestibular Vestibulitis, Postpartum depression, and body image issues. She takes immense pride and satisfaction in helping other women deal with similar challenges.

Through her practice Between Cheat Days, she offers one-on-one coaching, group programs and tailor-made solutions for her client's needs. She believes in the concept of bio-individuality: What works for one doesn't always work for another. While she's still available to her clients, her goal is to empower each client to become self-sufficient in creating their best life.

Sneha was born and brought up in the northern part of India, she graduated with a bachelor's in business and went on to pursue a successful career in one of India's leading private sector banks where she played a key role as a top- performer Investment banker.

In 2012, Sneha said goodbye to her rewarding career at the bank and decided to relocate to the USA with her husband to start a new life. Later, she became a stay at home parent to her adorable daughter, and while her road was a little bumpy in the beginning, she wouldn't trade it for the world.

Always a worker at heart, Sneha decided to plunge in a career that's in congruence with her heart, she started her second stint as an Integrative holistic health coach. What she considered a cliché- "Do what you love, and you will never work a day in your life"- is a reality for her today.

In 2019, she graduated from the Institute of Integrative Nutrition in New York City, and she looks forward to applying her education, training, and passion for helping people around the world live a life of health and happiness.

Sneha plans on advancing her knowledge of health and wellness with additional courses in functional medicine, Ayurveda and yoga.

When she's not helping clients, she loves experimenting with different cuisines in her New Jersey kitchen, writing journals and baking cookies with her daughter. Sneha loves traveling back to India to be with her family and admits that Indian street food is her big weakness!

Sneha lives in New Jersey with her husband Ashu and her 4-year-old daughter Aisha.

Contact Information

Sneha Sharma
Between Cheat Days
Website: betweencheatdays.com
Email: betweencheatdays@gmail.com

Chapter 19

Learning to Love Myself While Managing ADHD

By: Marc Almodovar

Where It All Began

Even as a child, I always knew there was something different about me. I still remember the feeling of embarrassment I felt like a third grader when I needed extra help with my school work. I always felt I was the only one who needed more help. Frequently, my teacher would stay with me after school to help me with math, and many of those times I was the only student in the room. I struggled to process information quickly in comparison to the other students and often felt I had been born into a world in which the odds were stacked against me.

During my middle school years, the motivation to perform began to drop significantly, and my grades were poor. There wasn't much appeal to doing well in school as I saw little reward. I attended the regular middle school during my sixth-grade year after I received my final grade report the decision was made that I would attend the alternative school the following year. Students were often placed at the alternative school due to poor behavior and attendance. However, I was placed there because of my lack of drive, poor test grades, and not turning in homework. Getting dropped off there every morning was mortifying. When the school district had special events such as field trips it was especially humiliating as our school arrived separately from all the other students. This further singled me out and led me to feel strongly that there much be something wrong with me. This thought frequently reappeared as the years went on.

When I was 16 years of age, a junior in high school, I was still receiving poor grades at school, lacking drive, and struggled to get up each morning. As teachers led class, my mind wandered from the present moment to things that were of more interest to me such as music. I had a strong interest in creating music those days and often had a beat or song on my mind instead of listening to what was going on in class. Organizational skills were also nonexistent as I frequently missed or lost things of value to me due to my messy room and poor scheduling ability. I would equate my mind to what Buddha describes as "The Monkey Mind," a mind that frequently wanders and takes a large effort to calm. I struggled to understand why I often felt I didn't belong and truly wanted to thrive in the same way I saw my peers thriving.

Throughout the school year, I made frequent visits to the guidance counselor to consult about my poor performance. The counselor repeatedly explained I needed to pay attention during class and complete my homework. Though all these things were true, my motivation was not increased by hearing these words over and over. Instead, this only increased my feelings that I was not normal. I often felt as if I had been born into a world that was against me at every turn. What happened next was a wake-up call that would change everything. My mom received a call explaining my poor grades, spotty attendance, and lack of drive had resulted in a need to repeat my junior year. I would not be moving to the twelfth grade with my peers. Infuriated, she began our conversation in much the same way as my previous conversations had gone with the guidance counselor. But this time something changed, I gained enough courage to be able to tell her how I was suffering. I shared that I felt depressed and insecure. We agreed that I needed help. My mom, being an incredible mother, acted and sought care immediately.

"According to Your Tests, You Have ADHD"

Soon began a series of doctor visits as we searched for answers. It was obvious upon meeting me that I appeared to be anxious which was confirmed by clammy palms and the way I spoke, often with my head down and a shaky voice. I was seated in front of a dull screen and asked to participate in tests that would help explain my brain's ability to focus. Some of the tasks were quite boring, but they provided valuable insight for the doctors and me. Doing different tests like this, they were able to see what's up with my brain. After all the tests and questions, I was given a diagnosis of Attention Deficit Hyperactivity Disorder, also known as ADHD.

Upon hearing that there was a reason for the challenges I was facing I felt an immediate sense of relief, especially when the doctor explained that it could be treated.

Once diagnosed, I learned the causes of ADHD remain unknown and are largely based on hypothesis. Genetics, screen time, refined carbohydrate consumption, and lack of exercise are thought to contribute to symptoms. Additionally, though many symptoms of ADHD are well known, the diagnosis also affects individuals in different ways. Some struggle with focus and others hyperactivity. While others, like myself, struggle with both. Many consider focus and hyperactivity to be the primary symptoms. However, those with ADHD may also struggle (or deal with) depression, anxiety, time management skills, moodiness, and lack confidence. I came to understand within the brain of an ADHD person two neurotransmitters, known as norepinephrine and dopamine are naturally low. Norepinephrine is both a neurotransmitter and a stress hormone that affects the brain's ability to concentrate and largely influences our brain's ability to stabilize mood. Dopamine helps regulate movement, attention, learning and emotional responses. Individuals with low dopamine activity deal with ADHD symptoms and may be more likely to engage in pleasure-seeking activities and run a higher risk of addiction. I struggle most with focus even if I am highly interested in the activity. Hyperactivity has also impacted me as I have always been a fidgety individual, struggling to sit still.

The Treatment Begins

After my diagnosis of ADHD, I began taking medication designed to improve negative symptoms I was experiencing and to decrease feelings of anxiety. I began with a non-stimulant medication known as a norepinephrine reuptake inhibitor. It was known to treat distractibility, hyperactivity, and impulsivity in children, teens, and adults with ADHD. The medication effectively improved my symptoms, but the side effects that resulted were not enjoyable. I began to see a therapist, arguably the most beneficial part of my healthcare journey. She helped me identify my strengths which provided me a much-needed confidence boost.

I also began to realize that I am not as lazy as I thought I was. There are certain odds against me. Growing up, I was never particularly efficient at sports and always pegged as a slow learner. I remember clearly, in middle school being told that I was not good at anything. Even in middle school, I went to a "normal" school for 6th grade and was sent to an "alternative school" for both 7th and 8th grade. In that school, I remember frequently being told that I didn't belong there, if I "paid attention more in class," I would be thriving like the other "normal" kids. I am certain these events influenced my lack of self-confidence. The counselor helped me understand that I am in fact, an intelligent individual. I needed to learn to explore my strengths and spend time with like-minded individuals. The diagnosis and a better understanding of my brain had been helpful.

I was fortunate to have a caring principal who helped devise a plan that would allow me to still graduate on time. I would have to go to summer school. I had more drive during my final year of high school, but my performance was still not at the level I was capable of.

Even so, I was getting by and gained some authentic and lasting friendships. I had better relationships with my teachers and was more consistent with completing homework and received much better grades. The combination of all these things allowed me to graduate on time with my peers. It was fantastic, but I don't think I realized the magnitude of it at that time.

Another important aspect of my life improved during that year. I reconnected with my father who has always been strong support for me emotionally. He believed in me during the hardest moments. We had grown apart during my teen years so having him back was very helpful. I went to visit him in Florida after graduation. I was still unsure of my next step but also wasn't concerned at the time. I was reeling from my high school experience and took some much-needed time with my dad to think and regroup.

An Introduction to Adulthood

I returned to New Jersey and began to apply for a job. This would be my first job. I was hired quickly for a job in a retail book store. The new sense of independence felt good, and the job gave me a good insight into my strengths. I had the opportunity to work in many areas of the store, such as the stock room, book floor, and as a cashier. It didn't all come easily for me. I needed an extra day of training on the cash registers even though others had picked it up quickly. This was disappointing for me, but still, I persevered. My self-dialogue was negative as I was still learning to understand and manage my challenges due to ADHD.

Awakening

Initially, I spent most of my time working in the stockroom. During some of my time at the cashier, the head cashier had noticed that was excelling at converting customers into members with a paid yearly card and encouraged the manager to put me on the floor to help customers. This was a tremendous confidence boost for me. Realizing that I was good at something and was doing gave me a sense of pride. My whole life felt like it had been focused on my weaknesses until now. Finding my strengths and accomplishing new things was an incredible feeling.

After a couple of months working at the store, I met a friend, Lisa, who also worked at the mall. She was easy to talk to, and we were instant friends. Eventually, Lisa and I agreed to go on a date. I was very excited, as we had flirted before but now, we were going to have an actual date.

A few days later, we headed to the movie theater, but the movie we had hoped to watch was no longer playing. We did decide on a different movie that neither of us enjoyed. To make up for the disappointing movie we had a delicious dinner. Dinner was fantastic, and we spent several hours just talking and getting to know each other. We connected during that time. What I remember most about that night was talking. It was the first time I had felt completely understood and accepted by another. It was a raw, liberating feeling to be able to be myself without hesitation. It was the first time I had felt this with another besides my family and therapist. Besides feeling accepted by her, we also shared many of the same interests in music, film, and fashion. It was freeing to be able to share these interests with her since I tended to become obsessive in my interests, as is common with ADHD.

Our Transformative Journey

As the days went on, we continued spending time together. I had the opportunity to share with her about my ADHD diagnosis, and she listened intently. She also experienced OCD and related to me due to her understanding of her struggles. Our relationship continued to grow, and we were excited. It felt wonderful to have a supportive partner to spend my days with. One experience has stuck with me. We were at a café; she was holding my hands, clammy palms and all. Feeling my anxiety, she looked into my eyes, free of judgment, and reminded me that she thought I was wonderful and there was no need to feel anxious in her presence. The feelings that I had when with her were comfortable, supportive, and exciting.

As is the case with many young relationships, things didn't stay happy and light for long. Lisa began to struggle personally which hurt our relationship as well. She was very sad which led to my becoming sad also. I wanted desperately to support her, but this wasn't what was to be. She needed space to give the necessary attention to and work through her struggles. It was hard, but I respected her decision and let her go.

It was my first break up, and it hurt. I had a difficult time letting go of the relationship, and it affected my wellbeing and began to hold me back. Her being sad would soon lead to me being sad, and then one day, we had a phone call where she mentioned that she needed a break from all the hanging out we were doing. There were other things that she needed to bring attention to in her life, and I, of course, was respectful of her choice, however, was hurt, as I couldn't help. It was without a doubt hurting as it was my first ever "break up" and I, in all honesty, was attached. For quite a while, I was down about this. I would show up to work noticeably unhappy, and my attachment to that relationship was holding me down.

Learning My True Power, Purpose and The Gift of Stillness

One day a chance in the book store changed my entire outlook and in turn spurred an interest in one of the most helpful tools in my journey to understand and manage my ADHD. While shelving magazines a customer recognized my dejected demeanor and asked for my help. Her question, and more importantly her answer, led me on a quest for further understanding and knowledge. She referenced a photograph that was in the magazine she was looking at and said she was hoping I could tell her what it means. She smiled and showed me a picture of a man rowing his boat comfortably while a killer whale stalked him directly below the surface, seemingly ready to attack. Though it appeared obvious, I described the photo to the inquisitive customer. She challenged me and persisted asking for more information about the photo. She agreed the man appeared comfortable but pressed for more. She dug deeper asking me why I thought he was comfortable or if I felt he should be worried. I could tell by her tone that she knew the answer to the questions she asked of me, which added to my annoyance. I responded rudely insisting I did not know the answers. After a brief smile and pause, she pressed one more time, "are you sure you don't know the answer?"

Sensing my frustration, she finally let me off the hook explaining her perception. As she put it, the reason the man was comfortable was that he isn't worried about the past or the future, rather he is simply enjoying the present. He is living the moment as it is, taking in all the beauty in his life while he still can. Up to this point, her questions did not make sense to me but when she said, "I think this is what you need to do also" it was powerful. With that photo, in a few moments, she painted a clear picture for me that began my journey to learn all I could about being in the present. When I returned home that night, I began to journal and wrote about my encounter. I was intrigued by the way she presented the philosophy of being present as an answer to happiness. Suddenly it dawned on me that all my life my happiness had been dependent upon others. I realized that instead of relying on others to create my happiness it was something that I needed to create for myself. I began to research and learn all I could. I immersed myself in books, my favorite being "You

Are Here" written by the Buddhist monk Thich Nhat Hanh. This book explained the philosophy of presence and powerful tools to allow me to incorporate mindfulness into my daily life. To my surprise, strong mindfulness practice is an effective tool for my ADHD brain. I learned of scientific studies including one by Dr. Lidia Zylowska whose results determined that participants who engaged in daily mindfulness practice showed a 30% decrease in the symptoms related to ADHD.

Armed with my new knowledge, I decided to take control of my future. I started by finding events in my area that I could attend. I felt it was important to build a support network and needed a sense of community. I came across a Buddhist meditation center near my home and signed up for a class. I still remember entering the building for the first time. One of the Buddhist practitioners bowed when I entered the building as a form of respect. It was unusual and felt very strange to me on this first visit, but I remained devoted to my goal and attended the class. The monk who led the meditation instructed us to be seated comfortably. He directed us to make our breath the anchor of our focus and told us that when we got lost in thought, we should gently bring attention our back to our breath. My ADHD brain could hardly stand it. It felt like an eternity before he rang the bell to end the meditation, but I made it. He then began to explain the goals of meditation and provided valuable insight to beginners.

That day I learned some valuable lessons that I carry with me to this day. The goal of meditation is not to silence your mind; rather it is to change your relationship with your mind As time went on it became easier to be present with my breath, and as a result, I noticed a tremendous change in how I showed up for everything in my day to day life. I was inspired and continued to attend weekly classes and later even meditation retreats. There I had the opportunity to learn from other monks and teachers who grew and developed my daily practice which has continued to this day. I have been practicing meditation for over four years now, and it has enhanced my ability to manage the symptoms of ADHD more than I could have imagined.

One of my favorite practices as a beginner was a short five to ten-minute sequence. Using a mantra was very helpful for me when I began my practice. As I learned to observe the breath, repeating to self "in" as my breath came in and "out" as my breath went out, rather than trying to alter the breath. I also learned to catch myself when I became lost in thought. My practice continued to grow. I learned I could even practice when doing daily activities such as brushing my teeth or when doing house cleaning activities. Doing this encouraged me to show gratitude for the little things in life and the benefits were amazing.

Once I had developed a consistent meditation practice, I began to make more changes. I began to exercise, participating in yoga and a variety of body weight workouts. I learned that exercise is easier to do when it is an activity you enjoy so I gravitated toward those activities. Daily movement is beneficial for an ADHD brain, and it enhances mood. Additionally, it has been proven to aid in norepinephrine and dopamine production. Yoga has been particularly helpful for me because it increases GABA levels in the brain which largely influences symptoms of anxiety. Finding an enjoyable exercise routine has made it easy to stay consistent, and consistency is important to reap the benefits.

The growth and improvement I have experienced because of all I have learned have affected me immensely. When I began to accept and take care of myself, it allowed me to fuel my body in a way that was best for me. This was when I began to truly live. Through my experience and using the knowledge I gained I found my career. I enrolled at the Institute for Integrative Nutrition and learned what it means to cause behavioral change not only for myself but others as well. I had the opportunity to learn from a variety of renowned health experts and came to understand several health theories. The knowledge I have gained has changed my life and provided me the opportunity to change the lives of others.

While not perfect, my life and experience with ADHD have significantly improved. Understanding that a person can create sustainable change to improve the quality of life has been the cusp of my transformation. I have been blessed to find my community and put necessary steps into action. I now love my ADHD brain and value all the challenges and victories gained thanks to my beautiful brain.

"To be beautiful means to be yourself. You don't need to be accepted by others. You need to accept yourself." - Thich Nhat Hanh

About Marc Almodovar

Marc is the founder and CEO of "Wellness with Marc," providing life and wellness coaching for individuals with ADHD and anxiety. With his work, including his coaching, blogs and frequent posts on social media, he's helping those with an ADHD brain overcome their limiting beliefs.

Marc is also a fanatic of health himself, combining both holistic health and modern-day science as he takes on his day to day life. From things like meditation, herbal teas, and breathing practices, all the way to using devices to track his sleep, measure his blood glucose and heart rate variability, you name it, Marc is on it.

Here's the thing though – Marc wasn't always this way. In school, he struggled. He was constantly distracted in class, struggled socially and at one point, even had severe depression. At the age of 16, Marc was diagnosed with highly inattentive ADHD. This, much to everyone's surprise, was a huge relief to Marc, as he always knew something was "different" about his cognition, however, didn't know what was going on until this diagnosis happened.

Years later, Marc had an "awakening moment" in his life where he realized enough was enough, and that it was time to take more control of his well-being. So, he did just that. He took part in things like meditation classes, attended mindfulness retreats with Buddhist monks, learned more about food and how gut health contributes to brain health from top leading doctors, he started meeting like-minded friends, changed his mindset and his overall life, as well with many practices, seminars, teachers and healthcare professionals, as well.

Soon, Marc would then transition his journey of healing to others who share the same struggle as him. He recognized that while there are certainly manageable downfalls of the unique ADHD brain, there are many strengths, as well. One strength is his patience and ability to motivate someone who feels "stuck" in their life as he knows the feeling all too well and the ability to "hyperfocus" which many don't know is a skill of ADHD.

Many ADHD individuals struggle far more than the average individual with adulting day to day tasks; however, have above average focus and passion when it comes to something that gives them meaning. Honing in on these skill sets, Marc studied coaching skills and several theories of wellbeing at the Institute for Integrative Nutrition® and has since then begun seeing clients one on one with great passion with his life and wellness coaching program, helping his clients see their true power, bringing awareness to their strengths.

Marc also recently dedicated his Instagram, @wellnesswithmarc to be a place of support for individuals with ADHD and a place to share his journey and has been having great success since doing so, and only wishes to let those with ADHD, despite how untrue it may feel, can be great, as well.

For those interested in working one on one with Marc, you can schedule a free initial consultation with him here, as he offers non-judging accountability, increased self-awareness in clients, guided meditation sessions and a whole lot more.

Contact Information

Marc Almodovar
Wellness With Marc
Website: www.wellnesswithmarc.com
Email: wellnesswithmarc@gmail.com

Chapter 20

Awakening of My Inner Healer

By: Shipra Alapuria

The Good Old Days

As I sit here with a coffee mug in my hand, contemplating my life in solace, my eyes are filled with emotions when I travel back in time, to the little girl growing up in India. Oh, how I'd love to relive the past, carefree, innocent days of my childhood. As far as my memory goes, I can recall each brick of my house, down to the unfinished walls of our home. I remember how I used to touch it, feel its strength and how it stood strong and tall with each passing season.

Life was celebrated in small but innocent ways, like when mom always bought the very first fruit of the season, on its very first day of arrival in the market. I feel deeply nostalgic when I recall the memory of my dad getting me ready for school and helping me make my braids. Another fond recollection is when my elder brother, who once gifted me a candy bought with his pocket money. I still cherish those memories.

My parents were there to fulfill my needs and give me all the love in the world and my grandparents were always ready to bridge the gap in which my parents may have innocently overlooked. To my advantage, they came with the wealth of a lifetime of experience behind them. They offered their support and stability while possessing an unlimited amount of patience.

School Days of Yesteryear

I was a sincere and dedicated student. You know that student in every class who is appraised by their teachers with regards to the quality of homework, class tests, etc. Yes, I was that girl. I would sincerely pay attention to what my teachers taught at school, and as a result, I was always the favorite. I was also very active, and my extracurricular activities were numerous. It was this active participation in interests such as dance, debate, badminton, and basketball that helped me to get selected as the school captain. I was always drawn to Bollywood dance, and as a result, I won many awards and was even chosen to represent my school for six continuous years on Independence Day; a day that was enthusiastically celebrated.

But as life tends to do, it moved on, and I graduated from high school. Transitioning to college was an exciting time for me because all I could think about was becoming independent. It was the first time I'd get to live on my own, but I was also feeling a little overwhelmed when I thought of the responsibilities, but nothing topped being on my own.

I was admitted to an engineering program in a technical college. To my surprise, it was love at first sight, especially with the scenic beauty of its location. Somehow, the beauty of nature took precedence over the technical specialization, and the mountains seemed to converse with me. I was thrilled and time stood still, Dehradun Institute of Technology brought me the best years of my life. Mussoorie was just a few miles away from my college which gave me ample time and opportunity to explore its beauty from time to time. In retrospect, I have bleak memories of the subjects and all I can recall is the time spent with friends; how we all went to Lord Shiva temple during our recess in search of free morsel and tea, and that lingering flavor and aroma of the tea that was specific to the temple. I remember standing in lines or sitting on the steps for hours enjoying the company of my friends. The journey from college to the temple was picturesque in its own way, full of curves, trees, and a groovy lane. It was a dreamy path, and it was a great time in my life.

The Health Struggles Begin

I graduated from college with good grades and moved to another city in search of a job, though there were few stressful and anxious moments, they were ignored. I soon got a job, and once again life started to sail smoothly. Suddenly, something very strange started to happen. I started feeling extremely exhausted and depressed with severe heart palpitations. I would sweat profusely every single day for no reason. The gastrointestinal issues I previously suffered from throughout my life, were now exacerbated from the stress and I felt overwhelmed. Things were moving beyond my control, and I started to lose weight at a tremendous speed, for no apparent reason. I started feeling low both physically and mentally. Things were "invisible" to everyone except me, as I was the sufferer. My hands developed extremely, pronounced tremors when left free. I felt pain in my wrists and bones. I was so riddled with anxiety that at times I would blow things out of proportion over trivial matters. All I could feel was a sense of breathlessness and imminent doom.

One morning, I went to the cosmetic clinic to treat my hyperpigmentation. Upon the doctor's examination of my face, he detected I may have an issue with my Thyroid. He then advised me to meet with the Endocrinologist. I consented, although I felt feeble at the doctor's grave expression. Just after a week, I got myself checked, and after the long-awaited reports came back, I WAS SHOCKED!!

My bloodwork, specifically T3, T4, TSH, was out of control. The doctor comforted and assured me that he would bring everything back to normal. For obvious reasons, I became nervous and hysterical and felt extremely helpless when hearing the doctors speak about radioactive iodine and surgery. Surgery? Radioactive? I was left shaken and terrified. I left the doctor's office and sat alone in the common area for nearly an hour. It felt as if my world was just shattered.

Because I refused the radioactive treatment, the doctors started treating me with medications. It started with a heavy dose of 100 mg/day of PTU. I did my best still keep up with the daily chores of life and manage my ailment, despite the overwhelming stress. Life still had to go on. I felt comforted when my reports showed considerable improvement in my health. I felt better, every time I viewed the progress. Nevertheless, fatigue, gastrointestinal problems, stress, and low energy accompanied the treatments.

Life kept on moving along, and I met and married my Mr. Right. He gave new meaning to my life. There was abeyance for that moment as we both stopped and were busy settling our nest. Medications kept me on my toes and luckily, we had enough help with the house in India. As time passed by, I became pregnant, and it was such a wonderful feeling. We were full of many beautiful emotions. The strength of the relationship developed as we went through the significant changes of becoming new parents.

A Baby is Born

During our first visit to the gynecologist, I never knew that my pregnancy would leave the nurse so surprised as she opinionated, "You can't get pregnant with this bloodwork." She reviewed my blood reports and raised her eyebrows in disbelief. My husband and I looked at each other's faces as this was not expected. With a few mixed emotions of happiness and fear, we decided to meet the senior endocrinologist at Apollo, India. He was God sent to us and with his calm and confident voice, he assured us that all would be fine. He referred us to another renowned gynecologist and told us that we just needed extra care. My husband and I felt relief by his promise. Nine months later, and with God's blessings and the utmost care, I delivered a healthy baby boy. He rejuvenated my spirits, and I felt alive and revived. The mid-night wake-ups, the crying, the diapering, and the nursing, was overwhelming at first, but I knew it was all normal. Now when I look back, I feel completely elated at how fast he grew.

I continued with my medications and life went on as I enjoyed tending to my baby's chores and cute moments. I felt blessed I had my family there to help and support me as well. When my son was 8 months old, my dearest husband got a job opportunity which required him to move to The United States of America. I was supposed to join him a little later because of my pending Master of Technology (Computer Science) exams. Once he was gone, I remained surrounded by my loving family, both his and mine and enjoyed their love and support as I stayed with each, alternating my time with them.

Not my Baby Too!

During October of 2012, my eight-and-a-half-month-old son caught a severe cold and cough. We took him to see a primary care physician who prescribed him some medications and antibiotics. His condition improved but, the cold and cough returned after a month or so. I returned to the same doctor to find out the reason my son relapsed but instead, he gave me a new dosage of medication and increased the dosage of antibiotics. To my frustration, this happened again a month later, and during this third visit, he referred us to another specialized doctor. This time, the new doctor informed me that my child, now 13 months old, might have sinus issues, as they were a little enlarged. At this point, I did not accept the doctor's conclusion. I knew that because he was born via c-section, his immunity could be weak. Whatever was analyzed, I was anguished, and it was not an easy moment for me. This time, the sufferer was MY CHILD, and as a concerned and protective mother, I was not going to allow the doctors to diagnose him with all kinds of different ailments. I couldn't succumb to the thought of him having sinus issues at such an early stage. I felt there was an over usage of antibiotics and I strongly believed that it was his weak immune system which could definitely be worked upon, naturally. I wanted to heal his issues with the right nutrition.

Enough is Enough!!

I moved to the US and wanted to gain control over everything happening with me and my son's health. He got a cold again, but this time I was prepared with the knowledge to conquer this problem with food, nutrition, and the right care. I gave him natural supplements and homemade syrups made with ginger, garlic, raw honey, and lemon. He needed a lot of rest, massage and care. The cold went on for about another 22-25 days and rarely came back after that. Whenever this issue did come back, I was always ready to face it with more natural healing techniques. He is 7 years old now, and I have never given him any cold or cough medicine to this date. He never had any sinus issues, he just needed his immunity to be strengthened.

Tapping into my Inner Healer

This was my affirmation. I wanted to take charge of my life. Also, I understood the importance of catching things on time and not allowing things to get to the point in which emergency medical attention is needed. I had both the time and zeal to work holistically, on my hyperthyroid symptoms and its associated side effects such as excessive sweating, brittle nails, fragile hair, extreme tiredness and difficulty sleeping. I wanted to evaluate as to why it was happening and began asking myself the important questions. Why was my immunity so weak? How could I make it better and how could I heal myself naturally? I was very much motivated with natural healing techniques as I already witnessed its effects on my kid's health. This is what embarked me upon my self-healing journey from Hyperthyroid and its associated symptoms.

The Journey of the On-Going Natural Healing

Having endured nine years of suffering from Hyperthyroid, Goiter, and Rheumatoid Arthritis, I was tired. I needed a permanent solution. I realized, I didn't know how to care for the flesh, blood, and bones I was living in, and I didn't know what my body needed from me to thrive on an intimate level, at that time. In turn, my body was also showing symptoms of tiredness, difficulty in sleeping, excessive weight loss, hand tremors, and rheumatoid arthritis. My immunity was weak, and my gut was giving the foreign invaders an easy way to enter my body. I even had tingling sensations and the occasional severe pain, in my hands.

I decided to start by improving my diet and lifestyle. I knew I had to work on not only what I ate but also how I enjoyed my life. I intuitively knew I needed to give my body the nutrition it needed to fight and to heal. Instead of destroying my thyroid with radiation, I needed to find another way. I had to reevaluate everything, even my relationship with food. Even though I thought I was eating nutritiously, I realized I wasn't absorbing properly because when we eat something, the effects should be demonstrated by the benefits appearing after that. That was not the case for me.

I always ate the standard Indian diet. It's good, but for me, wheat was acting like a slow poison. There was a lack of vegetables in my diet, and I could tell the amount of inflammation in my body was rising. I also had, succumbed to daily house chores and put aside my passion and love for dance, which was a way of self-expression before. I recognized it was the combination of the neglect I was doing to my soul along with the lack of confidence in my ability to heal myself that left me in such a state.

While evaluating the possible culprits, I found that I ate mostly high-carbohydrate meals with low-fat foods. My artificial sugar intake was very high. I was not keeping up with self-love and was living a monotonous routine. Also, unnecessary stress contributed to the acceleration of the existing symptoms. When I finally snapped out of that dieting mentality and instead focused on healing myself on all levels, I found that it was the best method of treatment, ever. I made changes on multiple levels and am still doing it to this day. I still take medication, but it has been reduced to

5mg/day which is a significant achievement for me. I focused mainly on curing my thyroid and improving my mindset by ignoring negativity and concentrate on life's bigger picture. I hope that I will be able to come off medication altogether. The journey continues.

Psychology Shift

When a problem exists, to solve the problem, one must first accept that there is a problem. Before the change, there needs to be a sense of acceptance. I accepted my true nature. I accepted my anxiety and looked at the bigger picture; that all emotions are equally important. I realized that anger, desperation, and sorrow are all real feelings and I stopped the blame game. I tried to explore the "why" behind everything. I realized that sometimes, negative emotions are the responses caused by the chemical reactions of the hormones in our body. I also learned that when we are stressed, maybe some part of our body needs relaxation, removal of toxins, meditation, hugs or merely to be heard.

I started working on my lost dreams and forgotten paths and worked to respect individuality, life, and valued the presence of people. I made my spirit contagious by helping myself and changing my attitude. Slowly and steadily, I changed my outlook and perceptions on life, gained control over my anxiety, and surrounded myself with positivity, fresh air, nature, and natural products. This procedure was strengthened by just five minutes of meditation a day, which helped me raise my consciousness and use powerful, cognitive-behavioral, coping strategies for transforming how I responded to the events of my life. I also started mind relaxation techniques like forest bathing. If you've never bathed in the forest, try it, I guarantee you will love it too.

There was a time I looked down upon myself as I was trying to fit myself in somebody else's shoes, as well as trying to fulfill the expectations of everyone around me. I acknowledged that one can't pour from an empty cup, so I wanted to take care of myself first. I honestly felt that to give love, you must first love yourself and to give respect, you must first respect yourself. So, I filled myself with love, respect, and self-care and simultaneously worked to be physically fit. This wholesome routine led to the path of fitness.

Whenever I was anxious, I would ask myself, "Is this issue going to be as important to me in a few days or months?" If the answer was no, I ignored it and instead of getting anxious over the matter, I placed my energy in finding the right solution for the problem. I also practiced positive affirmations, daily. I prioritized inner-peace above anything else.

Exercise

I have always loved dancing and sports. I felt instant excitement, the moment I started it. For me, dance is an excellent way of self-expression as it nurtures my body and soul. It's also a great mood enhancer and healing agent, for me. Exercise is so important to implement in your routine, and I suggest to everyone to find at least one thing that you enjoy doing, that involves moving your body, and commit to partaking in that activity daily. This will release happy hormones into the body, and your mood will be automatically transformed. It truly was a huge shift for me to return to physical activities I love.

Diet

This was a little tricky, but I tried and tested, what works for my body. This approach was completely trial and error. I have been working on balancing this part of my health for nearly five years. Although I have experienced some setbacks when I consume something too much that I know may not agree with me, I have always been able to dial it back and resume with a routine that I know works. Being Indian, "Roti" (Indian flatbread made up of wheat) is an integral part of my diet. Maintaining its intake to a point where my body tolerates it, was the key point. I knew its minimum inclusion was necessary to maintain the bacterial diversity in my gut, so I learned to eat it in small amounts.

Eating seasonal vegetables was also important. Crowding out/replacement was the best strategy. Dairy was replaced with almond milk. Millet tortilla (bajra roti), chana, millet were the primary replacement. Also, rice and quinoa became the major source of carbohydrates. When I ate the right foods, I could live a happier and healthier life. I loved the food which loved me back. I use this holistic approach to cure my problems. When I began taking all these steps, the inflammation in my body went down dramatically, and my thyroid function improved considerably. After realizing that love must not be one-sided, in every aspect of life, I found food items that were good for my body type.

As far as my love for food is concerned, I have always been a foodie. I want to eat nutritious, delicious food all my life. Invariably, I changed my preferences of taste and trained my mind to do so. I feel I am on my way as I keep finding the food that works for both my body and mind.

What Worked for Me

Food helped me fix the problem. I included high protein, healthy fats, low-glycemic carbs, optional, unprocessed, gluten-free starch (potatoes, sweet potato, and beans) and an unlimited supply of greens and vegetables. I have been consuming three meals and two snacks per day. I try to balance my diet according to my physical activities and include carbohydrates, protein, vitamins, and fats accordingly. For me, reducing weight was not the only criteria. One can get thin, even on the hospital bed! I was very thin at one point in my life but wasn't healthy. Now I'm active, fit and healthy. Hopefully, I will remain this way, as eating healthy helped me to keep my weight in check. I always consult my primary care physician and follow his advice before trying anything new. For example, during my second pregnancy, my platelet counts were getting really low. I did my own research and wanted to give papaya leaf juice a try. I consulted my hematologist, and when he approved, I added this along with many other things to my regime. Fortunately, it helped. I made the decision to become healthy. I choose it daily. I work on it daily and to achieve this mentality, I just had to look within myself and listen to my body.

Following My Path

It feels wonderful to work towards better health for myself and for those around me. I am still doing it, as I understand and accept that health is wealth! So, after a lot of contemplation, I decided to enroll in a Health Coach Certification program at the Institute for Integrative Nutrition in New York. It was logical as I had been practicing the natural healing process for the last 6 years and without my knowledge, it had become my passion too. What started out as a journey of recovery has now allowed me to explore my hopes and desires, create options for change and help people start their journey to achieve their own transformations. As an Educator and Health Coach, I want to help people overcome health problems with the help of an appropriate diet. Issues like gluten sensitivity are my specialty areas, as I have myself, tried experimenting through an elimination diet and witnessed the power of food.

Getting to the Point

To make a long story short, when I started working on my health, I realized that before the diagnosis of my thyroid issues, I had spent almost twenty years being disconnected from my physical, emotional, and spiritual self, and not supporting its needs. I didn't know how to care for the flesh, blood, and bones I lived in, and I didn't know what my body needed from me on an intimate level to thrive. I looked for a quick fix solution to every problem. In turn, my body couldn't support me either, as it was breaking down or started malfunctioning in subtle, and not so subtle, ways. I was an over-thinker. I was taking on unnecessary stress. I actually ruined my health because of stress. However, one thing was for sure, I wanted to thrive and wanted to live and laugh and love. So yes, I had to work on myself on many levels and changed my perception about things that were happening in my life. I finally followed my passion and chose to start dance once again, to give my self-expression a bloom. After nearly 7-8 years of suffering, I chose natural treatments and sure, they were slow, but they provided permanent solutions without any side effects. They let my body heal with the support of doctors and family.

My health improved but it was not an overnight success; it took a long time. It's an ongoing process, but I am sure about my destination and the path I have chosen. I truly believe that through healthy food choices, avoiding toxins, and taking steps to reduce stress, it is easier to achieve life goals and stay healthy. While exercising regularly and eating are no doubt important in restoring and maintaining one's health, perhaps the key factor is to be responsible for my own health.

The New Shining Me

Now, I have changed my mindset to devise effective strategies to solve problems, as I believe in the complete comprehension of a problem and working extensively for its solution. I am thankful for the hard times because they are the reasons I am stronger today. My joy is enormous, and I celebrate life. I have unlocked the door to my inner peace and healer. I believe in the power of the right nutrition. I have worked on the dark dreams of my subconscious mind, and as a result, things have been astonishing. Though there were some moments of failure, I did not fall apart; I stood again, walking tall and strong.

Our Transformative Journey

Most times, when a child is born, he is perfectly healthy, and I believe we should continue to be that way, remaining healthy, fit and strong. It is not fun to be sick. When I loaded my body with toxins, refined carbs, and unnecessary stress, I fell tremendously ill.

Now that I have gained control over my health issues, my curiosity leads me to look inside, to find out where I went wrong. I started taking the right food and nutrition which finally gave me control over it physically, spiritually and mentally. Then, I worked on my subconscious mind. I aligned my thoughts harmoniously with the creative principles of the subconscious mind. I eliminated the thoughts of fear, worry, anxiety, jealousy, hatred, and every other destructive thought. I calmed my mind using meditation and also worked on active breathing techniques. Through these techniques, my intentions came to fruition.

I paid attention to the food I kept providing my body, and when I worked on all these levels, the results were great. I could decide the direction of my life, and my health improved both physically and mentally. I learned to get in touch with the silence within and knew that everything in life has a purpose. I listened to my heart and found my true self-calling. All these efforts brought my thyroid medications down. No more suffering from rheumatoid arthritis, stress or fatigue and I could work very well under any stressful condition.

With each passing day, I want to be a better me. I love to come out of my comfort zone to test my limits. I want to keep myself happy so that I can encourage others to do so. I don't want to settle for anything less than my best. I love and value the encouraging voices of my support system, and I want to be positive. I love to refresh my self-image by speaking positive affirmations and faith-filled words. I have conquered my mind's and body's insecurities and have learned a great lesson with every setback. I am always determined to keep my thoughts positive.

The wings of transformation were brought out of patience and struggle. I am still working on my health and mind. I believe that each of us is born with a purpose in life. Identifying, acknowledging and working towards this purpose is the most important goal. I have found my purpose, and I am working towards it. I am still looking for wisdom. I am not looking for perfection, but I consistently keep monitoring every single move and its effects on my life. I will keep on going. I am evolving. You can too.

About Shipra Alapura

Shipra Alapuria is a certified New Jersey public school teacher, an integrative nutrition health coach and a stay at home parent to her two young kids. She is a health enthusiast and enjoys writing blogs on a wide array of health-related issues. She is compassionate about helping her clients and offers them one-on-one, group, and customized coaching programs. She firmly believes in the concept of bio-individuality: one person's food is another person's poison. She wants her clients to flourish not just on a physical level but also an emotional level.

Shipra's parents instilled a good work ethic and the importance of quality education in her. As a result, she was exceptionally bright in academics. She has earned bachelor's and master's in computer science from Dehradun Institute of Technology, India and Dr. A.P.J. Abdul Kalam University, India. Shipra excelled equally in sports as she did in academics and bagged several awards representing her school.

Her struggle with Hyperthyroid, Rheumatoid Arthritis, fatigue and anxiety coupled with her son's health challenges at an early age forced her to look for holistic measures rather than giving into strong radiations, surgeries and a lifetime of prescription drugs. After following a holistic nutritional approach, she saw a dramatic improvement in symptoms, both for herself and her son. In a way she could cure many problems with this approach. She was then automatically mesmerized by her passion for holistic approach, and the health and nutrition became a central interest in her life.

Shipra is a 2019 graduate of Institute of Integrative Nutrition in New York City. At school, she learned over one hundred dietary theories ranging from Ayurveda to Keto. She acquired a holistic approach to health where she was taught to treat the disease at its root level rather than symptomatically. She had the privilege of being guided by the experts: Dr. Mark Hyman, Deepak Chopra, Tom Malterre, and David Wolfe, to name a few.

Her journey, navigating through recommendations for surgeries and radiations to following her belief in holistic ways of healing, lead her to freedom from lifelong prescription medications. Her holistic, integrative approach has immensely helped her kid fight immune and abdominal issues.

Shipra is a strong advocate of Elimination diet to find out the real culprit for wide-ranging issues like weight gain, migraine, brain fog, depression, to name a few. She believes it to be a catalyst in losing weight and curing a plethora of other health issues. She swears by the benefits of a whole food-based diet. She witnessed a change in her health conditions following this lifestyle, which made her compassionate to help others find their true health and happiness.

Through her health coaching practice, Shipra aspires to educate and transform as many lives as she can. She teaches her clients to harness the power of their subconscious mind, using techniques like meditation and positive affirmations. She is a regular volunteer at various community events and believes in doing her share for the society.

When her clients do not occupy Shipra, she could be found enjoying gardening in her organic kitchen garden, dancing to Bollywood numbers, reading books on health & wellness or relaxing in nature.

Shipra currently resides in Woodbridge, New Jersey with her husband (Avinash), son (Arnav) and daughter (Avishi). She can be reached out via email at younaturallyhealthy@gmail.com

Contact Information

Shipra Alapuria
You Naturally Healthy
Website: https://www.quora.com/profile/Shipra-Alapuria/blogs
Email: younaturallyhealthy@gmail.com

Chapter 21

My Growing Space

By: Mandi Woodard

Battles. We all have them; we all know them. Some are a constant ebb, claiming your never ceasing attention with the slow burn of anxiety. Others are sudden, heart-wrenching battles that threaten to claim every ounce of our being in the span of a moment. It is not our place to judge and compare whose battles are worse. A battle is a battle regardless. Everyone deserves the chance to be heard and healed. I have always known that I existed to be of service to the world. I am here to help people any way I can to feel better and at ease. Born in a small town in Alabama the winter of '88 is where it all began.

Grateful:

The earliest memories I have from my childhood are of my dad, a man who was and still is everything a father should be. Around six years old my parents separated, and he became a single father to three young children; my older brother, myself, and my sister. Being a single dad and sole provider for us meant our kitchen was filled regularly with an inventory of frozen TV dinners and cereal; not exactly the picture-perfect representation of a nutrition-filled childhood. Despite the nutritional value, we were never short on food or more importantly, unconditional love. My grandparents lived close by and helped bridge any gap we had from an overworked father.

When I think of my mother, the phrase "loved us so much it hurt" comes to mind. Mom spent her life trying to find what would make her happy. She moved back and forth from her hometown in Delaware to Alabama every few years. My siblings and I saw her around three times a year, sometimes less. Her struggle with alcoholism and addiction can't take from us the very important life lessons we acquired from her. However, it also gave me a case of codependency still left to explore. The tears come now as I try to express the great qualities we inherited from her since there is a vast amount of pain attached to her memories. In her way, she knew leaving us in the care of my dad was what was best for all involved. She sought ways to take care of herself away from our household, mostly I thank her for it. Despite all that went on, growing up was filled with many happy traditions and memories.

I don't remember all the important details of my childhood; maybe a subconscious consequence of the deep traumas I experienced during it, but what I do know is what doesn't kill you makes you stronger when you utilize the right tools. Through our trials and tribulations, however big or small, we can come out on the other side better and stronger than we were before. Committing myself to this journey of health and wealth, becoming an expert space-holder for others, creating more flow in a muffled world, is truly one of the most important, life-saving choices I have ever made.

Resilience:

Stories like mine always start early. Elementary school was when I first experienced the positive impact that someone in a professional setting could have in an individual's life. We called her Mrs. Pickles because she had a small playful plush pickle in her office that, to this day, brings a smile to my face when I think about it. She was my elementary school counselor, and she was the first person that I remember I truly felt heard me. In a span of only a few years, beginning at the age of five, I endured the pain of my mother going to live somewhere else, leaving me with worries of how I could love both my parents equally but in different places at different times. My first experience with guilt was the day after two of my childhood friends died in a house fire. What if I had only told them how to stop, drop, and roll. Would they have lived? Guilt soon turned to confusion when my maternal grandmother committed suicide, and I watched as my mom fell apart even more. Trying to understand such big emotions while so young caused me to grow up quicker than expected. Mrs. Pickles listened to me and lifted my spirits during this darker time in my life. She created a safe space for me to sort my thoughts. She was a light needed in time or darkness. My time with her was evidence of the truth in the quote, "People may not remember what you did, or what you said, but they will always remember how you made them feel."

Through grade school I struggled with my weight, mostly staying on the heavy side. My friends were all that society would say was skinny, or "normal." The people that thought they were helping would instead teach us that size didn't matter. In an attempt to look like everyone else I spent a year on a slim-fast diet, counting every calorie. As hard as it was, I lost the weight. Once the results came, the diet stopped, and I went back to being a kid again. I spent time with friends, played sports, and ate whatever I wanted. You can imagine my surprise when I regained the weight and then some. I kept asking myself, "How did I let this happen? I was eating the same amount of the same food everyone around me was eating, if not less." Confused and just wanting to be like everyone else I always asked, "Why me?"

When I entered high school, my dad searched for tools to assist in my weight loss journey and found Weight Watchers. Dad bought the books and together we used the tools provided to begin our days adding up points of the foods we ate in hopes we had met our goals. We went to the meetings, stood on the scale, and watched as someone wrote down our weight loss over the past week. Did we lose weight? Yes. Did I feel any healthier? No. When the newness of the program wore off, we stopped going to the weigh-ins. There was a bright warning sign flashing in the back of my mind, "The weight is going to come back!

When I was 17, I fell in love. My first memories with him start around eight years old. He lived in Delaware, near my mom, so we saw each other when we visited. Fast forward eight years, we decided to make things official as boyfriend and girlfriend. Everything was perfect. It was a matter of months into our relationship when I received the call no ever wants, "Mandi, I have leukemia, and I've been admitted to the hospital." I will never forget the silence on the phone when he said those eleven words; I couldn't breathe. It was as if someone had ripped my heart out. I will spare you the depressing details of all the transplants, chemotherapy and radiation sessions that ultimately ended with his passing on November 3rd, 2005, only 26 days shy of his 19th birthday. It wasn't fair. I thought I would never heal from this one. I had dealt with so much already in my still developing mind and heart that it took everything I could to merely live life even as an empty shell for a very long time. I had tapered off communication with my friends and family;

I became a recluse before I even knew it. Within my desolate void of depression, food was the only thing that sparked a satisfied feeling. That was until I realized I was heavier than I had ever been, by at least seventy-five pounds. I felt defeated… again.

Another six months went by, and I was only getting worse. After trying several different kinds of counselors, I found my perfect match. This woman, who owned her practice with her husband, was so strong and inspirational and put me to work immediately! She gave me homework to do to bring me back to life. Simple things like making lists of what I was thankful for daily or spending fifteen minutes a day outside for no reason. My counselor's husband was the psychiatrist of the practice and experimented with different brands and doses of antidepressants, but given my mother's history, this sort of treatment didn't stick with me. She consistently held me accountable, and gradually the fruits of my labor paid off. I had put in all the work to heal myself from within; sweat and tears included. I took over the front desk position at their office. Although my brain was getting better, my body was still carrying the weight from my reclusive state. I knew in my heart that one day I would figure out how to take care of it.

Observed:

The uncertainty where life was taking me after my high school graduation led me to attend a college close to home. My family was my biggest support system, so it was important to stay close to them. A friend of mine had the idea of getting an apartment together. I took her up on her offer, and we found a place with a great pool and signed a lease. What more did we need? Our apartment was a communal living type. We shared common areas with two other girls who didn't know us or each other. When I registered for classes, it was more like a guessing game. Like a kid in a candy store, I explored different avenues of subject material yearning for a moment of clarity where my passion would unfold in front of my eyes, and I could begin to find out what life had in store for me. Introduction to Social Work immediately sparked my attention by teaching me something I couldn't believe I had not learned before. The words rolled off the professor's tongue as if she were speaking directly to me. She said, "When we experience intense trauma our brain changes shape. We physically become different." No wonder so many people feel so foreign in their bodies after a traumatic event. We are mentally and physically new. I began thinking to myself that I could make a living and make a big impact in the world. Without further adieu, I claimed my major proudly.

My father, being a skilled salesman, left a strong desire for me to go to business school, but everything happens for a reason, right? The coursework felt natural from day one, and when it didn't, I would spend hours reading every word, every chapter to understand it fully. At one point I even tried to take Crisis Intervention (a senior level course) my second-year. I ended up having to drop the class solely due to the fact I wasn't ready in the least. This was a very important lesson for me, and I feel like, for most others. It is imperative not to skip steps on your journey. You need to appreciate each one to the point you enjoy it. Later, I retook the class when it was time, and I passed with flying colors.

Crisis Intervention, as well as Cultural Diversity and Social Justice, were my favorite classes. They were taught by the two professors I learned the most from throughout my social work undergrad. A good professor teaches you both inside and outside the classroom; instilling within us the value of standing up for what one believes in, and my favorite lesson if you cry and the tears are real and sincere then you can let them out. This was a big deal to me since I cried about most things for as long as I could remember.

It's easy to get caught up in the idea that if I could go back and do things differently, I would. I know it crosses most people's mind, but the truth is, I wouldn't change a thing. Going with the flow of your wants and needs is important. I met more people in the first year of college than I made the rest of my college career. I built friendships forever and turned questionable decisions into unforgettable memories. The subject matter one pursues in college doesn't always follow through once you reach your adult life career path; however, the one thing you can take from it is the confidence that you can complete something. Even the tiniest act of making your bed everyday exercises your brain to be stronger, enhancing your ability to handle the harder times. The permanent goal was always to help people, but when I look back on my journey at Jacksonville State University, I see it not only as my education but more importantly, another step in my process of healing. Feeling better can come from a multitude of things though I may argue that truly getting to know yourself is the ultimate high. When Eleanor Roosevelt wisely said that you should do one thing every day that scares you, I believe she was telling us to explore different things to find out what inspires us the most, and when we do, only then will we find our place in the world.

While:

After graduating in May 2011, I headed to Alaska to visit one of my closest friends. We had met in college years before and bonded for life overnight. Molly had moved to Alaska a year earlier to finish her college degree. She invited me to spend seven weeks with her exploring the last frontier and then wrap up the summer with a week in Las Vegas. Molly was quite the planner. We spent over a year filling our schedules with dozens of activities within a reasonable distance from Fairbanks, all the while saving every penny for the adventures. A year of anticipation and excitement went by in a flash, and the day before my plane departed those emotions turned to anxiety and utter panic! Unexplainable thoughts of what if this happens or what if that happens circled in my head like a tornado. Eventually, the tears stopped, and I will be forever grateful I got on that plane.

One adventure led up to the Arctic Circle where we hiked so far into the wilderness that I had no choice but to be proud of myself and camped knowing bears could eat us if they wanted because we were no longer at the top of the food chain! If I had to choose one word to sum up my trip to Alaska, it would be humbling. I mention this trip because just how far out of my boundaries it pushed. There isn't enough time or space here to explain all of the teachable moments I was faced with, but I will tell you that traveling can be utilized as a major tool in one's personal growth. With every new location, you get the opportunity to experience and explore you are bound to learn something new about yourself.

After this once-in-a-lifetime adventure, my sister greeted me at the airport where suddenly I found myself crying in her car as we drove back to my house. I was overwhelmed, a word I knew far too well, with happiness to see my family combined with my desire never to come back. Maybe I just knew I had to be a grown up now but still did not know how I wanted to use my education. On top of that, I had spent all my money in Alaska. While there were no regrets, it did make getting on my feet a little difficult. There was an opening at the local mental health center for a rehabilitation instructor. My responsibilities were to oversee the staff members working in the group home, as well as to make sure the ten developmentally disabled adult males living there cared for according to state regulation. I couldn't believe I was in a position to make a difference.

The first day in this new position I stayed in the office so sure that I wasn't ready to take on these important responsibilities. A month went by, and I started to feel settled in life after college. Then, I received a phone call from my mom. She called me in the middle of trying to take her life. Calmly, I called 911. Astonished, I requested an ambulance be sent to my mother's residence in an entirely different state. Luckily, I had been trained and taught what to do in high crises, so after I made the phone call I continued with my day; there was nothing more I could do. She lived and was back in a recovery program, again.

Over the next year, I spent my days working on various plans ranging from menus and physical activities to medical visits, simply going through the motions of day-to-day life. I went to work, and I went home, usually picking fast food for dinner. I began waking up with stomach pain every morning. Several people suggested I see a doctor, but something inside kept me away. I figured it was the fast food I ate. I was stagnant and unfulfilled, still missing the intention and purpose I always craved. When it was time to file my taxes, I was left with defeated thoughts realizing I didn't earn close to what I thought I would earn after five years in college. Our professors had often reminded us not to go into social work for the money, and it was then I knew why.

A little over a year went by, the company went through budget cuts and ended up cutting my position from all the homes. God, Great Spirit, the universe, whatever you call your higher power, always has funny ways to remind you that change is inevitable. You must remind yourself that pain is optional. If you start asking for more from life it imperative to be prepared for the uncomfortable; to be open to whatever is about to head your way. If you choose to grow through the uncomfortable times, you will undoubtedly blossom into something so much better on the other side.

Transcending:

The time had come to pack up and leave my home town in Alabama. A friend of mine from college had a room open up in her home north of Atlanta, and I took my chance. After a few interviews, I accepted a job to be a nanny in a home. I immediately felt like I belonged at the moment

Our Transformative Journey

I stepped through the doors. Intuition is quite the superpower, and I learned early on to trust my gut.

January 31, 2015, only two months after moving to Georgia, I woke up to a call from my brother. He told me our mother had been found unresponsive in her home and it appeared to have been a heart attack. This was a pivotal moment for me; bittersweet almost. My mother was released of her demons at last. It was possibly the calmest I think I had ever felt. Her struggle with mental health, or lack thereof, was always present. It had been a chain around her waist, and now it was finally broken. No one should have to screen their mother's phone calls, but that's what we had to do. She was sick, and I was glad she was at peace. Although this was a painful experience, my philosophy is, "It's not what happens to you that matters, it's how you handle it."

During my mother's remembrance ceremony, I was eager to get back to my journey of breaking my chains before they got too tight to let loose. I was determined once and for all to become someone who felt good every day!

Almost instantly life started to change positively. I began to pick up on the healthy habits of the successful people I was employed by and was inspired by all the different family dynamics I was a part of. My new life was treating me good, yet something was still missing. It took me about a year to settle in my Georgia life, to feel like I knew my way around, and was finally ready to start on my next goal. Every night after work I spent hours researching what I could do with my life. I loved being a nanny, but I needed to make more money. I received a call for a high-profile nanny position. We set up an interview, and I got the job. No one could see inside my brain, but it felt powerful. One-by-one things were being marked off my lists of positive thoughts. I was truly creating my story one thought at a time. Through meditations and positive affirmations, I transformed my mentality to find the good in every situation. Fast food slowly started to phase out, and my mood improved dramatically. Ready for more, I decided to spend this time to focus on me finally.

I joined a local gym and got connected with a personal trainer. I was nervous. I felt embarrassed knowing I would have to sit in front of someone and tell them I gained seventy-five pounds ten years ago and was just now doing something about it. I cried in the first meeting.

However, once the results started to show I craved the space created at the gym and the process of becoming the best version of myself. For me, it was a place to forget about everything else; a place I could go and know only good things could come from that environment. Some days I wanted to quit, and some days I even backed out of sessions. Losing weight and taking control of your life is both empowering and devastating. You discover you are running towards a new version of yourself while mourning the previous version. My trainer shared the Paleo way of eating with me to get me back to a basic way of thinking about food. I was in the right place with the right people at the right time.

This is where I say my journey to effectively eating began. Having friends who have had similar goals as I helped, and we made a pact to try the blood type diet. I'm B Positive. After removing the suggested items said to have negative or not as positive effects on me I felt better and more clear-headed after just a few days. All of these positive lifestyle choices seemed to make the tears scarce and the anxiety to a minimum. After the allotted time in the plan, we slowly introduced food items back in to see their effect. Most people don't believe me when I tell them, but the next few times I ate chicken I was sick.

My stomach hurt and expanded with inflammation within thirty minutes to an hour. I stopped cold turkey, or maybe I should say cold chicken? My body started changing faster than I had ever before. My endurance increased, and my mindset was getting clearer. The child I was nannying at the time was a vegetarian, and I was expected to instruct him on nutrition. The number of meat products decreased, and I went on a quest for resources to teach and learn about nutrition. We started making up games like guess what's in your food or this food is good for what? It felt good knowing I may be equipping him with the tools he needs to have a nutritionally successful life. Not only was my body changing to the healthy version I had always wanted, but now I had to confidence to teach others how not to choose the unhealthy habits that become so easily adaptable in our busy lives. That's when I concluded that I wanted to further my education and certification so that I could coach others.

Health:

While looking up various things about health and wellness one evening, I came across the Institute for Integrative Nutrition. I enrolled in the course, not knowing how I would pay for it, just trusting if I concentrate my energy towards a task I could accomplish anything. The modules fueled me to keep going, and my vision got clearer and clearer. Sometimes I would have to pause the videos because I was overwhelmed with inspiration and excitement! That was the best feeling! The payments to the school were somehow paid effortlessly, and my journey to a Health Coach was well on its way. Throughout my experiences with healing and healers, counselors, psychiatrists, and falling witness to rehab, I noticed they all had one thing in common -- none of these interventions discussed into what we put in our bodies every day, and how we can change outcomes by being mindful of life in all directions. The more I learned at IIN, the more I wanted to teach. Did you know 90% or more of our serotonin, the chemical in your brain thought to contribute to feelings of well-being and happiness is created in your gut? I didn't either. Did you know a kiwi is high in serotonin? I didn't either.

If anyone ever tells you the process of change is easy they would be lying, but I'm proof if you press toward things that are uncomfortable you will grow from them. Making it to where I am today is a testament of determination, awareness, and staying true to the course. If I were to advise where to start, I would say right here, right now. Write down a goal and complete it. Then, write down another one, and another, until you run out of goals. My goal is to empower women to gain clarity of their goals and equip them with the tools to accomplish them. I also want to use my knowledge and passion for kids to cultivate different ways to teach nutrition early on. At any point in this journey, I've called life, and I could have given up.

What kept me on course was knowing the ripple of my actions, can and will have an immense effect on others. By making small adjustments day by day to becoming the best version of yourself we can all live a happy life. Life truly is about the journey and not the destination. Consistently seeking your balance in all areas of your life, including relationships, careers, spirituality, and staying active, is how one will make sustainable life changes. My journey to a health coach was the icing on the cake. The more energy I put toward my goals; the more opportunities have revealed themselves to get me closer to my dreams. Maybe it's some algorithm, or maybe it's fate, or maybe it's me simply trusting I can achieve anything I put my mind to. I'll leave you with this, one of my favorite mantras: "Every good decision leads to another good decision." If you can silence your mind and listen to your inner self, you will know which step to take next.

About Mandi Woodard

Mandi Woodard is the founder of Our Growing Space, a mindful approach to Health and Wealth for Women. Growing Space is a high-vibing, growth supporting space created to educate and empower women to go after exactly what they want. Mandi believes in adding in as many feel-good feelings as possible as a means to crowd out the bad.

Born and raised in Alabama, Mandi Woodard has the charm of a southern belle and the personality of someone who has seen the world. Having experienced her fair share of heartache during childhood and adolescence ranging from divorced parents to experiencing death in many different ways Mandi has a soft spot for those working to make it against all the odds.

After receiving her Bachelor of Social Work from Jacksonville State University in 2011 and overcoming spouts of anxiety and depression, Mandi moved to the Greater Atlanta Area where she hoped to utilize her degree in Social Work and relationship building skills to better her life. Almost immediately she began subconsciously surrounding herself with people who used food as a tool to fuel and energize the body. Mandi quickly learned that food could still be a comfort for her, but she needed help to figure out the right foods to do so. Once she was on the right path with a healthy diet and regular gym routine, she knew she wanted to take advantage of learning everything she could to teach others. Mandi discovered the Institute for Integrative Nutrition in 2017. After a year of asking questions and getting more information, she enrolled in their Health Coach Certification program. Overwhelmed with excitement as she completed her coursework to become a certified health coach, Mandi knew she'd found her calling. Currently living in the Greater Atlanta Area, Mandi is thrilled to begin her journey as a certified health coach by spreading knowledge on healthy habits and positive lifestyle choices.

Mandi has been a private and professional nanny for five years. Her time working directly with families and children, many of which are business owners, has developed her passion for helping families change the way they think about their time and their nutrition. Deeming herself a Family Dynamic Specialist, Mandi is confident she can help parents juggle a busy now for a better future as well as develop fun and new ways to answer the Why's of nutrition for children resulting in a healthier, happier life.

Mandi hopes to grow in her health and wellness career by private coaching, guest speaking at events, growing Our Growing Space, an online community as well as hosting retreats for women at various locations.

In her spare time, you will find Mandi utilizing her entrepreneur mindset. Mandi is the creator and founder of a successful event planning company, Sleepovers & Co. in her spare time. With her unwavering loyalty and compassion, Mandi is the person who will become that staple in your life you never realized you were missing."

Are you looking to get clear on your goals, kick those defeating thoughts and chase those feel-good feelings? Book a discovery session by getting in touch with Mandi at ourgrowingspace@gmail.com.

Join her community on Facebook to unlock your all-access pass to information, support, and LOVE in their journey to becoming the best version of themselves.

Contact Information

Our Growing Space
Website: www.mandiwoodard.com
Email: woodard.mandi@gmail.com

Epilogue

As centuries pass, the world evolves, and life on earth progresses. Where we once spent most of our lives in the very first level of Maslow's Hierarchy, directing all our energy and resources to secure the fundamental needs of food, water, shelter and rest, has now progressed to the masses capable of reaching the highest level of the pyramid; self-actualization. The need to achieve one's full potential and life's purpose is more of a deeper, inner-calling than a need to survive. The difference between one who strives to achieve self-fulfillment and one who settles in the psychological level of needs such as love, belonging and societal respect, is inner growth.

Transformations are about inner growth. The desire to grow past your current state because of the innate intelligence we are all born with that seeks to be better. As more and more of us find ourselves seeking to be better these days or to live a better quality of life with less suffering and more enjoyment, the more we desire transformation. The problem lies in the "How?" How do you transform your current state?

Despite the vast diversity of ages, backgrounds, ethnicities, levels of education, geographical locations, stages of awareness, and variety of situations and circumstances, our testimonies all share a common thread; the same blueprint for transformation. We stand united in encouraging a holistic approach, to formulate the most significant transformations.

Once you awaken to the need of transformation, understanding that you have unique mental, physical, and spiritual needs, requires that you perform a certain amount of self-study, to identify areas necessitating improvement and growth. Your mind, body, and soul need to be nourished, and where there is a necessity for healing, the wound must be restored. It takes courage, strength and, patience with yourself, to accomplish transformation but no more than you already have within you.

When each part of you is ultimately in harmony and balance, you will experience an immediate rise in quality of life, fulfillment, and happiness. Not only will you experience these things, but they will become your new normal as you continue to live with healthier habits. Performing more and more healthy habits over time, will replace the dysfunctional ones altogether, thus incrementally creating a healthier and happier lifestyle.

Our Transformative Journey

This book is our gift of healing to the world. We recognize we are all connected and surviving our own stories for the same purpose; in pursuit of happier lives. We are committed to creating the ripple effect in that touching and facilitating one transformation will create the momentum towards transforming our world. You are not alone, and you don't have to embark on this journey alone. We are here for you and in service to you. There is no greater way to transform than alongside someone who has been there, is uniquely qualified, and is dedicated and supportive of your goals.

As the *Our Transformative Journey* team moves forward in service to you, we welcome you to join our community online. The OTJ community is a wealth of knowledge, wherein all things relative to transformation, are shared through our daily posts, blog and upcoming conferences and events. We look forward to meeting you and hearing your story as we journey together towards your continued transformational success.

Best Wishes on Your Transformative Journey,

Kristie A. Alers
Co-Author

Our Transformative Journey

Bonus Material
The Transformation Process

7 Steps to Change

Scan the QR Code To Get Your Bonus Material

If you have any trouble downloading the material, please send an email to ourtransformativejourney@gmail.com.

www.ingramcontent.com/pod-product-compliance
Lightning Source LLC
Chambersburg PA
CBHW050855160426
43194CB00011B/2169